Hollywood on Stage

T0274931

STUDIES IN MODERN DRAMA
VOLUME 9
ROUTLEDGE REFERENCE LIBRARY OF THE HUMANITIES
VOLUME 2057

STUDIES IN MODERN DRAMA

KIMBALL KING, *Series Editor*

HOLLYWOOD ON STAGE
PLAYWRIGHTS EVALUATE THE CULTURE INDUSTRY

EDITED BY
KIMBALL KING

Routledge
Taylor & Francis Group

NEW YORK AND LONDON

First published 1997 by Garland Publishing Inc.

This edition Published 2011 by Routledge
711 Third Avenue, New York, NY 10017
2 Park Square, Milton Park, Abingdon, Oxfordshire OX14 4RN

First issued in paperback 2014

Routledge is an imprint of the Taylor and Francis Group, an informa business

Library of Congress Cataloging-in-Publication Data

Hollywood on stage : playwrights evaluate the culture industry / edited by
   Kimball King.
         p.   cm. — (Studies in modern drama ; v. 9)   (Garland reference
library of the humanities ; vol. 2057)
      Includes index.
      ISBN 0-8153-2823-0 (alk. paper)
         1. American drama—20th century—History and criticism.   2. Motion
pictures and literature—United States—History—20th century.   3. Hollywood
(Los Angeles, Calif.)—In literature.   4. Motion picture industry in literature.
5. Popular culture in literature.   I. King, Kimball.   II. Series.   III. Series:
Garland reference library of the humanities ; vol. 2057.
PS338.M67H65   1997
812'.509357—dc21   97-22440
                                                                              CIP

ISBN 13: 978-1-138-88407-6 (pbk)
ISBN 13: 978-0-8153-2823-0 (hbk)

Cover photograph by Donald Cooper Photography depicts Billie Whitelaw
(Nellie Mann) in The National Theatre production of Christopher Hampton's
Tales from Hollywood.

Publisher's Note
The publisher has gone to great lengths to ensure the quality of this reprint
but points out that some imperfections in the original may be apparent.

Contents

General Editor's Note

Hollywood on Stage: The Culture Industry was originally the title of a panel discussion at the Modern Language Association meetings in Chicago in 1995. The genesis of this book was four conference papers developed into essays included in this volume. The session was well attended and provoked interesting discussions. Eventually other scholars came forward with related essay topics. Stephen Watt, Professor of English at Indiana University, initially proposed the conference topic. I decided to collect the original conference papers and additional essays into a book. When the contributors to this volume and I tried to determine which stage plays about Hollywood were the most important, five or six plays by major contemporary writers immediately occurred to each of us. The topic not only proved fertile; it also threatened to become overwhelming. As we began to do research on our individual articles, we discovered an almost limitless number of legitimate stage plays with Hollywood settings.

In this volume there are fairly lengthy discussions of several dozen of these plays. Many more, though worthwhile in themselves and helpful in assessing the literary fashions of a particular decade, have not been included. I am hopeful that our study will stimulate an even more comprehensive analysis of the Hollywood-Broadway phenomenon, which may illuminate various aspects of American life and institutions in the twentieth century.

Kimball King
General Editor

Acknowledgments

I wish to thank Professor Stephen Watt of Indiana University for proposing the topic of this volume to the Modern Language Association. Thanks also to the University of North Carolina for providing me with funds for manuscript preparation and to Lanis Wilson and Jeffrey Campbell who served as my computer experts in coordinating the disks of our volume's many contributors. I also appreciate the help of Nina Wallace, who typed my own sections of the book, and of Garland Senior Editor Phyllis Korper, whose literary taste and wisdom are largely responsible for the best aspects of the Casebook series.

Finally I thank Professor Robert Gross of Hobart and William Smith Colleges for his willingness to read the first draft of this book and to share his many insights and helpful suggestions with me. Thanks also to the *Journal of American Drama and Theatre* for permitting us to reprint Katherine Burkman's article and to *American Drama* for Albert Wertheim's.

Introduction

Kimball King

Recently John Gregory Dunne published an account of screen writing with the provocative title, *Monster: Living off the Big Screen*. In it Dunne chronicles the tragic-comic assignment of Dunne and his wife, Joan Didion, to write a script depicting the life of the late TV network correspondent, Jessica Savitch. Although in real life Savitch was a controversial journalist who died young in a tragic auto accident, her story was transformed by Hollywood into a love story with Robert Redford and Michelle Pfeiffer, called "Up Front and Personal." Dunne and Didion wrote twenty-seven versions, collaborated with two more screenwriters and negotiated four new contracts with the studio before completing a final version which bore virtually no resemblance to the true Jessica Savitch story but which had followed studio directives to "keep it light," "keep the fun level up" and to "deliver the moment" (*NY Times Book Review*, March 2, 1997,8).

Dunne's account of the eight-year creation of a financially successful film, which was essentially a mindless star-vehicle, reveals a philistinism in Hollywood that almost defies satire. Yet from the early days of the movies, writers for the stage have, in fact, depicted Hollywood as a cultural desert and have demonstrated that industry profits, generally dependent on the popularity of a film rather than on its artistic merits, repeatedly alter scripts and pander to the lowest level of public taste. As early as 1931 John Van Druten in *Hollywood Holiday* described the absurd transformation of the biblical Jezebel story into a tale of Balkan royalty's excesses, to an epic about life in Antarctica, and finally to an exotic Moroccan romance. In his play Van Druten cleverly shows how ordinary people escaped their boring daily existences by succumbing to the glamour of Hollywood fantasies and celebrityhood. His unlikely heroine, an English spinster named Gladys Pinnet, who was once governess to the tempestuous film star, Hedda Maelstrom, is called to Hollywood by Hedda's director in hopes that she may instill some discipline in her former pupil. Gladys, who already shares her copy of *Screen Fun* magazine with the other tenants in a boardinghouse, enjoys her visit to America but preserves her innocence in the face of studio immorality and greed. Ultimately she forsakes the glamorous life and returns to England, uncorrupted except for a vocabulary of Hollywood slang expressions, which impress her old friends as a tangible sign of her encounter with the rich and famous.

A year earlier George S. Kaufman had collaborated with Moss Hart on *Once in a Lifetime*, still frequently performed as a classic comedy about life in Hollywood. Kaufman (who also wrote another satire of Hollywood, *Merton of the Movies*, in 1922 with Marc Connelly) and Hart focus on three out-of-work vaudevillians: Jerry, his girlfriend, Mary, and her friend, George. While the former pass themselves off as elocution experts, George becomes a movie director. He and his dim-witted girlfriend, Susan, shoot the wrong script and make a travesty of a film. However, critics proclaim George a daring and innovative director and he is consequently able to use his new-found influence to secure permanent jobs for his two old friends.

In the same "All's Well that Ends Well" vein, Bella and Samuel Spewack in 1935 wrote *Boy Meets Girl*, a gentle, witty, happy-ever-after satire of big studio machinations. Two screenwriters, J. Carlyle Benson and Robert Law, are in danger of losing their jobs; but when Susie, an unwed studio waitress, gives birth to a boy named Happy, the writers decide to feature the baby in a series of B-pictures with a has-been cowboy actor and borderline alcoholic, Larry Toms. Benson and Law, who are each described separately by the Spewacks as "a damned nice guy" (*Boy Meets Girl*, 11–12) are also genuinely intelligent and creative artists. They are seriously undervalued by the studio's producer, C. Elliott Friday, who is good-natured but pretentious and who claims to prefer Proust to Kipling—even as stage directions point to the uncut leaves of his copy of *Swann's Way*. Another time he sends Pirandello a letter, asking if he has any old material in his file drawer.

The Hollywood mogul's affectation of cultural superiority is endemic to a movie colony where feigned intellectual prowess is a badge of success. There are no vicious characters in *Boy Meets Girl*, and the vain and hypocritical ones are thwarted by the talented (Benson and Law) or the large-hearted (Susie). Using the gambit of a fake cablegram offering to buy the studio for five million dollars, Benson and Law consolidate their own positions in the industry, while Susie, in a real-life situation that mirrors the preposterous plots of film scripts, marries a stage extra who turns out to be an English aristocrat. Certainly the fragile artifice of Hollywood and the gullibility of movie audiences are scrutinized in this play, but the overall cheerfulness of the vehicle and its just resolution of personal difficulties make it a document of film land's "happy period" on the stage.

Following a series of successful comedies about Hollywood in the 1920s and 1930s, some of the same playwrights attempted to project the image of a zany but lovable Hollywood in the 1940s. George S. Kaufman, who had been so successful in *Once in a Lifetime*, chose Gilbert and Sullivan's famous *H.M.S. Pinafore* (1878) as the basis for his own *Hollywood Pinafore*. It opened on May 31, 1945, at New York's Alvin Theatre. This time Joseph Porter is no longer depicted as Admiral but has become a movie producer and Mike Corcoran is no longer a ship's captain but a movie director. His daughter has been transformed into a movie star in love with a lowly writer. The show only ran for 52 performances and more than half of the reviewers criticized the play severely. Citing *Hollywood Pinafore* as proof of Kaufman's declining writing skills, Steven Suskin argued that Kaufman's "two decades of comedic brilliance were over by World War II" (Suskin 316). Undeterred by audience rejection of Hollywood comedies, Broadway playwrights continued to exploit the genre. A generation later, Jerry Herman's *Mack and Mabel*, which recreated the era of Mack Sennet and Mabel Norman in musical form, fared much better, but Hollywood in the 1920s was Herman's nostalgic subject; he did not attempt to sentimentalize the cinematic milieu of his own generation.

Two major works, one in 1949 and another in 1959, made peripheral use of the Hollywood experience in challenging ways. T.S. Eliot's *The Cocktail Party* attempted to examine various approaches to spiritual salvation in a witty comedy of manners. One of the minor characters, Peter, is encouraged by Julia, ostensibly a casual acquaintance, but, on the spiritual level a "guardian" of his soul, to travel to Hollywood to make motion pictures. The play's suggestion is that in Los Angeles Peter will at last fulfill not only his earthy desires but also God's purposes. An audience responsive to this complicated but intriguing play would doubtless focus on the importance of the marriage of Edward and Lavinia or the martyrdom of Celia. But it is important to note that Peter is not dispatched to Hollywood out of plot necessity, but gravitates to it as a means of leading a useful and committed life. A decade later Tennessee Williams makes Hollywood an unseen force in *Sweet Bird of Youth*. The film actress, Princess, though loathe to relinquish her stardom, is fleeing from merciless camera close-ups. Her younger lover, Chance, is hopeful that his relationship with Princess will lead to his discovery by a talent scout. Ironically, Princess is lured back to Hollywood, while Chance's manhood and his dream of a movie career are gruesomely destroyed. By the late 1950s Williams grasped the darker truths of the movie-making world. One of the few dramatists whose plays were repeatedly made into successful films, Williams may have chosen deliberately not to condemn a community that was making him rich. Yet *Sweet Bird of Youth* exposes the perversities of Hollywood's influence on American life.

In the 1960s Claude Van Italie in his "Doris" plays, *Almost Like Being* (1968) and *I'm Really Here* (1965) (both of which were directed by Joseph Chaiken), poked rather savage fun at Doris Day fantasy movies. In the first of the "Doris" plays, Doris often addresses an unseen camera instead of the other actors during stage conversation. Furthermore, Doris has a "hurt mask" and a "cute mask" that are intended to be substitutes for genuine emotional reactions. Her "ideal lover" is mockingly named Rosanno Brassy (after Rosanno Brazzi). All the actors distort their facial muscles into artificial smiles at the conclusion of each scene. The second "Doris" play is even more horrifying; Doris is stabbed to death, bringing a totally incongruous note of violence to what had started out as harmless fun.

Four years later in 1969, Woody Allen's *Play It Again, Sam* featured Allen himself in his only Broadway appearance as a mousy film critic named Allen Felix. Deserted by his wife, Felix subsists on undefrosted TV dinners and memories of old films. Eventually he comes to believe that the spirit of Humphrey Bogart is his mentor, and circumstances in his personal life begin to merge with plot sequences in the movie *Casablanca*. More a commentary on the modern anti-hero than on the pernicious influence of movies, the conflict between the ordinary person's humdrum existence and the seductiveness of Hollywood's myths is inescapable in *Play It Again, Sam*. Blending the cynical comedy of Van Druten with Woody Allen's antic parody, Christopher Durang in 1976 wrote the *History of American Film* for the stage. Nominated for a Tony award, the play surveyed American perceptions of Hollywood from 1930 to the present, as a means of revealing the interests and obsessions of the American people during the same period. Covering two hundred movies, the play examined major Hollywood stereotypes: the gangster type (Jimmy Cagney), the innocent (Loretta Young), the sincere guy, the temptress, and the girl who never gets her man. Durang, who is an excellent parodist (at a recent Tennessee Williams festival, he presented an affectionate but entertaining satire of Williams's *The Glass Menagerie*), makes sport of the *Grapes of Wrath*, *Citizen Kane* and *Casablanca*. In an hilarious scene a group of showgirls dressed up as vegetables cavort in a big production number called "We're in a Salad." In another scene a character resembling (and named) Bette Davis refuses to smoke a cigarette, leaving Paul Henreid smoking two at a time. The black and white props in the play remind audiences of the impact which color film brought to the movie industry.

Following Durang in the 1980s and into the 1990s are a series of Hollywood plays by major contemporary dramatists: David Mamet, Sam Shepard, David Rabe, Arthur Kopit and Christopher Hampton, to name only a few. A substantial portion of this book is devoted to the way in which these authors deconstruct Hollywood myths and reveal painful social and psychological issues in American life. Most of the works which use Los Angeles as their primary setting could almost be classified as anti-Hollywood plays. One of the purposes of this volume is to show how audiences of films and stage plays began to reevaluate the Hollywood experience in hopes, perhaps, of understanding themselves and their culture.

The first stage play about Hollywood discussed at length in this book is *Merton of the Movies*, based on a 1922 novel by Harry Leon Wilson and adapted for the stage by George S. Kaufman and Marc Connelly the same year. *Merton*, although it followed another famous and successful Hollywood play, *Once in a Lifetime*, also by Kaufman, is considered to be the finest example of a satirical but largely positive view of Hollywood culture. William Hutchings, Professor of English at the University of Alabama at Birmingham, reveals the complexities and contradictions of the playwright's vision as well as accounting for the play's widespread acceptance and success. Hutchings has also edited *David Storey: A Casebook* for Garland in 1992 and has published *The Plays of David Storey: A Thematic Study* for Southern Illinois University Press in 1988.

Like Hutchings, Robert Gross is also an editor for Garland's *Casebooks on Modern Drama*. His volume on Christopher Hampton was published in 1990. Director of Theatre and Professor of English and Comparative Literature at Hobart William Smith Colleges, he is also the author of *Words Heard and Overheard: The Main Text in Contemporary Drama,* published by Garland Publishing, 1990, and *S. N. Behrman: A Research and Production Sourcebook,* Greenwood Press, 1992. Gross reveals in his essay that Behrman's vision of Hollywood is deeply ambivalent, that he values it as a place for people fleeing their pasts but worries that the price for its protection is the individual's loss of identity. Behrman's Jewishness and homoerotic subtexts are examined in detail.

With Albert Wertheim's article, in Odets's *The Big Knife* Broadway's demonization of Hollywood begins full scale. In what Wertheim describes as an almost suicidal act, in terms of his career, Odets sets up a comparison of the commercially debased art of Hollywood and the higher, purer art of the theatre. Professor of English at Indiana University, Wertheim has published many articles and books on contemporary drama and was one of the four original panelists at the Modern Language Association's December 1995 session "Hollywood on Stage."

Like Wertheim, Stephen Watt is also Professor of English at Indiana University and the moderator of the same 1995 panel on stage plays about Hollywood. Author of *Joyce, O'Casey and the Irish Popular Theatre* (Syracuse University Press, 1993), Watt has recently completed a manuscript on post-modern drama. In this volume he has constructed a densely allusive article which relates all the major living playwrights who have used Hollywood as a setting with their forebears in the theatre. He examines the breakdown of the stereotype of "low art" vs. "high art" in Hollywood and Broadway respectively as well as the misguided gender assumptions which affect contemporary culture so destructively.

Marcia Blumberg's article covers similar ground but focuses on Brad Fraser's compelling drama *Poor Super Man* (1994), which deconstructs the gender categories epitomized by the work of David Mamet and other modern playwrights. Blumberg is a Research Fellow at the Open University in England, supported by the Social Sciences and Humanities Research Council of Canada. She is collaborating with Dennis Walder on a book about the arts and AIDS in Africa; many of her publications in periodicals have dealt with similar issues. Like Wertheim, Blumberg was also a panelist on the 1995 "Hollywood" program in Chicago.

Following up on David Mamet's powerful exposé of Hollywood in his stage plays, Toby Silverman Zinman has written "So Dis Is Hollywood: Mamet in Hell." Zinman has produced two Casebooks for the Garland series, one on David Rabe in 1991 and the other on Terrence McNally in 1997.

Another two-Casebook author is Leslie Kane whose collection of essays on David Mamet was published in 1992, and her edition devoted totally to Mamet's *Glengarry Glen Ross* appeared in 1996. As president of the David Mamet Society, she brings a special authority to her analysis of Mamet's *Speed-the-Plow*.

Speed-the-Plow is compared to Sam Shepard's *True West* in Katherine Burkman's examination of the Hollywood-on-stage phenomenon. Long known for her studies of myth and its relationship to drama, Burkman is Professor Emeritus of English at the Ohio State University. Her books include *The Dramatic World of Harold Pinter: Its Basis in Ritual*, published by Ohio State University Press in 1971, and *The Arrival of Godot: Ritual Patterns in Modern Drama,* published in 1986 by Fairleigh Dickinson Press. She was co-editor with John Keindert-Gibbs of *Pinter at Sixty* and for Garland, she published *Simon Gray: A Casebook*. She traces various myths of Western experience that unite two very important Hollywood plays.

Robert LaVelle, visiting lecturer of Comparative Literature at the University of Seville, Spain, has also written an essay comparing Sam Shepard with another author, this time the novelist Henry James. His intention is to set two texts against each other which have different relationships to America's cultural history but are equally concerned with centering an individual in the context of American life.

Following LaVelle, Todd Lidh, a graduate student and teaching assistant at the University of North Carolina, has chosen Arthur Kopit's *Road to Nirvana* as a play which uses the picture of a corrupt, venal Hollywood as a metaphor for contemporary society. Lidh had the full cooperation of Arthur Kopit, who allowed him to see revisions he had made to the original play when it appeared in Europe in the summer of 1997. Kopit graciously visited the University in the Fall of 1997 and explained the origin and purposes of his own version of the Hollywood story.

While this volume has concentrated on English-speaking artists' reactions to film land, *Strindberg in Hollywood*, written by American Drury Pifer, at least fantasizes what a foreign-born playwright like the late August Strindberg would have thought of Hollywood. Pifer, anachronistically placing the Scandinavian playwright in Los Angeles, creates a timely satire of art debased by greed. William Kerwin, Professor of English at the University of Missouri, is actually a Renaissance specialist but agreed to do an essay on the Pifer play. He also edited a Casebook on Irish playwright Brian Friel, published in the spring of 1997.

Next, in "*The Last Tycoon:* Eliza Kazan's and Harold Pinter's Unsentimental Hollywood Romance," Christopher Hudgins has provided a detailed study of Harold Pinter's screenplay of *The Last Tycoon*. An adaptation of F. Scott Fitzgerald's last novel, *The Last Tycoon* is based in large part on the life of Irving Thalberg, an astute businessman and yet an artist in what was still the golden age of Hollywood. Hudgins's astute analysis is based on extensive research on the final screenplay and also on earlier drafts made available to him by playwright and screenwriter Pinter. An amalgam of the Englishman Pinter's and the American Fitzgerald's views of Hollywood, the film of *The Last Tycoon* reveals aspects of a society stage productions have often overlooked. Pinter's compatriot, Christopher Hampton also brings an English perspective to his analysis of Hollywood. My own essay explores Hampton's contribution to the topic of this volume in two plays, *Exiles in Hollywood* (1982) and *Sunset Boulevard* (1994), this time working with English musician Andrew Lloyd Webber.

The majority of essays in this volume mentioned so far have been devoted to relatively famous, mainstream playwrights who have also had their share of success in Hollywood. In the final three essays, attention has been directed to Hollywood as experienced by African American artists, gay writers and feminists, such as the author of *Etta Jenks*.

Barnsley Brown, an assistant professor at Wake Forest University, has provided insights into the Hollywood plays of Adrienne Kennedy, who has depicted the ways in which Hollywood has exploited African Americans. Although the cinema world has been hostile to black Americans, gay Americans have regarded movie culture quite differently. Robert Gross has always been aware that gay playwrights like Charles Ludlam or Charles Busch view Hollywood more positively than heterosexual playwrights. Together he and I have shared our insights into this particular genre of Hollywood plays. Finally, Leslie Frost, a Teaching Fellow at the University of North Carolina, who is currently involved in a history and analysis of the Federal Arts Project, has broached the issue of pornography in Hollywood. An organizer of a recent conference on feminist issues (Feminist Negotiations: Mergers and Takeovers), Frost is well qualified to contrast feminist attitudes toward pornography.

All of the other contributors to this volume and I have come to realize that the subject "Hollywood on Stage" is more vast and complicated than we had ever imagined. Individual authors and plays briefly mentioned or not at all in the volume deserve further exploration. No one understands fully what Hollywood represents to Americans or to the rest of the world. Assessments by those who write primarily for the stage may be biased, defensive or inadequate. Nevertheless, the legitimate stage has been curious about the movie-making establishment from its beginnings in this century. It has been and remains a watchdog and constant critic of what is possibly the world's most powerful cultural phenomenon.

WORKS CITED

Suskin, Steven. *Opening Night On Broadway: A Critical Quotebook of The Golden Era of The Musical Theatre, Oklahoma! (1943) To Fiddler on the Roof (1964).* Foreword by Carol Channing. New York: Schirmer Books, 1990.

HOLLYWOOD ON STAGE

"Engaged in the Art of Photodrama": *Merton of the Movies*

William Hutchings

When, in 1935, Gertrude Stein was touring California, she was asked by her host in Monterey what celebrities she would like to meet. As she recorded in *Everybody's Autobiography*,

> any celebrity can choose whom he wants to meet and that is a pleasure and he mentioned several and I said no, no, but I had heard that one was there that to me would be a pleasure and that was the author of Merton of the Movies about the best description of America that has ever been done. (287)

That author—though now largely forgotten—was Harry Leon Wilson, a best-selling novelist of the day as well as a favorite (and frequent) contributor of short stories to *The Saturday Evening Post*. *Merton of the Movies*, which Stein also praised as "the best book about twentieth-century American youth that has yet been done" (288), had been published in 1922 and was adapted for the stage by George S. Kaufman and Marc Connelly the same year, opening on November 13 at the Cort Theatre in New York City and quickly establishing itself as Broadway's biggest comedy hit of the year. It is the first American novel to depict the world of Hollywood and the still-new commercial art of movie-making—and it was also the first to earn its author a fortune—$100,000—for the motion-picture rights (Leutrat 20). The film, directed by James Cruze and released in 1924, starred Glenn Hunter, who had created the title role on Broadway; it was remade in 1932 under the title *Make Me a Star* and again in 1947 under its original title (but from a new script by George Wells and Lou Breslow) as a vehicle for Red Skelton. Wilson's protagonist—Merton Gill, a clerk in a small-town general store who goes to Hollywood to become a star—is a classically American character type, no less readily recognizable than Jay Gatsby and Nick Carraway would become when *The Great Gatsby* was published in 1925. In adapting the book for the stage, Kaufman and Connelly remained faithful to the outline of the novel's farcical plot but made it not only a more topical satire but also a gentler, less physical comedy than it was heretofore.

As a dry-goods clerk at Gashweiler's General Store in Simsbury, Illinois, young Merton Gill lives for—and through—the movies, which show him a world far wider than his counterparts only a few decades earlier could ever have seen. With typically adolescent disdain for the domestic mundane that surrounds him, he reads assiduously the fanzines that glamorize Hollywood and its stars; adopting the stage-name of Clifford Armytage, he secretly acts out scenes with the store's mannequins, poses for photographs in elaborate costumes, and completes a correspondence course in acting from a school in Stebbinsville, Kansas. Mustering as much Luck and Pluck as any Horatio Alger hero had a generation or two before, the young man went West—as Horace Greeley (and, earlier, John Babsone Lane Soule) had urged. Having a carefully-saved two hundred seventy dollars in his pocket and a train ticket in his hand, Merton heads to Hollywood in search of Fame and Fortune, as countless thousands like him have done before and since. Once there, however, a harsh reality sets in: three weeks are spent standing outside the studio gates, then days pass by as he waits inside the casting office, where he is repeatedly told there are no opportunities today as his funds dwindle away. Enamored of screen star Beulah Baxter, he wants to work only at the studio that employs her—and perhaps someday to act in one of her pictures; however, he disdains the slapstick comedies that do not "uplift the screen art" (Kaufman and Connelly 70), even if they might provide him a job.

Befriended by an actress known as the Montague Girl, Merton eventually lands a one-day job as an extra, where he overplays his part, annoys the director, and gets fired. Sleeping secretly on the movie lot when he runs out of money, going without food for several days, Merton wends his way onto the set of Beulah Baxter's current film, meets her briefly, and is astonished to learn that the Montague girl is her stunt double. His disillusionment is acute: his screen idol is married (to her fourth husband, the director) and—despite what he read in the magazines—she has not performed the feats of derring-do that he so admired. When the Montague girl notices Merton's resemblance to leading man Harold Parmalee, she convinces the director of the Buckeye comedies that Merton so despises to cast him in a parody of Parmalee's films—without ever allowing the young actor to realize that he is starring in a comedy. With an earnestness matched only by his innocence, Merton becomes the unwitting star of a hit farce—as he is shocked and humiliated to learn at its premiere. He overcomes his initial outrage at the director and the Montague girl, is offered (and declines) a far higher salary from a rival studio, reconciles himself to his success, grants an interview to one of the fan magazines, and plans to marry the Montague girl as the play ends.

In adapting Wilson's novel for the stage, Kaufman and Connelly constructed a four-act play containing a total of six scenes, each of which requires a separate set: the rear of Gashweiler's general store; the waiting-room outside the casting office of the Holden Studios lot in Hollywood; a movie stage on the Holden lot, where Merton gets his first job as an extra; a second part of the studio stage, containing a boat floating in a glassed-in tank of water; the office of comedy director Jeff Baird; and the living room of Mrs. Patterson's boarding house, where Merton is a lodger. The most technically daunting of these is, of course, the boat scene—in which, on stage and in full view of the audience, the Montague girl, as a double for Beulah Baxter, escapes from a gun-firing villain by seizing a rope from the boat's riggings, swinging out over the water, and plunging into the waves during a rainstorm. After observing this scene as a bystander, Merton realizes for the first time that his screen idol does not perform her own stunts—a crucial moment in his disillusionment, although in most productions (unlike the original Broadway one) the cliffhanger escape from the boat necessarily takes place entirely offstage.

Since so much of the humor of Wilson's novel involves the ineptitude of Merton's acting and the elaborate deceptions through which he is made the star of two comedies, it is surprising that the theatre audience sees none of Merton's actual acting apart from the scene in which he is an extra—unable to master the simple act of descending a staircase, picking up a book from a table, and noticing its title. This evening-dress scene, part of a high-society adaptation of *Robinson Crusoe*, is an invention of Kaufman and Connelly; in the novel, Merton fares somewhat better as an extra, playing an utterly jaded urban sophisticate in a film titled *The Blight of Broadway* and being given several close-ups by its director. The cleverly inventive ruses through which Merton acts his way through two farces without ever realizing he is in even one are almost entirely omitted in the play, referred to only relatively briefly in Act IV, scene i, the shortest of the play's six scenes. Although the theatre audience sees Merton enter in an elaborate western outfit of chaps, sombrero, and spurs, only two sequences from the movie are described: in one, Merton shoots a villain by aiming at the bad guy's reflection in a mirror; in the other, he wears such outlandishly oversized spurs that it is impossible for him to walk upright for long. The novel, however, includes scene after scene travestying the already long-familiar conventions of the genre: the card game that turns into a saloon-smashing brawl; the hero's leap from a second-story window onto his horse's back; the doting gray-haired mother who is perennially mopping (on the ranch, in the town saloon, on a rock in the desert). Even when blatant anachronisms and conventions from other genres are incongruously added in, Merton never has doubts for long:

> If at times he was vaguely disquieted by a suspicion that the piece was not wholly serious, he had only to remember the intense seriousness of his own part and the always serious manner of Baird in directing his actors. And indeed there were but few moments when he was even faintly pricked by this suspicion. It seemed a bit incongruous that Hoffmeyer, the delicatessen merchant, should arrive on a bicycle, dressed in cowboy attire save for a badly dented derby hat, and carrying a bag of golf clubs. . . . But Baird explained carefully that the old man . . . was demented, like the poor old [endlessly mopping] mother who had gone over the hills after her children had left the home nest.
>
> . . . There was the tense moment when a faithful cowboy broke upon the festivities with word that a New York detective was coming to search for the man who had robbed the Hoffmeyer establishment. . . .
>
> The detective was the cross-eyed man, himself now disguised as Sherlock Holmes, with a fore-and-aft cloth cap and drooping blond mustache. (Wilson 236–237)

Whereas theatergoers have only a general impression of the film in which Merton stars, readers of the novel "see" it virtually scene by scene.

As inept and inexperienced in his love scenes as he is in the rest of the action, Merton Gill is one in a series of uniquely American comic figures: the all-American Innocent, good-hearted but hopelessly naive, genial and earnest but prey to the worldly-wise. As one of the latter, the Montague Girl has a surprisingly complex and difficult role: she is, on the one hand, Merton's best friend and his eventual romantic interest, thus doubling for his screen idol Beulah Baxter in real life as in the movies; she is also his foremost promoter in the business, helping him secure his first job as an extra and teaching him the basics of his new profession. Moreover, she becomes literally his protector and nurturer, a virtual Angel of the Backlot, rescuing him from his desperate hunger and his stowaway status on the set: she provides him money, food, and endless encouragement—and even refers to herself repeatedly as "Mother" in the final scene as he *"falls into her arms, sobbing"* with shame in his initial humiliation over the ludicrousness of his film debut (Kaufman and Connelly 93). The scene's maternal imagery is even more detailed in the novel:

> Quickly he knelt beside her while the mothering arms enfolded him. A hand pulled his head to her breast and held it there. Thus she rocked gently, the hand gliding up to smooth his hair. Without words she cherished him thus a long time. The gentle rocking back and forth continued.
>
>   . . .
>
> "There, there, there!" she whispered. "It's all right, everything's all right. Your mother's got you right here and she ain't ever going to let you go—never going to let you go."
>
> She was patting his head in rhythm with her rocking as she snuggled and soothed him. . . . Then she began to croon a song above him as she rocked, though the lyric was plainly an improvisation.
>
> "Did he have his poor old mother going for a minute? Yes he did. . . . But oh, he won't ever fool her very long, very long, because he can't fool his dear old mother very long, very long: and he can bet on that . . ." (324; cf. Kaufman and Connelly 93)

"Dear old mother" the romantic lead has, of course, been able to fool *him* for quite a while, since she devised and instigated the entire deception that eventually makes her man-child a star, enabling him to fulfill his ambitions in ways that he would never have wanted or accepted. Overcoming the fact that "[she] said [she]'d always been afraid of men" (Wilson 298), she readily becomes Mrs. Merton Gill, bringing the action of the play (and novel) to the traditional close for a comedy—even if the audience is apparently presumed to be untroubled by the unmistakably Oedipal implications of the imagery.

The films in which Merton Gill appears would have been readily recognizable to moviegoers of the 1920s: Jeff Baird's Buckeye Comedies, the knockabout farces that Merton so disdains, are clearly based on Mack Sennett's Keystone comedies; Bert Chester, the cross-

eyed comedian whose slapstick antics Merton considers especially low
(and whose co-star he eventually becomes), is the fictional counterpart
of Sennett favorite Ben Turpin, whose eyes were reportedly insured
against ever becoming uncrossed (Bergan 92). Though Sennett is now
remembered primarily as the creator of the knockabout Keystone Kops,
he also created a number of "parody" films like *Teddy at the Throttle*
(with Gloria Swanson and Wallace Beery), *A Small Town Idol* (with
Ben Turpin), and *Her Torpedoed Love* (with Louise Fadenza), which
lampooned the popular melodramas and other genres of the day in
much the same way the films that Merton stars in do. Indeed, as Walter
Kerr has observed in *The Silent Clowns*, "it is often difficult to tell . . .
just when comedy is intended and just when the presumably parodied
melodrama is actually being played straight" (68). Wilson's clever
variation on this theme, of course, is that it is impossible for Merton to
tell that any comedy is intended, though it is unmistakably clear to
everyone else.

If Jeff Baird is based on Mack Sennett, then the Montague Girl is
the fictional counterpart of Mabel Normand, whose movie *The Diving
Girl* (1911) was the first film that Sennett directed. The first
advertisement for the Keystone Company (1912) referred to her as "the
beautiful diving Venus" in a film titled *The Water Nymph* (quoted in
Slide 150); the on-stage dive in Kaufman's and Connelly's adaptation
clearly echoes such films. Unlike more traditionally "feminine" film
heroines (and more serious dramatic actresses) like "America's
Sweetheart" Mary Pickford and sisters Dorothy and Lillian Gish, Mabel
Normand defied the conventional gender roles given women in her day.
As Gene Fowler observed in his biography of Mack Sennett, Mabel
Normand

> could swim, dive, ride, shoot, and played only with boys. Girls were
> too frail; they bored her. . . . She was an arrant tomboy and a jokester
> unable to excuse dignity. . . . Possibly she was an authentic genius.
> Perhaps Isadora Duncan was the only other woman of [her] time to
> possess beauty, charm, ability, soul and courage the equal of Mabel's.
> (Fowler 81–83)

Even so, as David Thompson has remarked, "she was one of the first
proofs that a good-looking girl could succeed in the movies without any
special pretense to acting" (441). Her close relationship with Sennett,
which reportedly included plans of marriage that were disrupted by her
jealousy over Sennett's attentions to Mae Busch (Slide 147), may help

to explain the otherwise surprising degree of familiarity that enables the Montague Girl to suggest plot lines to Baird and to bring Merton to the director's attention during a visit to his office—a scene that might seem implausible for a stunt double and an extra in his films. While at Keystone, Mabel Normand had, in fact, made just such a discovery in bringing Helen Holmes to the attention of J. P. MacGowan, who was so impressed with her screenplay *The Girl at the Switch* that he filmed it with her in the lead role (Slide 161–162).

While such success stories were part of the legend that drew the likes of Merton Gill to Hollywood, specific movies and series are also deftly parodied throughout the novel and play. Among the most prominent of these are the (melo)dramatic serials that were quite popular with moviegoers throughout the previous decade. With their always alliterative titles and perpetually endangered heroines, the best known of these multi-part cliff-hangers were *The Perils of Pauline* (in twenty episodes) and *The Exploits of Elaine* (in thirty-six), both of which starred Pearl White and were released in 1914; White's final serial, *Plunder*, was released in 1922, the same year that *Merton of the Movies* was published. However, the novel's serial, *The Hazards of Hortense*, starring Merton's idolized Beulah Baxter, is probably based on *The Hazards of Helen*, produced from 1914 to 1916 by the Kalem Company in 119 thrill-packed episodes that starred Helen Holmes, who was succeeded in the role by Helen Gibson as well as, at times, other actresses—like the Montague Girl in the novel—when the stars "were unavailable due to illness or the like" (Slide 164). The Montague Girl's stunts—described in the novel as having "to climb down ten stories of a hotel elevator cable, and ride a brake-beam and be pushed off a cliff and thrown to the lions, and a few other little things" (79)—are typical of the serials' ever-wilder feats of derring-do. The novel also contains an extensive parody of Rudolph Valentino's *The Sheik* (130–136), which had been enormously popular since its opening in 1921; Sennett's own travesty of it, *The Sheik of Araby*, was filmed the following year and starred Ben Turpin, though its release was delayed until 1923.

Whereas Wilson avoids naming actual actors and referring to specific events in Hollywood, Kaufman and Connelly added references to western star William S. Hart (8) and to "the world-famous authors who go out there[:] Rex Beach, Elinor Glyn, Maeterlinck and Rupert Hughes" (15). The original stage production was also much more topical in reference to censorship and to Will Hays (29), head of the film industry's newly instituted "self-regulating" body, the Motion

Picture Producers and Distributors of America, which had been created in 1922 amid a number of scandals that had made Hollywood seem much more debauched and sinister than it ever appears in Wilson's novel. Hays, formerly Postmaster General under President Warren Harding, sought to assure the public that films would offer only wholesome and totally inoffensive family entertainment. Kaufman and Connelly's most explicit riposte came at the end of *Merton of the Movies* when, as the reviewer for *The New York Times* indicated, they added

> . . . at least one new [satiric] stab that Mr. Wilson overlooked, and it is as good as anything he did. At the end of the play a former Secretary of Agriculture, who is now the head of the picture industry, comes in and makes speech or speeches [sic]! He is something to hear! (Corbin)

Although no such character appears in the text that is currently available from Samuel French, the scene is included in the excerpts from the original version of the play that was published in *The Best Plays of 1922–23* and the *Year Book of the Drama in America* (1923).

Suddenly, a Mr. John Wheaton, "who has been wandering mysteriously about the studios of Hollywood for several days," is introduced by the Montague Girl as the "former Secretary of Agriculture, now head of the Motion Picture Industry"; he tells Merton that "it's men like you that the motion pictures need" and solicits his help so that "motion pictures are to be put upon a higher plane" (Mantle 301–302). Such a proposition has always appealed to Merton, and—despite his inadvertent success in the "low" comedies he disdains—he finds an immediate ally in America's foremost censor. That Wheaton would "like to hear [Merton's] ideas" is the scene's ultimate joke: an imminent meeting of the minds between one naive, sanctimonious, humorless, hopelessly provincial, earnest but inept idealist and another. Clearly, Merton was—and still is—"so innocent he doesn't know a close-up from a censor" (Kaufman and Connelly 77); insofar as he is concerned about censorship in Wilson's novel, he would direct it toward Buckeye comedies (as affronts against his notions of cinematic artistry) rather than what a friend of his describes as excised "scenes of dignified passion like they did in Scarlet Sin" (Wilson 20). If he and Wheaton become allies, they can no doubt try to suppress both laughter and passion, but such an enterprise would seem to be ultimately as futile as the *other* form of prohibition attempted by the all-American killjoys at the time. With someone as gullible as Merton in charge, the audience can laugh at the pretensions of the censors, thus subverting— as comedy has always done—the sanctimoniousness of those in power, ominous though they might otherwise be. In fact, however, Will Hays remained in office until his retirement in 1945, and the so-called Hays Code (formulated in 1930) was not seriously challenged until the mid–1950s and after.

The scene that Kaufman and Connelly substituted for Mr. Wheaton's brings about a surprising reconciliation between the generations. Quite unexpectedly (and quite implausibly), Mr. Gashweiler, the store owner from Simsbury, happens to be passing through Hollywood on vacation and sees Merton's movie at its premiere; the following morning he visits the new celebrity and announces that his home town is "goin' to honor her illustrious son the way he ought to be honored . . . [with] a brass plate made for the front of the store" (Kaufman and Connelly 90). Merton is thus restored to and reconciled with the community from which he has been separated, but whose values he has never left. Equally importantly, however, Gashweiler—who has been, in effect, Merton's surrogate father— admits that he "never knowed what [he] was talkin' about when [he] said you hadn't ought every [sic] try to get into the movies" (Kaufman 89). With the generations thus reconciled and the comic hero's triumph over adversity confirmed, he is ready to marry the Montague girl, providing a traditional ending for the comedy. No such reappearance of Gashweiler appears in Wilson's novel, though it too ends with the announcement of plans for the marriage.

Hollywood's legendary (mis)treatment of literary works is deftly satirized in both the novel and the play. Plans for a screen adaptation of *Robinson Crusoe* involve characters and situations that Daniel Defoe never imagined:

> The way we work it is this. . . . Friday has a sister, see—only she can't be his real sister because she's white. . . . We'll work it out later. She's the daughter of an English Earl that was wrecked near the Island, and Friday's mother brought her up as her own child. She's saved the papers that came ashore and she has the Earl's coat-of-arms tatooed [sic] on her shoulder blade. . . . [F]inally, after Robinson Crusoe has fallen in love with her, along comes the old Earl, her father, in a ship that rescues them all. (Kaufman and Connelly 35; cf. Wilson 112)

The motive behind such alterations was exactly the same then—censors and the Hays office notwithstanding—as it is today: "In that way," the director remarks, "we can get the sex into it" (Kaufman and Connelly 35). This line is Kaufman's, not Wilson's; it would have been too racy, presumably, for readers of *The Saturday Evening Post* but not for the Broadway stage. In the novel, however, still further changes are made in *Robinson Crusoe*: though it begins as a "good, clean, censor-proof picture," it is soon transposed into the twentieth century, turning Robinson Crusoe into "a rich young New Yorker" whose comic valet is "one of these stiff English lads, never been wrecked on an island before and complains all the time about the lack of conveniences" (113). When objections arise that "you got a story there, but it won't be Robinson Crusoe" after such extensive changes (and more) are made, the solution is vintage Hollywood:

> "Call it Robinson Crusoe, Junior! . . . We get the value of the name and do the story the way we want it, . . . in evening dress and everything. Can't you see it? If that story wouldn't gross big then I don't know a story."(113)

While Wilson may well have had such concerns about the adaptation of his own novel for the stage and subsequently for the screen, he was in fact well pleased with Kaufman's and Connelly's work—and autographed a copy of the script for producer George S. Tyler, noting that "I wrote the book, but you people did the play. I merely bought a cheap lot and sold out at an enormous profit after the town grew—me sitting around playing checkers while it was growing" (Meredith 111).

Ridiculous as the produced scripts are, those of Wilson's would-be script-writers manage to surpass them in outrageousness. Even the Montague Girl has a project under development, which she tries to sell to a director:

> I'm this Hawaiian princess and my father, Old King Mauna Loa, dies and leaves me two thousand volcanoes and a billiard cue. . . . And every morning I have to go out and ram it down the volcanoes to see if they're all right. . . . The *villain* is very wealthy, and owns one of the largest ukulele plantations on the island . . . (Kaufman and Connelly 33)

Told that her story is "Absurd, absurd!," she replies that "no one ever listens to you until you break into the magazines" (Kaufman and

Connelly 33) of the kind that Merton used to read back in Simsbury. There too aspirations for screenwriting flourish as heartily as Merton's ambitions to become a star: his friend and confidante Tessie Kearns, a mild-mannered dressmaker and milliner by day, churns out scenarios with lurid titles like "Passion's Perils," all of which are promptly returned, rejected, by the studios to which they are sent (Kaufman and Connelly 16; cf. Wilson 18–19). Yet when, in the revised ending of the play, Gashweiler tells Merton that Tessie is considering coming to Hollywood herself as they had once discussed (15), Merton demurs, explaining that

> It's a pretty stiff game, the movies. You've got to have a certain amount of what they call hokum to get your scenarios over. Tessie's an awfully nice girl and all that, but I don't think she could get away with it. It might break her heart. (Kaufman and Connelly 90)

Merton's views of cinematic hokum are merely parroted from the cynical remarks of a businessman at the studio, who contends that "the public wants hokum" rather than "satire, which is over the heads of most of the public" (Kaufman and Connelly 86; cf. Wilson 317–320). Though Merton's own heart has clearly been broken—at least temporarily—by his experience, whether he has actually learned from it or whether he is merely acting (convincingly, for once) is left decidedly ambiguous at the end of the play and the novel. He may or may not be a sadder and/or a wiser man as a result of his experience—but in either case he has at least convincingly learned his lines, creating an image for public consumption in the very fan magazines that he once so credulously devoured.

In the later chapters of the novel and in the final act of the play, surprisingly grandiose claims are made for Merton's comic artistry, both by the studio head whose harangue he overhears and by Merton himself. By giving Merton a self-description as a "Tragic Comedian," Wilson would seem to align him most clearly with Charlie Chaplin and Buster Keaton, but the phrase is undercut when Merton acknowledges that it is the title of a book he saw but did not read in the library in Simsbury (326). Although he overhears—and later parrots—a discussion about "the real pathos [that] is there" in his performance and is reassured that "there never was a great comedian without it" (320), his forte remains parody rather than pathos, and there is apparently none of the kind of sentimentality associated with Chaplin's Little Tramp, for example. Instead, Merton's unchangingly earnest facial expressions as chaos swirls around him suggest the stoicism of Buster Keaton, though the "something peculiar [that] even while he's imitating a bad actor you feel somehow that it isn't all imitation" (319) sets him apart from all of the major actual film counterparts of his time.

More important than any similarities to the screen comedians of the day is the fact that Merton Gill is an exact embodiment of the "myth of the Good American," which has been especially well defined by Walter Kerr in *The Silent Clowns* in his discussion of Harold Lloyd:

> The good American, still devoutly believed in during the 1920's, was two things: he was aggressive, and he was innocent. . . . "Up-and-at- 'em," "do-or-die" were still the mottoes of the day. But whatever had been done aggressively, or was being done aggressively, had been and was being done from the noblest motives. . . . [He was] A boy whom nothing could defeat, or even deter. Grit, sand, spunk—the whole lot. . . . And all the while a shy and awkward boy, one who might cry in his room at night, a boy whose very naivete stemmed from an excess of good will. . . . Naivete, after all, went arm in arm with innocence. Defensively or no, America began to take pride in its decency. Decency might make mistakes but at least they would not be indecent mistakes. . . . It was there already in every American boy who rose from shoe clerk to national hero. (190–191)

One of popular culture's foremost purveyors of this myth had long been *The Saturday Evening Post*, for which Wilson wrote regularly and in which *Merton of the Movies* had been serialized in ten installments. The impact of this myth—as it intersected with the myth of becoming a movie star virtually overnight—has been thoroughly analyzed by Alan Havig, who notes that with remarkable rapidity "movie studios, Hollywood mansions, and fan magazines replaced prairie homesteads, discoveries of yellow or black gold, and factories as symbols of American success" (167); by 1924, an estimated 200,000 aspiring actors came west each year in search of stardom (Leutrat 21). Although he is more naive than most and far more fortunate than all but a few, Merton Gill embodied the aspirations of many—whether they actually ventured west or merely stayed home and dreamed.

The mythic pattern of Merton Gill's experience is far older than that of the "good American," however: to a surprising extent, his travails in the film community constitute a classic pattern of initiation and recapitulate many elements of the "monomyth" that Joseph Campbell would later describe in *The Hero with a Thousand Faces*

(1949). Separating himself from the comforts of home and his (surrogate) family in Simsbury, Merton sets out on a quest for fame and glory, acquires a mentor/helpmate (the Montague girl), and endures multiple privations and humiliating (slapstick) indignities during his period of initiation into the industry (a symbolic hell-descent); eventually, he emerges triumphant over these adversities, gains a boon (success and/or insight into the nature of the world), is reintegrated into the community (i.e., gains public acclaim), and proves himself worthy to marry the woman he loves. Although Kaufman and Connelly's adaptation recapitulates all of these phases from the novel and even enhances a few of them (e.g., with Gashweiler's visit in the final act and reconciliation with his surrogate son), it elides Merton's elaborate initiatory hell-descent—which occupies forty-two pages in five chapters of the novel—into a stage direction:

> . . . There is nothing debonaire about him just at present. He has been sleeping on the lot for a week, most of the time in his clothes. He has not shaved for four days, nor eaten for two. The result of his starvation is that his thoughts are jumbled and confused, and most likely to pour forth irrelevantly. He is, in fact, almost on the edge of delirium. (Kaufman and Connelly 64)

Convinced that he must be willing to suffer and sacrifice for the sake of his art (a belief that is itself another myth, having its origins among the romantics), Merton eventually runs out of money and is therefore exiled from his room at Mrs. Patterson's boarding house. As if to prove himself worthy of being in the movies, he must clandestinely live in them, subsisting on the set among the false-fronted buildings that he once had mistaken for realities, enduring cold and deprivation in solitude. During this period, too, "the most important of all his visions had been rent to tatters," as he learns that his beloved Beulah Baxter is doubly false and thus unworthy of his esteem, since she is married and does not perform her own stunts (177). "Menaced by a complete emotional overthrow" (183) of a kind that besets every initiate during the process of his ordeal, Merton is reduced to literally eating garbage and grubbing among ashes: he subsists on two-day-old moldy beans that were dumped into an ash-pile at the completion of a scene in a miners' cabin. Recognizing that "he must move from this spot, forever now to be associated with black disillusion" and thus like hell itself (180), he is hailed by the Montague girl—an unmistakably angelic "beaming, joyous figure of one who had triumphed over wind and wave" (181), a redeemer offering both food and money, restoring him to health and returning him to the world.

That so much of Merton's initiatory sufferings (and so many of his humiliations during the filming) have been omitted in the stage adaptation fully justifies the claim by the reviewer for *The New York Times* that "Messrs. Kaufman and Connelly have softened the original story somewhat," though that does not necessarily lead to the conclusion that "their Merton is a more sympathetic character than Mr. Wilson's (Corbin). Like Don Quixote with his books of chivalry, like Emma Bovary with her novels of romance, Merton Gill believes what he reads as well as what he sees on the screen; like them, too, he seeks such a reality in his own life, an alternative to the mundane world that surrounds him. Like Gerty McDowell in the "Nausicaa" chapter of *Ulysses* (also published in 1922), Merton has so thoroughly absorbed the popular culture reading material of his day that his very consciousness itself is structured by it—a fact that is deftly revealed in the novel's style which, though in third person, reflects Merton's impressions of the world and his point of view. Repeatedly, but especially in the early chapters of the novel, he experiences day-to-day life *in terms of* scenes from the movies; reality as he lives it is framed in terms of scenarios, scripts, stock character types, and the rhetorically heightened style of silent films' printed dialogue as it appears on screen:

> What to him meant the announcement that Amos [Gashweiler] expected a new line of white goods on the morrow[?] . . . He wished to reply in polished tones, . . . [to] register the emotion that would justly accompany such a subtitle. (Wilson 12–13)

While working behind the counter, he presumes that "No one could have thought that . . . the clerk was mentally parting from Amos forever *in a scene of tense dramatic value* in which his few dignified but scathing words would burn themselves unforgettably into the old man's brain" (Wilson 7; emphasis mine). Wilson's parodic style, like Joyce's, assimilates the already-cliched discourses of popular culture as a means of characterizing its consumer/"fan"; the films, like Gerty's romance novels, are part of the uniquely modern commodity culture, show *business* (mis)taken for art (mis)taken for life. As a result, Merton is already wholeheartedly "of the Movies" long before he ever leaves for Hollywood.

Such parodic narrative strategy and the subjectivism that it conveys could not, of course, be transferred from the novel to the stage—a loss that is no less significant than that of the details of Merton's initiatory hell descent and the slapstick comedy scenes in which he appears. Nevertheless, the transformation that Kaufman and Connelly wrought does preserve the crucial and uniquely American myth of *Merton of the Movies* that so appealed even to as sophisticated a high modernist as Gertrude Stein: the prospect of fame and prosperity—of transformation if not transfiguration—achieved through the good fortune of the good-hearted, however innocent, however naive. Quaint though such ideas now seem seventy-five years after the novel and play achieved such popular success and critical acclaim, they are parodied as well as perpetuated both then and now; that *Merton of the Movies* did so when the movie industry was still so young makes it all the more remarkable, unduly neglected though it remains today.

WORKS CITED

Bergan, Ronald. *The United Artists Story.* New York: Crown Publishers, 1986.

Campbell, Joseph. *The Hero with a Thousand Faces.* Bollingen Series 17. 1949, rev. 1968; Princeton: Princeton University Press, 1973.

Corbin, John. "'Merton of the Movies' A Joy." *The New York Times,* 14 November 1922, 16.

Fowler, Gene. *Father Goose.* 1934; New York: Avon, 1974.

Havig, Alan. "Hollywood and the American Heartland: Celebrities, Fans, and the Myth of Success in the 1920's." *Journal of Popular Film and Television* 4.4 (Winter, 1987), 167–175.

Kaufman, George S. and Marc Connelly. *Merton of the Movies: A Dramatization of Harry Leon Wilson's Story of the Same Name.* 1922; New York: Samuel French, n.d.

Kerr, Walter. *The Silent Clowns.* New York: Knopf, 1979.

Kummer, George. *Harry Leon Wilson: Some Account of the Triumphs and Tribulations of an American Popular Writer.* Cleveland: The Press of Western Reserve University, 1963.

Leutrat, Jean-Louis. "Merton Gill, un homme ordinaire du cinema des annees 1920." *Revue francaise d'etudes americaines* 9.19 (February 1984): 19–31.

Mantle, Burns, ed. *The Best Plays of 1922–23 and the Year Book of the Drama in America.* 1923; New York: Dodd, Mead and Co., 1969.

Mason, Jeffrey D. *Wisecracks: The Farces of George S. Kaufman.* Theater and Dramatic Studies 53. Ann Arbor: UMI Research Press, 1988.

Meredith, Scott. *George S. Kaufman and His Friends*. Garden City, New York: Doubleday, 1974.

Pollack, Rhoda-Gale. *George S. Kaufman*. Boston: Twayne Publishers, 1988.

Slide, Anthony. *Early American Cinema*. New York: A. S. Barnes & Co., 1970.

Stein, Gertrude. *Everybody's Autobiography*. New York: Random House, 1937.

Thomson, David. *A Biographical Dictionary of Film*. 2nd ed., rev. New York: William Morrow & Co., 1981.

Wilson, Harry Leon. *Merton of the Movies*. New York: Doubleday, Page & Co., 1922; rpt., illus. with scenes from the play, New York: Grosset and Dunlap, n.d.

What Makes Sammy Run?: S. N. Behrman and the Fugitive Kind

Robert F. Gross

I

In 1941, as Samuel Nathaniel Behrman's *The Talley Method* was about to open in a Philadelphia, pre-Broadway tryout, under the title *The Mechanical Heart*, an anonymous member of the Playwrights' Company (perhaps even Behrman himself), sent out a parody of a press release describing the dramatist as a man in flight:

> In fact, Mr. Behrman is probably the most famous, runner-away from practically every business and social responsibility in contemporary America. He runs away to start a play. He runs away to finish it. He runs further yet from his first night, and furthest of all from its last. Even at home he runs from the phone. He has been labelled a living fugue. (Publicity, 1)

This comic description had a strong basis in fact; Behrman was known for being private and elusive, and for dropping out of sight when a production became tense and unpleasant. Preparing to work with the playwright on a new project, Lynn Fontanne admonished him "try to refrain from that 'first you're here and then you're not' game so often" (Fontanne, Letter). For director and critic Harold Clurman, Behrman's evasiveness was the predominant feature of his style, causing him to address his readers through a mask, and often tell another story than the one he actually had in mind (36). In our current age of talk shows and tell-all autobiographies, these impulses toward indirection and self-effacement are distinctly unfashionable, and demand that we scrutinize any textual traces that might be signs of the author's "fugal" existence. For Behrman, Hollywood became a major image of the flight that characterized so much of his behavior; it was a place in a highly

personal and carefully guarded personal mythic system—perhaps even
guarded from the author himself.

Behrman first traveled to Hollywood in 1930, and was put to work
on the film adaptation of Ferenc Molnar's *Liliom* "*See*FerencMolnar".
Over the next decade, he divided his time between the two coasts,
writing some of his most successful plays for the Broadway stage—
Biography, *Rain from Heaven*, *End of Summer*—and collaborating on
screenplays for Janet Gaynor, Al Jolson, and, most notably, Greta
Garbo, for whom he helped to write *Queen Christina*, *Anna Karenina*,
Conquest and *Two-Faced Woman*. With the end of Garbo's career in
1941, Behrman was absent from Hollywood for a decade, and then
returned only rarely during the 1950s. His experiences in Hollywood
provided material for two stage comedies—*Wine of Choice* (1938) and
Let Me Hear the Melody (1951)—an essay, "Zion Comes to Culver
City," a novel, *The Burning-Glass* (1968) and several chapters in his
memoir, *People in a Diary* (1972).

II

Behrman's two comedies of the film industry, *Wine of Choice* and *Let
Me Hear the Melody* are among his most ill-fated pieces for the stage.
Wine of Choice suffered greatly in its pre-Broadway tryouts, during
which both the original director and leading lady quit the company, and
Behrman's original intentions were subverted in a mass of rewrites.
Meeting largely unfavorable reviews, it ran only 43 performances on
Broadway. *Let Me Hear the Melody* fared even worse. Behrman began
the play in 1946, but the play did not find its way to the stage until
1951, where it suffered from directorial and casting problems, and
closed in Philadelphia. Behrman's notes indicate that he considered *Let
Me Hear the Melody* a reworking of the central idea of *Wine of Choice*,
and the two plays are best considered as a single, prolonged attempt to
find a successful dramatic form to express Behrman's very personal
vision of Hollywood.

Wine of Choice treats Hollywood from a distance—the distance of
a continent, since the play is set on a Long Island estate. The estate is
presided over (though not owned) by Binkie Niebuhr, a man for whom
intrigue is a way of life. Armed with his notebook, which contains "the
social and sexual history of New York, of London, of Paris" (7), he
arranges marriages and divorces, brings together wealthy homeowners
and interior decorators, influential editors and aspiring authors. The
most important of his current projects, however, is to bring together
Wilda Doran, an exotic beauty from an impoverished background and

Laddy Sears, an amiable young playboy with no purpose in life. Binkie persuades Laddy to try his hand at film production, starring Wilda in an exotic potboiler about a Javanese princess, based on a plot invented by Binkie himself. Laddy, though momentarily torn between film production and an expedition to discover the headwaters of the Orinoco river, chooses the former, mostly because of his attraction to Wilda, and is easily controlled by Binkie.

Wilda, however, proves more resistant to control. Once model and wife to a brilliant, self-destructive, and egotistical painter and now romantically involved with a maverick Senator from New Mexico, she believes that a career in the movies might finally give her the freedom to understand who she really is and what she really wants. She explains:

> I saw that I've always instinctively reflected what people wanted me to be. That I myself have never been anything—not really. That's why I want this chance, Binkie—so I can find out what I really am— what I really might be—not for your reasons—but for my own. (19)

For Wilda, Laddy Sears figures only in her professional plans, not her personal ones. Resisting both Binkie's matchmaking and Senator Ryder Gerrard's proposals of marriage, she falls under the spell of Dow Christophsen, a hard-bitten proletarian novelist, who embodies all the genius and all the ruthlessness of Wilda's ex-husband. She rejects her other suitors in favor of Dow, only to be rejected in turn by the young Communist, who will let no one compromise his dream of absolute independence. Alone, and with her new film received only tepidly by a Hollywood mogul, Wilda is left wondering if she is really at all free to make choices.

Wilda's pursuit of self-knowledge and freedom are poorly served by the film industry. Rather than offering her a sense of self, it further alienates her. Wilda reports on her screen test:

> It was good but it wasn't me. It was like watching somebody else— another creature who didn't have my thoughts, my griefs, my doubts, my ups and downs—just a cool creature wearing a pretty frock and being agreeable—yet she was good—she was effective.

What Wilda sees on the screen is Wilda reduced to mere appearance and bereft of subjectivity. Transformed into a virginal Javanese princess, she becomes an ingredient in a drug that addicts people to

escapism and renders them incapable of coping with reality. As Senator
Gerrard explains:

> I like fairy stories as much as anybody but "The Princess of Java"
> isn't a fairy story. They dish it out to you as fact, as possibility, even
> as probability. Any girl may be the Princess of Java—any boy may
> love the Princess of Java—any boy may marry the Princess of Java.
> (183)

Both Wilda and the public are cheated by cinematic fantasies of self-
transformation, which do nothing but cut them off from their selves and
their actual circumstances. In a Platonic attack on the degenerate effect
of art on the populace, Behrman presents Hollywood as a place that is
characterized by an ontological insufficiency—it can only convey
appearance, not reality—and seduces the public away from difficult
realizations and hard facts.

The rough cut of Wilda's film, we are told, needs further editing,
because it still exhibits moments of wit and, most dangerously, a point
of view. The director plans to excise the intellectual content of Wilda's
lines. "You can read lines, but you cannot express ideas," he explains to
her. "I shall cut out the ideas and leave the lines" (109). Just as Wilda's
appearance has been alienated from her subjectivity, Traub's lines will
be divorced from any significance.

Wilda, the sole woman in *Wine of Choice*, is the quintessential
Hollywood creature. Once an artist's model and night club dancer, she
realizes that she has never known herself, but has only been the Galatea
to a succession of Pygmalions. But what would an authentic self be,
away from the gaze of the Other? The men in *Wine of Choice* generally
anchor their sense of self in an intellectual position, whether communist
(Dow), liberal (Ryder), reactionary (Charlie) or cynic (Binkie,
Michael). Only Wilda's most infatuated suitor, Laddy, lacks an
intellectual position, and he shares in Wilda's lack of self. He has no
desire of his own, only a mimetic desire. As film director Michael
Traub explains to him:

> You're a suppressed exhibitionist, Laddy. You can only fall in love
> with an object of universal desire. You succumb to the aura of
> reputation. (186)

The magic of the movies resides in its ability to render all images and
all desires inauthentic.

At first glance, the oppositions at the heart of *Wine of Choice* seem as old as Western metaphysics: masculine self-sufficiency versus feminine dependency, ideal versus imitation, Socrates versus the Sophists. But as Gilles Deleuze has brilliantly demonstrated it is "the anti-Platonism at the heart of Platonism" itself (128), which renders these oppositions unstable. For, even if Hollywood is the Platonic cave, there is no space exterior to it in *Wine of Choice*, no escape from the realm of imitation and errancy. The dynamics of the movies merely foreground the sense of insufficiency that is found everywhere. Wilda may be drawn to Hollywood, but Dow, Ryder, Binkie and Laddy are all drawn to Wilda, and all fail in successfully shaping her to their ends. *Wine of Choice* occupies a skeptical position, in which all projected narratives, whether an exotic screenplay, a Marxist view of history, or an amorous intrigue, all run aground against the surprising and inexplicable peculiarities of individuals. Ryder and Laddy come from the same backgrounds, we are told, and yet no one seems to be able to account for the great differences between them. Binkie Niebuhr's life was spared in a pogrom in Lithuania because the Military Governor appreciated his mother's cooking. Chance and contingency rule here, and all totalizing statements are undermined.[1] Behrman's epigraph for *The Burning-Glass*, taken from philosopher David Hume, could easily preface *Wine of Choice*—"The powers by which bodies operate are entirely unknown."

III

Between *Wine of Choice* and *Let Me Hear the Melody* comes an essay of Behrman's own experiences in Hollywood, "Zion Comes to Culver City." Originally written as the introduction to a biography of Chaim Weizmann, the essay presents itself as a paean to the humanity and vision of the Zionist leader, but also is Behrman's most personal essay on his experiences in Hollywood. Here we see Behrman as a laborer in the Platonic cave, with Zionism offered as a possible route of escape. Surprisingly, however, Behrman chooses to remain in the cave, not because he has reservations about Weizmann, but about himself. While praising Weizmann and embracing the Zionist cause, Behrman nevertheless isolates himself from both—a modern Moses who contemplates, but does not enter into, the Promised Land.

Behrman's essay begins with an odd distortion of fact.[2] Behrman describes how he is sitting in his office at Metro-Goldwyn-Mayer, working on a script in which Greta Garbo is being made to do what she does best on the silver screen—suffer. He summarizes the plot of the

film, which sounds suspiciously like that of one of Garbo and
Behrman's most successful collaborations, *Anna Karenina*. But *Anna
Karenina* had been made in 1935, not 1941, as Behrman would have us
believe. The Behrman/Garbo collaboration of 1941 caused Garbo to
suffer, yes, but in quite a different way. The film was the comic *Two-
Faced Woman*, a critical and box-office fiasco that not only hurt the
careers of Behrman and director George Cukor, but also proved to be
Garbo's last film appearance. Behrman certainly had clear personal
motives for repressing memories of *Two-Faced Woman*, which had
been marked by more than its share of off-camera tensions, climaxing
in the need for massive rewritings, reshootings and editing to keep it
from being condemned not only by the Roman Catholic Legion of
Decency, but by Cardinal Spellman himself.[3] Behrman thus rewrites the
events of June 1941 to make them coincide with Garbo's days of glory
as film tragedienne (and Behrman's most popular screenplays). He also,
however, casts Garbo in a tragic role to strengthen the essay's
fundamental oppositions. For, in "Zion Comes to Culver City,"
Behrman opposes Garbo to Weizmann, and Hollywood to Palestine.
Hollywood becomes a second Babylonian captivity, in which Behrman
languishes; "What was I doing in the Thalberg Building? Why wasn't I
in Moab? How did this displacement come about?" he laments (99).
Here the rabbi does not remind Behrman of the "patriarchal, learned
and patient" (104) rabbis of his youth, but is a businessman who sprays
"thickly the heavy oil of platitude—fortissimo" (104). The leaders of
the Chosen People have been lead astray, as priests were earlier lead
astray by the cults of Baal and Astarte.

    In Behrman's essay, Greta Garbo is the pagan idol. She exists only
in a disembodied form, like Wilda in her screen test. She is not a real
person, but a cinematic phantasm whose beauty exists in direct
proportion to her fictive agonies:

> She must suffer, yes, but exquisitely. She must endure, yes, but with
> an enhanced vulnerability. She must die, yes, but unravaged by
> mortality (96).

Behrman's office in the Thalberg building becomes a wry parody of the
Sadean torture chamber, in which it is more strenuous to be torturer
than victim. Here, Greta Garbo's legendary beauty is not an attribute
deriving from herself, but the result of the pain Behrman inflicts on her.
In fact, she is given no physical attributes whatsoever, but is
transformed into a rarefied quintessence of feminine pathos, distilled by

Behrman, who deliberates, "What further agonies could I invent through which she had not already passed, what refinements of torture that would also be *photogénique?*" (96). Although Garbo's ability to suffer masochistically seems to be boundless, it is, rather, her torturer who has reached the limits of his endurance. Captive rather than captor, the shadows of the office's Venetian blinds lie across his desk in bars, and he shivers from some obscure cause (96). He labors, he admits, "with a faltering sadism" (96). The sardonic point of the essay's opening quickly becomes apparent; Behrman's sadistic fantasy is a self-mocking fiction, in which his macabre wit only points up his lack of any real power.

Like Garbo, no woman is physically described in the course of the essay. Mrs. Weizmann is mentioned, but is given no physical or behavioral properties. Behrman's own wife is never mentioned—a salient feature of all his autobiographical writing. Women are effaced from the history of Zionism altogether. Rather, Behrman reserves physical description for the men: the "very handsome, somber-eyed, black-bearded" Theodor Herzl (97); and the "fascinating" and "alluring" Chaim Weizmann"*See* SamuelNathanielBehrman" (97) with the "beauty of his head, massive and sculptural" (97). This attractiveness, however much rooted in physicality, transcends it. Although Weizmann's beautiful head summons up Behrman's adolescent memories of Roman busts in his high school Latin textbooks, this Jewish head, unlike the "sightless," marmoreal Gentiles, can speak with its eyes, eyes that both express and elicit "yearning" (98). As a scientist, Weizmann creates "absorptive capacity" (111), and it threatens to absorb Behrman as well.

Descriptions of the "alluring" Weizmann briefly give way to Behrman's memory of sharing a maisonette with another alluring Jewish man, George Gershwin, whose performance of his songs becomes, in Behrman's description, a serenade:

> Gershwin sang for me what were to be his last melodies, with that transparent eagerness to please which was one of the most engaging of his qualities. (111)

The attractiveness of Jewish men in general, and Weizmann in particular, proves more seductive than the Nordic screen goddess. Thoughts of Weizmann interfere with Behrman's work, and render him completely incapable of furthering his heterosexual, sadomasochistic "work" on Miss Garbo. Behrman's masculine "dominance" of Garbo, presented ironically from the first, is undermined as Behrman becomes feminized in his infatuation with Zionist leaders.

Weizmann is able to spirit Behrman away and lessen the distance between him and Jewish history. As Behrman listens, he begins to become aware of the enormous attraction that Zionism holds for him. That attraction, however, is repeatedly met, not by a political argument, but with repeated evasions on Behrman's part, evasions that leave him, at the end of the essay, still in Culver City, working on the Garbo script. These evasions have been suggested from the first. Behrman recounts his earliest memories of Zionism as repressed memories, which return to consciousness as he goes to meet Weizmann for the first time. He insists that he knows little about Weizmann and even less of Zionism. He remembers his neighborhood decorated with banners, and wants to believe it is an American holiday, only to learn that the visit of a Zionist leader is being celebrated. The meaning of this visit is repressed as well. "If my father explained to me what that [Zionism] meant I do not remember what his explanation was," Behrman tells us (97). Thus, Zionism becomes a forbidden knowledge for Behrman, a knowledge somehow associated with a repressed knowledge about Jewish men. Thus, both the construction of masculinity and Zionism are marked with signs of desire and prohibition. The household photograph of the handsome Theodor Herzl, after all, depicts him "with his arms folded prohibitively across his frock-coated chest" (97). What does this stance prohibit? The physical intimacy for which his attractiveness makes Behrman yearn? In this essay, Zionism is so completely identified with latent homosexuality that Behrman cannot choose the former without accepting the latter as well. There is "something terribly intimate in the pull of all this" Behrman admits, anxiously (108), and the intimacy comes from the confluence of ethnic and sexual identity.

Behrman does, however, try to configure homoeroticism independently of Zionism. He refers to his childhood in Worcester, Massachusetts, in which the Gentile section of town did not contain an anti-Semitic oppressor, but his Gentile counterpart, the humorist Robert Benchley, "who, I was to find out many years later, was as wistful on his side as I was on mine" (108). The yearning that Weizmann both expresses and inspires finds its echo in the mutual wistfulness of Behrman and Benchley. Yet this youthful wistfulness of Behrman and Benchley's remains solitary, lacking the powerful eye contact of Weizmann, which communicates:

a yearning, touched with an intimation of futility, to cross the limitless areas that insulate in loneliness even those most desirous of communication (98).

The fact remains, however, that Behrman and Benchley do not find each other in the Worcester of their boyhoods. There is a boundary between Jew and Gentile in Worcester that remains in force, even if over the boundary one finds a wistful Robert Benchley rather than a threatening Tsarist officer. While Behrman's use of Benchley is ostensibly there to minimize the existence of anti-Semitism in the United States, the example simultaneously reinforces the sense of Behrman's isolation from Gentile America. Thus, the example, pulls two ways, with Behrman simultaneously refuting and succumbing to the Zionist vision.

The longer Behrman listens to Weizmann, however, the more he feels an intense, formless anxiety:

> And yet there was something. There was something. I thought back. Wasn't there, from earliest childhood, a sense of not belonging with the unconsciousness of others, an anxiety, a distress, a feeling here and there of tentativeness, a sensation like the sudden fall of an elevator, a sense altogether, even anticipating any outward slight, of the penumbral, the unresolved? (108)

Behrman's usual penchant for elegant phrasing and concrete particulars disappears here, and is replaced with a murky turning back of consciousness upon itself, as it unsuccessfully gropes toward the ground of the thinker's anxiety. Just as Zionism was earlier presented as a repressed childhood memory of the prohibitive Herzl, so here, the presence of Weizmann sends Behrman back to "earliest childhood" and a primal anxiety. The fact that Weizmann is able to awaken such anxiety creates an ambiguous response in Behrman. It could validate Zionism, or it could be a sign of demagoguery. Weizmann's power is that he can awaken deeply personal emotions, and is precisely that which Behrman fears. Worrying that he will be unable to respond consciously and rationally to Weizmann, the Zionist leader's very seductiveness causes his admirer to panic: "Was I merely yielding to the immense persuasion of Weizmann's personality? I must be on my guard!" (109). The awakening of eros is here marked by an awakening of anxiety and a heightened awareness of vulnerability so intense as to cause the recoil of the lover into himself, and an awakening of defensive mechanisms.

For Behrman, Weizmann's strength is both attractive and sinister; the absorptive capacity of the visionary threatens to absorb the narrator himself. Throughout his writing, Behrman's acute awareness that insecurities render us particularly susceptible to manipulation caused him to attribute the success of fascist dictators to their abilities to play on the weaknesses of others. In his 1936 comedy, *End of Summer*, he presented a suave psychoanalyst, Dr. Kenneth Rice, who could exploit the insecurities of others for his own profit. This drawing-room fascist can easily be seen as the demonic version of the visionary Weizmann:

> Some men are born ahead of their time, some behind, but you are made pat for the instant. Now is the time for you—when people are unemployed and distrust their own capacities—when people suffer and may be tempted—when integrity yields to despair—now is the moment for you! (200)

For Behrman, singlemindedness and power are to be feared, while the divided mind is both more virtuous and more vulnerable. As Miguel explains to Ferne in *Dunnigan's Daughter*, "Evil is mobilized. Goodness not. Goodness is like you—mixed up, not resolute"(156). In other words, for Behrman to retain his virtue in the presence of Weizmann, he must remain resolute in his irresoluteness, fixed in his inner divisions. The more he is tempted with a unified psyche, the more he must resist, and yet it is the unified, purposeful psyche which is associated with Weizmann and masculinity.

This inner division manifests itself throughout the essay, up to the very end. Behrman tells us that he found Weizmann irresistible, and overcame his scruples about him. He admits, "I was—as the ultramodern musicologists have it—sent" (118). Yet he does not follow Weizmann. He returns to Culver City, back to M-G-M, and to his illusory and sadistic marriage of convenience to the fantasmatic Garbo. Behrman's words point toward a whole-hearted embrace of Zionism, his actions to a rejection of it, and there is no mediating element between the two impulses. The repressed existence of Garbo's *Two-Faced Woman* is replaced by Behrman's *Two-Faced Man*, slipping out of his Thalberg Building office for a clandestine meeting with Weizmann, and slipping back to his domestic routine.

Even more disturbing is the macabre turn that life seems to have taken in the Behrman/Garbo *ménage*. "Meantime," the essay concludes,

"I dug my scalpel into Miss Garbo" (119). At the beginning of the essay, Behrman had been unable to think of *photogénique* tortures for Miss Garbo. Now, he is ready to work, but his image is one of violence and disfigurement. The sentence remains ambiguous: has he gone back to work on Garbo as he was supposed to, or has he become a violent renegade, gashing the face that is Garbo's glory? The fact that Behrman was actually working on Garbo's last picture at this time makes one wonder whether this essay is communicating some residual guilt that Behrman felt for his part in the difficulties with *Two-Faced Woman*. More importantly, however, for our purposes, the violence of the final image indicates that Weizmann has affected a change in Behrman. If Behrman was unable to torture Garbo at the end of the essay, he certainly feels no inhibition now. Garbo—whether Garbo the woman or Garbo the Gentile—has become the object of anger and violence, and digging the scalpel into her has become the single decisive action that Behrman takes. In the course of the essay, Zionism and its homoeroticism has been presented as healthy and expansive; Hollywood and its heterosexuality have been exposed as perverse and confining. Yet the very attractiveness of Weizmann's Zionism sends Behrman back to Culver City, to a Platonic cave in which figures are ever "toiling toward dissolution" (119).

In one sense, Behrman has been the dweller in the Cave throughout this essay. Rather than deliberating on Weizmann's story in terms of political action, he has always seen it as the stuff of great moviemaking. In his imagination, he is always turning it into shadows and light thrown upon a screen. In choosing Garbo over Weizmann, he shows himself choosing the fantasmatic over the real, the female over the male, illusion over substance. Thus, Behrman ultimately judges himself unworthy of Weizmann's vision, perhaps because it precipitates in him a crisis of sexuality too intense and disorienting for him to accept. This failure, in turn, is manifested in a heightened moment of misogyny, as a resentment towards a heterosexual norm.

"Zion Comes to Culver City" invests Zionism with such a strong homoerotic charge that Behrman's presentation of it is at once fascinated and phobic. This presentation leads to a disturbing subcurrent as Weizmann is presented as a man who can draw on the same obscure, existential anxieties as can fascist dictators, thus leading to a destabilizing moment in which Zionist leaders and anti-Semitic dictators can grow dangerously close. Behrman's fear is not Weizmann, but the weaknesses in Behrman that Weizmann elicits. "Zion Comes to Culver City," becomes a narrative in which the protagonist's major fear is his own desire, a fear that isolates him from others, and confines him in a prison of violent and resentful fantasies—a prison that is Hollywood.[4]

IV

With *Let Me Hear the Melody*, Behrman returns to the high comedy stage, and to a dramatic structure reminiscent of *Wine of Choice*. Its leading lady, Esme Smith, is Wilda grown older, more experienced, and a star. Partly modeled on Paulette Goddard, Esme was discovered by a comic genius (Charlie Chaplin) and rose to fame, only to become box-office poison. Re-discovered by Alvin Connors, a macho, fascistic film director, she is now being launched as a dramatic actress, playing Pauline Bonaparte in an lavish but hopelessly inert costume drama about Napoleon. Like Wilda, she becomes the attractive center of the play, about which swirl a host of men, not only Alvin, but also (in various drafts) a young musical genius, a nuclear physicist, a British screenwriter modeled on Christopher Isherwood, and a burned-out American novelist, à la F. Scott Fitzgerald.[5] Like Wilda, Esme wants an opportunity to exercise choice, and the Bonaparte film becomes the battleground for her choosing. Unhappy with her role in the film, and dissatisfied with her lover/director, Alvin, she insists that an intellectual and celebrated novelist rewrite her role, for which her contract gives her script approval. Furthermore, like Wilda, Esme is a Galatea, who works to extricate herself from one Pygmalion, only to fall under the spell of another, and she casts her new screenwriter into the role of her latest mentor, a role to which he reluctantly and only briefly assumes. A more humane Dow Christophsen, he casts off the role of Pygmalion in favor of his art, leaving the Napoleon film in shambles, and Esme planning to star in the next work of her new Pygmalion, Vincent Bendix. His musical, *Drive-In Girl* will take the place of the Napoleon film. On one level, *Let Me Hear the Melody* is a reworking of *Wine of Choice*, shorn of the liberal versus communist debate that had obfuscated the earlier play. "It's a *Wine of Choice* idea really—only this time it will be clear" an enthusiastic Behrman writes in his notes.[6]

On another level, however, the play can be seen as a wishful, comic reworking of themes from "Zion Comes to Culver City." There are more autobiographical details here than in *Wine of Choice*. The overblown Napoleonic epic is an obvious allusion to one of Behrman's less congenial scriptwriting assignments, the 1937 box-office dud, *Conquest*, in which Greta Garbo played Maria Walewska to Charles Boyer's Napoleon. In his memoirs, Behrman explains his antipathy to the project, an antipathy that Sayre Nolan, the screenwriter in *Let Me Hear the Melody*, will share:

> I wished to convey my personal feeling that the existence of Napoleon, "the archaic little man," as H. G. Wells calls him, was a disaster for the human race. But it was not easy to get sympathy for that point of view from a group of men who had busts of Napoleon in their offices, since he represented their secret wish—dreams of conquest. (162)

In *Wine of Choice*, Napoleon was mentioned as the prototype for twentieth century authoritarian leaders. In *Let Me Hear the Melody*, he finds his comic equivalent in the ruthless and egomaniacal captains of the film industry. The dangerously eroticized figure of the Zionist leader in "Zion Comes to Culver City" is reconfigured here, with his power embodied in the egomaniacal, homophobic and seemingly Gentile Alvin Connors, and his attractiveness incarnated in the young, attractive, guileless and Jewish Vincent Bendix, a thinly disguised version of George Gershwin, who had made a brief, beguiling appearance in Behrman's earlier essay. Here, however, Gershwin does not die, but survives the Second World War, remains youthful, and, thanks to the interventions of the Behrman-like screenwriter, wins Esme, the girl of his dreams. Bendix is a rarity in the Behrman *oeuvre*, a character undivided, yet totally innocent.

Sayre Nolan's brief infatuation with Esme is a mimetic desire. Finding himself enchanted with Vincent's genius, his unassuming qualities, and his vulnerability, he resolves to use his influence over Esme to separate her from Alvin, and plead Vincent's case to her. Attracted to Vincent, he temporarily mistakes Vincent's desire for his own. Leaving Hollywood and yielding the field to Vincent, Sayre retreats from the object of his attraction, much as Behrman himself turned his back on Israel in "Zion Comes to Culver City."

In fact, the major theme of Behrman's essay nakedly rises to the surface of a 1947 draft of the play, in which Nolan vehemently takes Esme to task for trifling with Zionism as a cause, and not understanding the gravity of the issue. Once again, the screenwriter is caught between the female star (Garbo, Esme) and Zionism, and takes out his frustration on the star, without following the call of Zionism. This scene only survives in a single draft of the play, but indicates the nature of Behrman's personal investment in this material.

In an interview that appeared before the Philadelphia opening of
Let Me Hear the Melody, Behrman reveals a further dimension of his
personal experience in Hollywood that colored the writing of this play.
In "Hollywood a Heartbreak Town for Artists, Says Author," Behrman
describes Hollywood as a place artists flee to when confronted with
crises—he himself had fled there. In the play, Vincent Bendix takes
refuge in Hollywood after the box-office failure of his first opera
(shades of *Porgy and Bess*). Alvin Connors became a director when he
realized he did not have the makings of a first-class painter. Sayre
Nolan, a novelist who suffers from writer's block, goes even further.
He explains to a recent acquaintance:

> You have an odd look on your face—as if you were seeing a ghost. In
> a sense you are. Obviously you thought I was dead. In a sense I am.
> (1–1–4)

Behrman's flight to Hollywood came in the midst of professional
and personal problems. His drama, *Meteor* "*See* SamuelNathaniel
Behrman", had failed to find favor with either audiences or critics on
Broadway, and his close friend and mentor since boyhood, Dan Asher,
had committed suicide in a mental hospital. Asher, as Behrman tells it,
was to Pygmalion to young Sam's Galatea; it was he who first decided
that the young writer should be a playwright. It was Asher who
arranged for Behrman to transfer to Harvard, in hopes of becoming a
playwriting student of George Pierce Baker's, and it was Asher who
objected to Behrman's taking a teaching job in Minnesota, rather than
staying in New York to pursue his playwriting career. "It was Willie's
choice as much as mine" Behrman reflects (*Worcester*, 235).[7] Asher
emerges in Behrman's writing as another Weizmann, attractive,
mesmerizing, and able to overwhelm a divided mind and rob it of its
freedom of choice. Unlike Weizmann, however, he also carries within
himself impulses toward madness—schizophrenia, depression and
suicide (*Worcester*, 236–239). It may well be that the deep ambivalence
of Behrman toward dominating males reached a crisis with Asher's
suicide. For Behrman, the trip to Hollywood was a flight from the
specter of personal disintegration.

In *Let Me Hear the Melody*, Nolan comes to a similar conclusion
as Behrman. Hollywood is a washing machine:

> where people come to dump their hurts, to wash away their failures,
> their limitations—a great laundry of frustration. (3–20)

The only answer, Nolan decides, is not to write about Hollywood, but to write about himself. He can only come back to life as an artist by refusing to run and facing himself.

The specter of disintegration haunts the drafts of *Let Me Hear the Melody*. In early drafts, the presence of a nuclear scientist leads to discussions of the atomic bomb and Hiroshima; Nolan, in an Isherwood-like moment, talks how he wrote tales of the misery in Berlin between the Wars, but was unable to take any purposeful action; Esme, traumatized by her experiences on a wartime USO tour, laments "My God, I saw the world with its throat cut—and I find myself turning out the same old machine-made product" (1947 draft, 1–38). In later drafts, the specific references to the war largely disappear, and the studio executives fret about the film industry being forced out by television, but the crisis of the artist remains an important theme. Nolan theorizes that the loss of melody in contemporary music is due to a loss of belief; in the modern world, we cannot find the melodies of Bach and Mozart because we lack their faith. Literature and film are plagued by a similar disintegration of form:

> There are no happy endings any more. There aren't, in fact, *any*
> endings. The endings we put in are arbitrary just like the ones stuck in
> by the statesmen, the economists and the philosophers. (2–2–40)

Let Me Hear the Melody becomes the story of a film that is never completed. The vast, Napoleonic enterprise grinds to a halt as director and leading lady, screenwriter and producer, quarrel and conspire. All that is left, ultimately, is "a great unread pile of scrap-paper, a monolith of anonymity" (2–1–9). The classic Hollywood studio system is not only an evasion, it has begun to become an anachronism, a city of ghosts.

V

With *The Burning-Glass*, Behrman returns to Hollywood, but moguls and moviemaking retreat to the background in favor of a deeply introspective examination of ethical values. This Hollywood is a place for people in flight—primarily refugees from Nazi persecution. At the center of the novel is a young writer in flight from himself. Although he is known to the world by an Anglo-Saxon name, "Stanley Grant," his real name is "Jacob Ben Sion-Trynin." The path from Stanley to Jacob is a circuitous one, as he moves from Salzburg to Hollywood and Manhattan, through a dense, labyrinthine plot of artists and socialites, psychiatrists and sociopaths, and only finds its destination in the book's final paragraph, as the playwright finally writes his Hebrew name on the title page of his new play. Along the way, there are lightly disguised sketches of Franz and Alma Werfel, Max Reinhardt, Ina Claire and Henri Bernstein, as well as more complex portraits that may be composites or inventions of the author.

The Hollywood chapters comprise the darkest and most violent section of *The Burning-Glass*, the most filled with a bitterness and sense of betrayal that makes the cruelties of "Zion Comes to Culver City" pale by comparison. Sardonically described in one chapter heading as "The Promised Land," it is, once again, a false Jewish state, estranged from its own values and traditions. Here Jacob's Catholic wife, Eileen, studies Judaism and Hebrew, which often annoys her agnostic husband, and it is Eileen, not Jacob, who eventually emigrates to Palestine.

The society of Behrman's novel is as distinguished by the prevalence of male homosexuals as of Jews (though lesbians are absent), leading the male heterosexuals to good-naturedly wonder whether they are indeed in the majority. Moreover, as groups who are the object of prejudice and are tempted to submerge their identities, the Jews and homosexuals tend to be seen as similar. Jacob cites Proust in this regard; "Proust segregates Zionists with the homosexuals as two groups which arouse hostility" (360). Once again, we are back in the Hollywood/Zion/homoerotic nexus of "Zion Comes to Culver City," but in a far less disguised form. In this case, however, Behrman resolves the tension by making Zion the site of heterosexuality (Eileen goes to live there with her child by Jacob and her second Jewish husband), while Hollywood becomes the city of male homosexual desire. Eileen's Palestinian family finds its Hollywood contrast in the household of Stephanie, a drug-addicted actress (Wilda/Esme in a desperate reincarnation), Ian, her murderous, bisexual husband, and Vincent, his charming and good-hearted lover, whose first name is that of the idealized Jewish genius of *Let Me Hear the Melody*. In one of Behrman's most memorable variations on the theme of flight, Jacob comes upon Vincent on a beach in Santa Monica, exercising vigorously. Jacob learns that one of Vincent's best friends was just murdered in a gay-bashing incident, and Vincent works out to keep himself ready to defend himself in the inevitable event of a similar attack. As Jacob leaves, he looks down, where "Vincent had resumed his running as if the dark angel were after him" (259). None of this physical regimen, however, is able to keep Vincent safe, and he is stabbed to death at a bar in Watts.

Despite their similarities as objects of persecution, however, Behrman's treatments of Jews and homosexuals are not identical. Although the major characters in *The Burning-Glass* are sympathetic to homosexuals, and speak against stereotyping and in favor of toleration, the dynamic of the novel works to purge homosexuality from the novel in favor of a model of Jewish patriarchy. After Vincent's violent death, all the overtly gay characters drop out of the novel, and Jacob leaves Hollywood, the novel's site of the most overt homosexual culture. At the novel's climax, Jacob is finally able to put an end to his flight from himself as he scrutinizes a watercolor of a Jewish cemetery, and tries to decipher the name on one of the tombstones:

> He was determined to ferret out the identity of at least one of the deceased. But he couldn't. He applied his hand glass. With a kind of painful shock he managed to decipher one word in one name: ben— the son of. But he couldn't make out anything else.—he couldn't decipher who the son was the son of. He looked and looked at the sharply angled memorial of the son of somebody. It was part of his own name: ben. (407)

Unlike Vincent, Jacob confronts death in the form of the cemetery. There are no disconcerting eroticized, male Jewish bodies in sight here; the bodies have been replaced by text, and the only discernible word in the text is one that has no individuality, but is a marker of patriarchal succession. This succession, which relies on heterosexual activity, has no place for homosexuality. Jacob can confront death and find, not only a *memento mori*, but a cultural commonality which is reflected in the "ben" he shares with the deceased. In the pre-Stonewall sensibility of *The Burning-Glass*, there is no sense of a gay identity that can transcend the individual male and his mortality. For Behrman, Hollywood and homosexuality exhibit a Heideggerian flight from death, which results in an inauthentic existence.[8] It is the acceptance of Jewish patriarchy that leads to authenticity and an end to flight.

Yet Jacob's moment of recognition also has its disconcerting side. Discovering his identity among the tombstones, he echoes both the theme of ghostliness in *Let Me Hear the Melody* and Wilda's self-alienation in *Wine of Choice*. He is reduced to mere relationality—a textual 'son' without body, desire or sexuality. The alternatives posed in *The Burning-Glass* bear an interesting resemblance to the oppositions in Behrman's essay on Dan Asher in *The Worcester Account*, "Point of the Needle." There, "Willie Lavin" (Asher) stands for impulse, rebellion, speculative thought, and the embodied world of the stage. Behrman's father, on the other hand, is a Talmudic scholar, who reverences the written word, tradition and limitations. The dichotomy is almost Nietzschean, with the energy and irrationality of Asher's Dionysus confronting the Apollonian world of the patriarch. *The Burning-Glass* ends by accepting the the Apollonian values, but at a cost. There is no flight, but no longer any narrative movement; Jacob accepts his identity within the patriarchy, only for the novel to come to an end. As in Behrman's other Hollywood fictions, the space outside the cave remains elusive.

Behrman's Hollywood is a Platonic cave of insufficiency, a place for people fleeing persecution, their pasts, their talents, their ethnicities, and their sexualities. It is a flight into the unreal, and Behrman is best able to counter its falsity with a public acceptance of Jewish identity, which finds its noblest form in the Zionist movement. This acceptance, however, is dogged by the shadow of male same-sex desire, which functions as the shadowy Other of Jewish patriarchal bonds, and can only be extricated with difficulty from Behrman's vision of Jewish patriarchy. Behrman's relationship to Hollywood is deeply ambivalent. He both castigates it for its false values, cowardice and ontological insufficiency, but he also sees it as a place that encapsulates his own inadequacies. For what is he if not an Esme or a Wilda—a Galatea who embodied the choices of his Pygmalion, Dan Asher? The dark angel that pursues Vincent on the Santa Monica beach may easily be that of Behrman's youthful mentor, carrying with him the combination of desire, resentment and fear that can make up the conflicted relationship of mentor and pupil. Male identity is fragile in Behrman's Hollywood, and always aware of its vulnerability. In Behrman's Hollywood fugue, Jewish identity and male same-sex desire are two voices that restlessly pursue each other, and never resolve in a harmonious chord. There is only flight and death.

NOTES

Part of this paper, in an earlier form, was delivered under the title, "Between Zion and Garbo; Eroticism and Identity in an Essay by S. N. Behrman" at the Conference of the Philological Association of the Pacific Coast, San Francisco, 5 November 1994. My thanks to Stephanie Barbé Hammer, Andrew Moss, and Jim Gulledge for their help on this project.

1. The final confrontation between Ryder and Dow, in which Ryder wraps himself in the American flag and vows to fight communism, seems to be a last-minute attempt to stabilize the play's scepticism. It is interesting that this scene is a later addition, and was the result of the Theatre Guild's insistence that Behrman make Ryder a more attractive character, and repudiate Dow. See Gross, 76–77. Any attempt to reconstruct *Wine of Choice* along the lines of Behrman's personal intentions needs to examine earlier drafts of the play, at the Wisconsin Center for Theatre and Film Research.

2. Behrman's autobiographical writings tend to swerve away from unpleasant memories. In his volume of memoirs, *People in a Diary,* unsuccessful productions and unhappy collaborations are censored. For example, neither *Wine of Choice* nor *Let Me Hear the Melody* are ever mentioned.

3. For the story of *Two-Faced Woman,* see McGilligan, 165–167.

4. It is not my intention to "out" S. N. Behrman in this essay. First, biographical information on this timid playwright is scant, and the occasional rumors in the theatrical community of his homosexuality have not ever, to my knowledge, been substantiated. More importantly, neither the appellations "gay" nor "straight" do justice to the anxiety-ridden texture of much of Behrman's work. As the analysis of this essay shows, the homosexual and homophobic, the heterosexual and the misogynistic can interact within a single text. My interest here is in what Kaja Silverman has identified as "the author inside the text" (161–162). Regardless of the private details of Behrman's life, his work repeatedly manifests conflicted feelings about sexuality and intimacy.

5. Unpublished and without a Broadway premiere, there is no definitive text of *Let Me Hear the Melody.* Early notes and drafts can be found at the Wisconsin Center for Theatre and Film Research, and typescripts from 1951 are available in the Theatre Collection, New York Public Library at Lincoln Center. Unless otherwise indicated, I will refer to the 1951 version, since it was the sole performed version, even though I am not convinced that it is necessarily the most satisfying draft of the play. Since some names change from draft to draft, I will refer to all characters by their 1951 names.

6. Notes on *Let Me Hear the Melody,* 20 April 1950. Wisconsin Center for Theatre and Film Research.

7. In *The Worcester Account,* Behrman refers to Dan Asher under the alias "Willie Lavin."

8. See Heidegger, 251–255.

WORKS CITED

Anonymous. "Hollywood a Heartbreak Town for Artists, Says Author." *Evening Bulletin,* 20 March 1951.

————. Publicity Piece from The Playwrights Company for *The Mechanical Heart*. Theatre Collection, Philadelphia Public Library.

Behrman, S. N. *The Burning-Glass:* A Novel. London: Hamish Hamilton, 1968.

————. *Dunnigan's Daughter:* A Comedy. New York: Random House, 1946.

————. *End of Summer:* A Play in Three Acts. New York: Random House, 1936.

————. *Let Me Hear the Melody.* Typescript. Theatre Collection, New York Public Library.

————. Notes and drafts for *Let Me Hear the Melody.* Wisconsin Center for Film and Theatre Research. University of Wisconsin-Madison.

————. Notes and drafts for *Wine of Choice.* Wisconsin Center for Film and Theatre Research. University of Wisconsin-Madison.

————. *People in a Diary: A Memoir.* Boston: Little, Brown, 1972.

————. *Wine of Choice:* A Comedy in Three Acts. New York: Random House, 1938.

————. *The Worcester Account.* New York: Random House, 1954.

————. "Zion Comes to Culver City." *The Suspended Drawing Room.* New York: Stein and Day, 1965: 95–119.

Clurman, Harold. *Lies Like Truth: Theatre Reviews and Essays.* New York: Macmillan, 1958.

Deleuze, Gilles. *Difference and Repetition.* Translated by Paul Patton. New York: Columbia University Press, 1994.

Fontanne, Lynn. Letter to S. N. Behrman. 5 April 1937. Wisconsin Center for Film and Theatre Research. University of Wisconsin-Madison.

Gross, Robert *F. S. N. Behrman: A Research and Production Sourcebook.* Westport, CT: Greenwood Press, 1992.

Heidegger, Martin. *Being and Time.* Trans. by John Macquarrie and Edward Robinson. London: SCM Press, 1962.

McGilligan, Patrick. *George Cukor: A Double Life.* New York: St. Martin's Press, 1991.

Silverman, Kaja. *Male Subjectivity at the Margins.* New York: Routledge, 1992.

Hollywood as Moral Landscape: Clifford Odets' *The Big Knife*

Albert Wertheim

No name is more associated with New York agitprop theatre of the 1930s than that of Clifford Odets. As Odets confronted a "me first," acquisitive capitalism that left a generation of workers starving, unemployed, and shattered, his anger was both profound and dramatic. And particularly during 1935, which marked at once the nadir of the Great Depression and Odets' *annus mirabilis* as a playwright, that anger found its voice. In that year Odets had four major works produced in New York: *Waiting for Lefty, Awake and Sing!, Paradise Lost* and *Till the Day I Die*, each of them imbued with Odets' hard-hitting vision and impassioned language meant to open the eyes of Americans so that they would see something larger than their immediate and personal distress. For Odets, society was a moral landscape, and the Depression an event that rendered men and women as actors in a modern morality play. In his dramas, Appetite and lupine Greed were encountered not only by the saints and martyrs, but by the Everymen, the Joe and Ednas, the Ralphies, who were driven into their roles and sometimes to their enlightenment by the direness of the times. Odets was a playwright who discovered in the Depression a dramatic occasion to teach people how to become better, an occasion for moral and political education.

What must it have been like for this playwright, so imbued with Marxist idealism and the political ideology espoused by his beloved 1930s Group theatre, for a man so much a product of the hard-bitten New York and Philadelphia he knew so well and where he had grown up as a young man and come of age as a playwright, to fall headlong, during the subsequent decade, into the soft, seductive, West-Coast arms of the motion picture industry; into a Hollywood environment as alluring and erotic as Jean Harlow or Betty Grable or Frances Farmer who beckoned amorously to millions of enthralled viewers seated in the fantasy land and darkness of local movie palaces?

In many ways, it could be said that Hollywood as Siren, as Pacific Coast Lorelei, shipwrecked Odets; and if it did not altogether destroy his talent as a creative writer, it doubtless blighted it. He was never again to capture anything close to the success he had enjoyed during the 1930s. Certainly Odets himself had intimations of this, and his consequent love-hate relationship with Hollywood was an open secret during the 1940s. He recognized Hollywood as the Tinsel Town it was and is, he saw beneath its shallowness, and he knew and understood it as an incarnation of corporate capitalism in its most glamorous and seductive form.

Thus when, in 1948, Odets's *The Big Knife*, a drama set in Hollywood, hit the stage, critics understandably saw it—and continue to see it—as his intensely personal dramatization of his own tragic situation in America's movie capital. After seeing a preview performance of *The Big Knife*, Allan Lewis wrote Odets a warmly enthusiastic letter (*Odets Papers*, box 14, February 1949), in which he warmly extolled Odets' play for using Hollywood as a bellwether of American life:

> As to the play—it is written with dynamite, words explode with fury and hate. The play has the power of deep personal experience, the cry of a man that must be heard, that has got to be said, and stridently. And this is good, for the passion and venom must out and if it can do so with the fuming rage that this play has it makes strong theatre. It is nonsense to talk of the writer being removed, preserving objectivity, for he can better keep his balance in the heat of an honest fight. Objectivity can lead to a sterile liberalism. You have created a violent attack on a corrupt and corrosive industry, and through what you say of Hollywood comes the picture of an American scene where cultural decency and honest artistry are submerged in the greed and inhumanity of a movie magnate or the preservation of a bank balance. . . . The one adverse comment would be that the audience may not make the transition from Hollywood to themselves, may not see that values being torn to shreds here are the same forces that destroy their own creative needs. . . .

In his book (Lewis, 112), published 21 years later, however, Lewis ungenerously and, I believe, short-sightedly utters the more common assessment of the play:

> When Odets returned to Broadway with *the Big Knife,* his first play after many years of financial success in Hollywood, he retreated to the personal drama. Charley Castle seeks to escape from Hollywood's erosion of his artistic integrity, but he really wants the physical comfort that Hollywood offers. The drama never reaches beyond Odets' own dilemma. Everyone attacks Hollywood, particularly those who have been its best-paid hirelings. No one has yet made the attack significant. Satire would be a more effective weapon.

Lewis not merely forgets his initial and well-founded enthusiasm for the play, he surely as well neither read Nathanael West's *Day of the Locust* nor properly understood what Odets was about in writing *The Big Knife.* And John Mason Brown's vitriolic review of the play saw it as nothing more than Odets's mean-spirited attack on Hollywood (Brown, 34–35).

To see Odets' play as a castigation of Hollywood is to misunderstand it, to see it as less than it is, to reduce it to a melodrama penned by a man bent on biting the hand that generously fed him, a man at odds with himself for having "sold out" (Murray, 162 and Miller, 80ff) Clearly *The Big Knife* and its main character, Charlie Castle, are not completely separable from Odets' personal situation. Like his infamous relationships with women, Odets' love affair with Hollywood was filled with a commingling of passion, ardor, anger, disgust, and at once great amorous energy and revulsion. His letters to his wife, Bette, are filled with warm solicitude and words of genuine affection which alternate with vitriolic charges about her insufferable infringement upon his creative energy and talent. As with Bette, Odets loved Hollywood even as he saw the sacrifice of his talents to her seemingly all-consuming needs. But finally *The Big Knife* is not about Hollywood or Odets or even Charlie Cass, the idealist actor who came to Hollywood spouting about FDR and who became Charlie Castle, the sybaritic, politically disengaged, Hollywood matinee idol. What the critics seem determined not to see is that in *The Big Knife*, Hollywood was simply a cipher for larger moral and existential issues.

For Odets, Hollywood, that city of movie sets, was itself an appropriate set design; not so much for film as for a morality drama of Elizabethan stage grandeur. Long before he even thought of writing *The Big Knife*, Odets kept a file of personal observations about Hollywood. Among the notes he wrote during the 1940s is one that reads, "Hollywood, like carbon monoxide, is colorless, odorless gas; and like carbon monoxide has 100 times the affinity to blood that oxygen has"

(*Odets Papers*, box 10). He saw as well the several familiar types and parasites of the film-making industry in much the way that the seventeenth-century allegorist John Bunyan saw the creatures and caricatures who populate his Primrose Path and Vanity Fair. Caricaturing the Hollywood agent, for example, Odets writes in his notes:

> The agent is sinister because, as in certain Hitchcock movie scenes, you think you are talking to a friend working on your side until you discover with horror that he is all the time working for "them." The agent's principal job is to keep you in line for the studio. This is understood by everyone concerned, except the client. What a client can really get is previously understood, too.

That sense of Hollywood as a landscape or backdrop for a modern morality play is there when, in a letter to his most trusted friend, producer, director, critic Harold Clurman, Odets outlines some play ideas. The letter, dated 5 August 1947, well before Odets set pen to paper and 18 months before the opening of *The Big Knife*, nicely reveals the zygote that Odets would develop into a full-length stage play:

> ... a more recent idea about a public figure of a man (most likely a Hollywood star) who kills a child as a hit & run driver and reveals the whole sickness of modern life in the struggle to reach a decision as to confess or not his guilt. (*Odets Papers,* box 3)

And three weeks later (27 August 1947), in a 15-page letter to Clurman, we can recognize a rapidly developing embryo taking shape:

> I want this play to be Elizabethan in brutal, excited feel. For many years now capitalism at its extreme, and Hollywood in particular, have been as ghastly murderous and terrorizing as anything Shakespeare or Webster wrote. That sinister feeling, that total disregard of human life, I want to get in this play. So what I want to write is an Elizabethan tragedy and if my luck holds, and the quality of my talent is intense enough, that is what will come out. (*Odets Papers,* box 3)

Rather than write a nasty insider tragedy about Hollywood, Odets clearly wished to use the Hollywood setting, much the way Jonson and

Webster used Italy or Shakespeare used Denmark and Scotland, as an image of the noisome world that corrupts and tests its inhabitants. Indeed, Odets' protagonist, Charlie Castle, comes to see himself as Macbeth, "in blood / Steeped in so far that, should [he] wade no more / Returning were as tedious as go o'er." And that Shakespearean connection is made absolute when Charlie Castle views his plight and exclaims, "I can't go on, covering one crime with another. That's Macbeth" (Odets, *The Big Knife,* 70).[1] He sees himself as well as a Hamlet surrounded by evil who, in the midst of his despair, asks his friend Hank, "Why don't you stay here, Hank—be my Horatio?" (59).

Even more, Charlie reminds one of a Faustus who has already made his fatal choice prior to the play's first act. And as in Marlowe's *Doctor Faustus* or late medieval moral temptation plays, *The Big Knife* provides a corrupt, satanic antagonist for its present day Everyman. At the moral—or rather immoral—center of Odets' Hollywood is Marcus Hoff, the Mephistophelian movie mogul, whose histrionics and blandishments bring out the worst in susceptible men like Charlie Castle. Marcus Hoff is every bit as witty, shrewd, comic and manipulative as any Titivillus or Mephistopheles. And reminiscent of Faustus' signing his pact with Mephistopheles, Charlie Castle signs his Hollywood contract with Hoff Federated Studios. And Marcus' satanic henchman and general factotum wryly comments to Charlie, "Just keep in mind that the day you first scheme . . . you marry the scheme and the scheme's children" (61). These are words that could as easily have come from the pen of Christopher Marlowe as from Clifford Odets'. Furthermore, like the world of *Doctor Faustus* or the world of morality drama from which Marlowe liberally drew, Hollywood seemed for Odets populated not merely by archetypes such as "the agent" he described in his notes, but by classic physiognomies that go with those archetypes. Indeed Odets, from the 1930s until his death, kept a clipping file of Hollywood photos and classic faces that included the profiles of female and male models and performers as well as of producers and directors. That file, which Odets labeled "Hollywood Types," contains facial shots of Laurence Harvey, Milton Berle, Warren Beatty, Charles Laughton; and mug shots from *Operation Bikini,* including the posed faces of Tab Hunter, Frankie Avalon, Scott Brady, Jim Backus, Gary Crosby, Michael Dante, Jody McCrea. There are as well photos of Shirley MacLaine as Gittel in *Two for the Seesaw* as well as of Edie Adams, Paul Newman, several Hollywood producers, Burt Lancaster, Fay Spain, Jane Fonda, and Fay Wray and her ex-husband John Monk Saunders clipped from Saunders' obituary (*Odets*

Papers, box 10, 11 March 1940). During his Hollywood years, Odets was a painter as well as a playwright, and his canvases of *Diva, Italian Movie Star (Sophia Loren), Smoker, Burlesque Girl, Actress,* and *Straight Man* all again show his admirable talent for caricature (Odets, "In Hell + Why," 8, 24–25, 28–29).

In *The Big Knife,* Charlie Castle is a character reaching for Elizabethan tragic dimension, a Faustus or Macbeth who has made irremediable choices, has essentially sealed his fate, yet wishes to retrieve his moral rectitude. It is important that this play set in Hollywood never show Charlie Castle acting in a movie set or in the business offices of a film studio. To pun on the medieval theatre term, *The Big Knife*'s only mansion is the one in Beverly Hills owned by Charlie Castle; and all of the play's action takes place in its one and only set, the so-called "Playroom" of that mansion. It is in that appropriately named playroom, which features a much-used bar, that Charlie, like a morality play protagonist, is visited by the grotesques and demons of Hollywood: Patty Benedict, the insidious conflation of Hedda Hopper and Louella Parsons; Dixie Evans, the blowzy would-be starlet; Connie Bliss, the lustful wife of the man who went to jail in Charlie's stead for the hit-and-run fatality; Nat Danziger, Charlie's agent who is really working for the studio; and of course those incarnations of unvarnished Evil, Marcus and Coy.[2] There he is also visited by the play's incarnations of Good: Charlie's wife, Marion, whom he frequently calls "angel," and by Hank Teagle, his friend and better self, to whom he says, "But where the hell do you stash your angel wings?" (38). And at the rear center of the set there is a prominent iron spiral staircase leading to the upper regions of the house. Those private and unseen upstairs areas seem to be the areas of grace from which Charlie has fallen. It is theatrically appropriate that it is there he commits suicide by slashing his wrists while running the water in his bathtub. And it is appropriate, too, that the first sign of Charlie's suicide is marked by the bathwater dripping from upstairs through the ceiling and down into the playroom.

What *The Big Knife* is meant to be is not a castigation of Hollywood but Odets' powerful portrait of the American post-World War II wasteland, devoid of the ethics and ideals that had sent Americans to the battlefields of Europe a few years before. And it is a wasteland replete with untrammeled acquisitiveness. What has happened to Charlie Castle in Hollywood is Odets' terrible image of the sickness besetting American life. A heartsick Hamlet-like Charlie seeing what is rotten in the state of California and in America, feelingly laments to his Horatio friend, Hank: "When I came home from Germany. . . I saw most of the war dead were here, not in Africa and Italy. And Roosevelt was dead. . . and the war was only last week's snowball fight. . . and we plunged ourselves, all of us, into the noble work of making the buck reproduce itself!" (58).

Hollywood is likewise a particularly apt linguistic setting for Odets' purposes. Edward Murray suggests an undertone of homosexuality as he checks off the vocative uses of "darling," "lovely," and "boyfriend" among the male figures in the play or of Smiley Coy's calling Charlie "Ella" (Murray, 169–170). Murray notices as well the feminine, subaltern imagery of lines like "I'm like a girl in a summer-time canoe—I can't say no!" (26) recurs throughout the play. Odets' aim in writing this language is not at all to imply homosexuality but to deepen his portrait of a world structured, as is its representative language, to create emasculated denizens. It is the studio bosses like Hoff and, ironically, the women—Marion, Patty Benedict and Dixie Evans—who wield power, who are the doers. Without wishing to exaggerate the importance of Odets' title, one could argue that the Hollywood of studio producers like Hoff is the Hollywood phallically represented in the play's title. Certainly men like Charlie, who are powerful male figures in on-screen cinematic fictions, are courted, seduced, and overpowered like females off screen. Charlie has lost his virginity and is whored in Hollywood; and that kind of passivity or disempowered masculinity is very much in keeping with morality play and post-morality play structure. A passive Everyman or Human Genus, or the archetypal figure of emasculated man, Samson in Milton's *Samson Agonistes,* is fixed on stage in one spot to be visited by the men and women who wield power over him. In Milton's drama this is particularly clear as a bound Samson is faced with the power of Harapha and of Dalila. R. Baird Shuman in criticizing *The Big Knife* says, the play "revolves around Charlie Castle, who, peculiarly enough, is probably the weakest character in the play"; and in so saying, Shuman unwittingly touches the plays structural essence (Shuman, 122 and Miller, 80).[3]

But what transpires in plays structured like *The Castle of Perseverance* or *Samson Agonistes* is also what Odets allows to transpire in *The Big Knife*: the central and emasculated character reclaims, heroically and sometimes tragically, his masculine power by moving from a passive to an active state. For Odets, the emasculation of the central character by Hollywood is a sign of the times. It is what has happened to the American public after the anger of the Thirties and

the war of the Forties. Speaking of Hank Teagle's novel about
American society, Charlie says, "You're right, Hank. Your hero's half a
man, neither here nor there, dead from the gizzard up. Stick him with a
pin and see, psst! No feelings!" (58). Obviously, Charlie is that
moribund, desensitized half-man, and he is so because in post-war
America the captains of industry are threatening the spirit of American
individualism, of the classic American Everyman, who is reduced to a
receptive female role. And for Odets, Hollywood movie moguls are just
one glaring example of the satanic captains of contemporary industry
and Charlie Castle is just one victim, one example of oppressed
American individualism. Odets uses Hollywood almost metonymically.
It is his shorthand for a more general American post-war fall from
grace. When Charlie Castle makes his one exit from the stage and the
play, he ascends the staircase not merely to his death but to what is the
only way he can reclaim grace.

It was Odets' closest friends, Harold Clurman, and director Jean
Renoir, who saw exactly what Odets meant to dramatize in *The Big
Knife*. After reading a first draft of the script, Clurman wrote in a letter
to Odets (15 October 1947):

> The core of your play is a bitterness which people today want to gloss
> over in platitudes, in sentimental evasion, or in the subterfuge of
> calling such bitterness "confusion," "neurosis," and "craziness." In
> other words they will try to suggest that you are writing about special
> people, whereas you are really writing about everybody. You are
> writing about the fundamental base of middle-class America.
> (*Odets Papers,* box 3)[4]

And reading a later draft, Jean Renoir wrote (15 November 1948):

> Your Hollywood background becomes as rich as the court of
> Denmark or Venice in the 15th century. And your hero is the brother
> of all those kings, generals, great lovers, who talk in the Latin or
> Greek verses we had to translate in school. (*Odets Papers,* box 4)

Likewise, critic John Gassner, clearly saw the flaws of *The Big
Knife*, but also saw its strength, when he wrote of Odets, ". . . he
deliberately chose Hollywood as a symbol for everything deteriorative
and unscrupulous in our society: he returned to the 'Golden Boy' theme
of how a materialistic, success-worshipping world corrupts the soul"
(Gassner, 26).

Move important, we have among Odets' papers, his own words about *The Big Knife*. In a seven-page letter of rebuttal (24 March 1949) to critic John Mason Brown, who had written very deprecatingly of *The Big Knife* in *The Saturday Review of Literature* (Brown, 34–35), Odets defends his play against the charge that continues to dog it, that it is an anti-Hollywood play written by a man who, as Allan Lewis was to say, had been all too willing to become one of its best-paid hirelings. Odets must have been particularly stung by Brown's high-handed, savage and personal attack, for Odets' letter is dated just five days after the Brown diatribe appeared. In his unpublished letter, Odets passionately writes:

> As for intention, "The Big Knife" is not about an actor and it is not about Hollywood. It is a morality play about a certain kind of modern *Prince of Success* and some of the human problems which come in the wake of his elevation. The Hollywood background was chosen because the author knew it from more than hearsay; and because, secondly, Hollywood is the very glass and symbol of high success the wide world over. . .
>
> The better part of Charlie Castle is represented in my play by his wife, Marion, a woman who, as he says, is "the iron hoop that keeps my rotten staves together."
>
> Well, in conclusion, I must tell you that I wrote "The Big Knife," not because I have personal pains, but exactly because so many people in Hollywood (and in the other high places of the land) are so utterly "realistic" about their work and so unmoved morally by the rotten fruit of that work. Much of the work is demeaning and degrading to themselves and to the millions who later view it. Hollywood is purveying a steady diet of bon-bons to a great people who are hungering for the simple bread of a spiritual life, that's all.
>
> Forced from time to time to make a living from Hollywood (and giving honest, skilled work in return), I am unable to remain "realistic" about the enormous abuse there of human possibilities. Let me lose my writing hand when I stop writing out against the abuse of human talent and aspiration in any shape or form, in this, my native land! (*Odets Papers,* box 4)

Odets' eloquent and, alas, unpublished response lucidly suggests the tenor of his thinking as he wrote *The Big Knife*. Odets' reply should also serve as one for the rather unfair treatment of *The Big Knife* given by Gerald Rabkin, who argues:

The Marxist eschatology provided the dramatist with a structural
referent, for implicit in the dialectical struggle is an essential drama,
the vanquishing of the old class by the new. . . The structural failure
of *the Big Knife* lies in Odets' inability, after the loss of political
commitment, to substitute a suitable unifying dramatic metaphor.
(Rabkin, 199)

Odets makes clear in his letter to Brown that fifteen years and world
wars have created new issues for America, for which the Marxist
rhetoric and vision of the Depression era is no longer apt. It is,
moreover, precisely the loss of that ideological and social clarity in
American life that Odets is writing about in *The Big Knife*. In the 1930s
New York world of oppressed taxi drivers against corrupt unions in
Waiting for Lefty, it was "us against them." But in the new, late 1940s
world, a world epitomized by a Hollywood imbued with seductive and
duplicitous saccharine euphemistic language, luxury, and sweetheart
deals, the issues and the lines of combat are blurred, even as the
characters' thinking is blurred by the alcohol they imbibe from the
centrally placed bar, itself euphemistically referred to as "the lemonade
stand" (7). In 1935, people were starving, children were stricken with
rickets, lives were shattered by the economic hard times. The times
were tough and the issues clear. In 1949, however, the times were good,
post-war affluence has come to the United States, and, consequently,
social issues and moral decisions were both less pressing and less
clearly delineated.

   In a world of oppression heroism is relatively easy, but how, Odets
ponders through the figure of Charlie Castle, can one retain the hard
edge of heroism and moral rectitude in a soft world of near sybaritic
ease? Castle's malaise stems from his failure to name an enemy. It is
natural to call "Strike!" against indigence and human indignity
unleashed in the 1930s. But, as Charlie Castle finds and Odets knows, it
is far less easy to tilt against a world of swimming pools, parties,
beautiful people, million dollar contracts, elegant clothes, beach houses
and expensive cars. It is precisely the loss of political commitment and
the need for political commitment in the United States, Hollywood, and
Charlie Castle's life that comprises the central issue of *The Big Knife*.
Classic tragic character that he is, Charlie is so corrupted, "in blood
steeped in so far," that when he has his moment of tragic insight, his
Aristotelian *anagnorisis*, it is already too late for him to reform, and
suicide is his only way out. It is, however, for the other characters, for
Odets' Macduffs and Horatios, for Marion and Teagle among others

and of course for the audience, to learn from Charlie's tragedy, to see the moral issues behind the seductive facade of the new American post-war affluence, to recognize filth in a silk stocking, and to act so that commitment to social and political ideals in America does not die a death induced by a surfeit of riches.

The shrewd and jaded characters of Odets' play understand Charlie Castle and in so doing understand America as Odets saw it after the war. Charlie's agent Nat, explains, "Everybody has a delusion that you're very tough—they mix you up with the parts you play. But I know you better. You're a special, idealistic type. The only thing— business and idealism don't mix—it's oil and water. Darling, you expect too much from yourself" (20). Nat's is an image of Charlie Castle and of America. Hank Teagle, a writer and Charlie's best friend, telling Charlie of the book he is completing, says, "I still try to write out of Pascal's remark: 'I admire most those writers who tell, with tears in their eyes, what men do to other men.' This book is about a man like you . . . It's a fable about moral values and success" (57). *The Big Knife*, too, using Hollywood as its backdrop and symbol, is also a fable about moral values and success.

NOTES

1. Parenthetical references refer to the Dramatists Play Service 1949 edition of *The Big Knife*.

2. Brooks Atkinson curiously put his finger on the morality play texture when he wrote in his review of *The Big Knife*, "Always a vivid writer, he [Odets] has put together a whole company of authentic individual people, characterizing them brilliantly and displaying them in a series of scenes." *The New York Times,* 25 February 1949, 28.

3. Miller recognizes Charlie as the person who is continually on stage and at the center of the action but who never leaves his playroom. "It as if," Miller says, "everyone has access to the world outside the stage except Charlie, who is confined to the Hollywood castle that his own name betokens." Miller goes on to compare the play to Ibsen's *A Doll's House*.

4. One can only wonder what Odets must have felt when he read his friend Clurman's essentially negative review of the play in *The New Republic* (14 March 1949), 28–29. There Clurman writes, "As a mechanism for conveying a definite theme, idea or emotion, 'The Big Knife' is misbegotten. . . . The ostensible point of this is that a good person in our society becomes the prisoner of forces that will manipulate him as a commodity. Unless he is a saint or a revolutionary he can live only by dying. Apart from any judgment as to the validity of this thesis, the play fails to demonstrate it."

WORKS CITED

Atkinson, Brooks. *"The Big Knife,"* The New York Times (25 February 1949), 28.

Brown, John Mason. "The Biting Hand," *The Saturday Review of Literature* (19 March 1949), 34–35.

Clurman, Harold. *"The Big Knife,"* The New Republic (14 March 1949), 28–29.

Gassner, John. *"The Big Knife,"* Theatre Arts 33 (July 1949).

Lewis, Allan. American Plays and Playwrights of the Contemporary Theatre. New York: Crown Books, 1970.

Miller, Gabriel. *Clifford Odets*. New York: Continuum, 1989.

Murray, Edward. *Clifford Odets: The Thirties and After.* New York: Frederick Ungar, 1968.

Odets, Clifford. *The Big Knife*. New York: The Dramatists Play Service, 1949.

Odets, Clifford. *Clifford Odets Papers.* The Lilly Library, Indiana University.

Odets, Clifford. "In Hell + Why": Paintings on Paper from the 1940's and 1950's. New York: Michael Rosenfeld Gallery, 1996.

Rabkin, Gerald. *Drama and Commitment.* Bloomington: Indiana University Press, 1964.

Shuman, R. Baird. *Clifford Odets*. New York: Twayne, 1962.

Weales, Gerald. "Awake and Paint," *American Theatre* 13 (September 1996), 56–57.

Hollywood on the Contemporary Stage: Image, Phallic "Players," and the Culture Industry

Stephen Watt

> "This whole movie thing is a murder of the people. Only we hit them on the heads, under the hair—nobody sees the marks."
>
> Charlie Castle in Clifford Odets' The Big Knife

> "Movies and radio no longer pretend to be art. The truth that they are just business is made into an ideology in order to justify the rubbish they deliberately produce."
>
> Max Horkheimer and Theodor W. Adorno
in Dialectic of Enlightenment

> "You gotta be a man to do this job."
>
> Buddy in Swimming with Sharks

Some fifty years ago, two German intellectuals writing in Los Angeles and a successful New York playwright working in California launched their respective critiques of what the former, Horkheimer and Adorno, disparaged as the "Culture Industry." The latter, Clifford Odets in *The Big Knife* (1949), in an early example of what is now an impressive canon of mostly American plays about Hollywood, attempts a realistic, if finally melodramatic, representation of both a medium and an industry whose myriad corruptions confirm Horkheimer and Adorno's indictments in *Dialectic of Enlightenment*.[1] Both book and play attack what Horkheimer and Adorno term the "false identity of the general and the particular" in mass culture (121); both attend to the manner in which "real life is becoming indistinguishable from the movies" (126); and both explore the limits to which the culture industry disciplines its consumers (not to mention its own workers). Both the Marxian critique and play, therefore, are premised on a number of crucial oppositions, the most important being that between art and mass culture, or "high" and "low" art. As Adorno disparages it elsewhere, "The culture industry intentionally integrates its consumers from above. To the detriment of both it forces together the spheres of high and low art. . . ."[2]

To what extent this may (or may not) have been true in the 1940s is of less interest to me than the ways in which contemporary dramatists represent—and, in rather different ways, critique—Hollywood. There is, for example, little question that depictions of Hollywood like Odets's overestimate both the civilizing benefits of drama and the rebarbative liabilities of movies, a separation or "great divide" as vast as the distance between Broadway and the backlot of Republic Studios. The Odets protagonist, Charlie Castle's allegation that movies "murder" their audiences is paralleled by his wife's plea for him to tell the powerful studio head Marcus Hoff that he's leaving Hollywood "for good," returning to the more dignified and literate world of "the theatre." In *The Big Knife*, much as in Christopher Hampton's play about film studios in the 1930s *Tales from Hollywood* (1981), Hollywood is ruled by dictatorial producers (appropriately named Charles Money in Hampton's play) with near absolute power and equally conspicuous vulgarity. And even while George Abbott in his Foreword to Bella and Samuel Spewack's earlier play *Boy Meets Girl* (1935), which Abbott directed in New York, attempts to rebut what had by the 1930s become stereotypes of "crass and illiterate producers" and dim-witted actors, the Spewacks' play demonstrates the difficulties enlightened filmmakers inevitably confront.[3] By contrast, like the late-capitalist economy of decentralized authority that analysts like Daniel Bell describe, contemporary Hollywood as viewed from the stage scarcely resembles that industry in which despots led and actors servilely followed. Power is much more diffusely circulated; conceptions of identity and gender are placed under vastly different pressures in such an economy. The Culture Industry today, in short, goes about its interpellating work quite differently than Odets imagined.

Or so Sam Shepard, David Mamet, Arthur Kopit, and others have suggested, for in its collective vision of the Culture Industry—and, whatever differences obtain between these instances of "Hollywood on Stage," such a shared vision *does* exist—American drama sees a postmodern media desert aptly theorized by such various commentators as Jean Baudrillard and, a more recent critic of postmodernity, Edward Bond. My principal occupation here is to adduce the attributes of

"Hollywood on stage" within the broader contexts of this postmodern desert. At the same time, however, in its misogyny and copious nihilism, Hollywood on the contemporary stage and screen is resolutely *anti*-postmodern in the more politically resonant ways outlined by such different cultural critics as Huyssen and Robyn Wiegman. I intend here to address this paradox—to read this drama as postmodern and not postmodern at the same time—by juxtaposing plays from the contemporary theatre with examples taken from such recent films as Robert Altman's *The Player* (1992) and George Huang's *Swimming with Sharks* (1994), and to foreground in my reading issues of gender, the instauration of a normative heterosexuality, and what I might term the revenge of a threatened phallocracy. Stated in another way, contemporary playwrights seem to have glimpsed Baudrillard's America and, through their representations of Hollywood, have either partaken of his nihilism or blithely shared in his eccentric, even perverse, joy and humor.

By "resolutely anti-postmodern" I mean just this: most plays about contemporary Hollywood reinscribe, often with a vengeance, the "great divide" between High Art and a mass culture of instant consumability. Yet Art isn't so easily located in New York or on Broadway in such plays, the theatre's virtue having been compromised years ago. Moreover, there is little evidence in these dramas of what Huyssen delineates as an uncritical "populist" trend in 1960s social commentary of a mass culture that will fulfill "the promise of a 'postwhite,' 'postmale,' 'posthumanist' world."[4] Wiegman is right, I think, to query (queery?) this hypothesis, to interrogate the implication that women and minorities serve "as the difference that posts the modern" and its reliance "on the other *as other* for the politics of the postmodern to be achieved." This binarity and form of identity politics are of particular concern for Wiegman, who in pondering the definition of a "lesbian postmodern" cautions against our forgetting "modernity's political investment in categorical identities as well as the disciplinary function they have served only too well."[5] Fair enough. But when we resituate this caveat within Baudrillardian simulation and gender politics, even when ignoring the ubiquity of the image and bracketing the problem of recognizing anything beyond its vast domain, we are faced with one of two assertions. First, if one accepts the hypothesis advanced by such cultural theorists as John Tomlinson, Fredric Jameson and of course Baudrillard (and his recombinant son, Arthur Kroker) that under the imperial regime of the media—and the image—all of us are becoming more homogenous, more monadically isolated in front of televisions,

computer screens, and slot machines,[6] then it's only one more step to
the erosion of gender difference in contemporary culture (Kroker's
Toni Denise, the "man-made woman. A woman made from a man").[7]
This homogenization/erosion is somewhat more delicately rendered by
Baudrillard in the rise of "gender benders" (Michael Jackson, Boy
George) in popular culture and "muscle girls," the monadic raised to
the nth degree:

> What does sexual difference consist [of]? Liberation has left
> everyone in an undefined state . . . No one knows where they are.
> That is why there's so much love-making . . . here at least you still
> have proof that two people are needed *so difference still exists.* But
> not for long. Already the 'muscle-woman,' who simply by using her
> vaginal muscles, manages to reproduce the effect of male penetration
> exactly, is a good example of self-referentiality and of getting along
> without difference . . . [8]

Given the narrowing beam of categorical identity with which Wiegman
is concerned, such confusions might initially appear as both
emancipatory and "post" modern, and perhaps this is one reason why
Neil Jordan's film *The Crying Game* (1992) has received so much
critical attention of late. But, second, the "lightning-flash" of
"seduction" that can mutate or alter the process Baudrillard describes
can only do so through by restoring gender, a restoration that is more
than metaphoric:

> The feminine. . . suggests a challenge to the male to be *the* sex, to
> monopolize sex and sexual pleasure, a challenge to go to the limits of
> its hegemony and exercise it unto death. Today, phallocracy is
> collapsing under the pressure of this challenge . . . (*Seduction*, 21; my
> emphasis)

And what, other than the "feminine," is the gravest threat to this
phallocracy? Plenitude or sexual freedom, which means the blurring of
identities and the endorsement of practices that exist outside what
Wiegman terms the "normative heterosexual script." For Baudrillard,
then, as for Harold Pinter in his latest "political plays" and several of
the playwrights I shall discuss here, a homology exists between sexual
and capitalist economies, both of which rely upon a patriarchal
management of sexuality and its ability to maintain an acceptable level
of scarcity—acceptable to the ruling phallocracy, that is. The

maintenance of scarcity, for Baudrillard, is where seduction begins: "Economic reason is sustained only by penury. . . ; [d]esire too is sustained only by want" (*Seduction*, 5). But what happens when the authority of patriarchal management is challenged? The "un"-postmodern and ultimately retrograde politics of Hollywood in much contemporary drama portrays such a challenge—and the politics of gender reinscription, heterosexuality, and acute misogyny that often results. For what is at stake in mass culture, as Mamet, Altman, Kopit, and Shepard, among others, have shown us, is the recuperation of phallic prerogatives and the creation of images that facilitate this recuperation. This means, inevitably though not always successfully, the attempted vanquishing of the "feminine challenge" and all that she represents.

This is scarcely a revelation insofar as Shepard and Mamet are concerned, for impotence and the role of imaging in either masking or ameliorating male impotence typically lurks somewhere in their writing. Take, for example, Sam Shepard's autobiographical *Motel Chronicles*, in which he bemoans the primacy of the image and its effects on selfhood: "Men turning themselves into advertisements of Men. . . . Women turning themselves into advertisements of Women."[9] Or consider the nostalgia that permeates Shepard's writing: a nostalgia for old movies, cowboy actors, and '57 Chevies. Not so pessimistic as Baudrillard, Shepard still believes that Nature, the real, and sexual desire exist—or so his brief paean to the "natural woman" implies:

> I've about seen all the nose jobs capped teeth and silly-cone tits I can handle I'm heading back to my natural woman. (*Chronicles*, 102)

To recapture the real in Shepard, Kopit, and Mamet—to name but three theatrical and filmic chroniclers of contemporary American culture—one also frequently confronts the power of the phallus and the "reality" of violence against or the marginalization of women. "Heading back" to "nature" thus isn't always pretty (or categorically "pure") in Shepard, but the journey typically is—or, rather, *was*—something a man *can* (could) handle and from which he might regain some sense of phallic renewal.

"Was" appears to be the operative term here, the difference between the 1960s and 70s in Shepard's America and today—and tomorrow, in the case of *States of Shock*. In an *oeuvre* so replete with examples of this problematic as Shepard's, it's difficult to privilege one instance over another. Yet few works present stronger evidence of a

dominant phallic regime than *Hawk Moon* (1981), a collection of
poems, monologues, and stories that celebrates a 1970s of gender
difference, promiscuous heterosexuality, and phallic reveries in which
an erection could be realized in stick shifts, gun barrels. and the
subsequent violent penetration of women. In "Back in the 1970's," the
monotony of unemployment and gangfights sends young people into an
orgy of "fucking and sucking and smoking and shooting and dancing
right out in the open" (12). Then, "[f]ull-blown color pages of cock and
pussy" circulated through small towns; motorcycle gangs and the "bad
boys" of rock, the Rolling Stones, were touring America. Young men
queued outside "The Phantom Trailer" to have sex with young girls,
one of whom, it is rumored, in a fit of passion induced by Spanish fly
impaled herself on a stick-shift, and in "Montana" a woman is violated
by an "old Buntline Special with an extra long barrel" (21). Then, it
seems, difference ruthlessly enforced, which is why the film cowboy in
the short prose piece "Hollywood" falls to his knees at the end begging
Utah for forgiveness. A *real* cowboy cannot wear "white make up" or
lipstick for the camera (40); it's not just that he appears foolish—
Shepard describes the make-up as clownish—but that he has crossed
lines of gender difference. It's little wonder that he is deprived of an
"extra long" Buntline to brandish.

The dystopic nightmare of *States of Shock* foregrounds this
malady, as Stubbs, whose perpetually flaccid "THING" hangs "LIKE
DEAD MEAT" (34), seeks companionship from Glory Bee. Like the
nomadic Lee in *True West* who finds "home" only when he eats—and
the sanctity of this return home is something he vigorously defends—
Stubbs tells Glory Bee, who is supporting him as he staggers and raves,
to keep focussed on "home," on a "better time. Truman, maybe. County
Fairs! Ferris wheels," but the project is extremely difficult:

> STUBBS: Hold to an image! Lock onto a picture of glorious, unending
> expansion! DON'T LET YOURSELF SLIP INTO DOUBT!! Don't
> let it happen! You'll be swallowed whole!
> GLORY BEE: I can't keep this up!
> STUBBS (*staggering badly*): Lock onto an image or you'll be blown
> to KINGDOM COME!! (38)

Seconds later, their congress concluded, both fall into a pile,
"exhausted and breathing hard." Images of an America of the past, of a
"better time" before a multi- or transnational present and its

emasculations, sustain these characters and render a facsimile of sexual potency possible, if only for a moment.

But one need not venture into such "nightmare" futures as that of *States of Shock* or Margaret Atwood's *The Handmaid's Tale* to find an "ideological quilt" stitched together of a diminished male potency and declining individual agency in late capitalism, waning national superiority, and the power of the image.[10] The present moment is rife with such ideological elements, and Hollywood has provided the raw materials necessary for piecing them together. Mamet has been stitching such a quilt, fixing these otherwise "free-floating" elements, for some time now in *Edmond* (1982), *Glengarry Glen Ross* (1983), and *Speed-the-Plow*. My reading of the obvious deceptions, misrecognitions, and betrayals in Mamet, it should be said, differs from those like C.W.E. Bigsby's which are based upon a kind of *modernist* notion of subjectivity and agency. For Bigsby, Mamet's films *House of Games* (1987) and *Things Change* (1988) form a primer of human behavior with which one might read the plays:

> Just as advertising, pornography or Hollywood make fundamental human needs serve the purpose of commerce, so Mamet's confidence men do the same. In doing so, of course, they thereby acknowledge the reality of those needs as they do the equally powerful impulse to exploit them. They also show the power of the imperial self, which wishes to subordinate other people, to colonise their imaginations as do Madison Avenue and Hollywood.[11]

But is it certain that Mamet's "salesmen/priests" in what Bigsby terms the "postindustrial age" *possess* "imperial" selves or, given Bond's concerns about the confusion of wants and needs in the reign of the image, that "fundamental human needs" always pre-exist the manipulations Bigsby enumerates? Does, say, Mamet's Edmond, who feels as if his "balls were cut off" a "long, long time ago" fit this description?[12] Do the real-estate men in *Glengarry Glen Ross* or low-level mob figures in *Things Change* possess anything like the transubstantive power of priests—or even the self-autonomy and agency of bourgeois "individuals?"

More to the purposes of this essay, what does it mean to assert that something essentialized as "Hollywood" does anything? What exactly *is* Hollywood? For Robert Altman, as he emphasizes in a 1992 interview on *The Player,* "Hollywood is something that really doesn't exist. These corporations have nobody running them—that's the change."[13] Exactly—and in Mamet's case, Hollywood producers like Bobby Gould and Charlie Fox are not nearly so imperious modelers of the consumer's desire as Bigsby implies, nor do they resemble the nearly omnipotent producers of Hollywood's Big Studio era (Marcus Hoff in *The Big Knife* and Charles Money in *Tales from Hollywood*). From the play's opening lines, Mamet establishes Gould's positionality on the boundary between—and midst the confusions of—"Art" and "Entertainment": "If it's not quite 'Art' and it's not quite 'Entertainment,'" Gould explains, "it's here on my desk. I have inherited a monster."[14] The play's narrative demands that Gould negotiate between the Scylla of "art"—always dangerous when the bottom line of profit is to be assessed—and the Charybdis of mere "entertainment," the kind Odets's high-minded Castles deplore. Fox brings to Gould's attention an example of the latter variety, a "buddy film" complete with the possibility of a bankable star for the lead, and his secretary Karen promotes the former: the "radiation" script of an Eastern intellectual with the power to "speak to" its audience, to *change* them. In depictions of the Culture Industry, the film that can effect an immediate transformation of an audience, enlightenment dispensed with catastrophic suddenness, is frequently offered as a counter to the vastly more typical, mind-numbing two hours of entertainment, the "commodity," as Gould explains, that gets "The Asses in the Seats" (53). Such is the project, for instance, of Martin Mirkheim in Howard Korder's *Search and Destroy* (1990): to adapt the novel *Daniel Strong* which, albeit laden with "commercial potential," will bring its author's "message to millions of people in a simple way they can understand."[15] Never mind that the "Art" film's premise seems far-fetched, as it is in *Speed-the-Plow*—or is an adaptation of an adventure novel penned by a late-night television psychologist-huckster, as it is in *Search and Destroy*. Making history by making the monumental film, not the mere movie, Mirkheim's "pitch" to the novel's avaricious author, is more important. Or so, in fleeting moments of megalomania or rare high-mindedness, film producers on the contemporary stage are fond of proclaiming.

Of course, these films seldom get made, for Karen and those like her fail to recognize the extent to which the masculinity of producers like Gould are connected to the "commercial potential" of buddy films and "slashers."[16] This point is underscored with pointed irony in George Huang's *Swimming with Sharks*, as a beautiful and thoughtful writer, Dawn Lockhart (Michelle Forbes), attempts to induce the ruthless Buddy Ackerman (Kevin Spacey), Senior Vice-President at Keystone

Pictures, to make a film entitled *Real Life*. But the competition is formidable: a powerful, if invisible, executive's grandson wants the studio to make the "hippest, hottest thing" going (something like a rock video) and Buddy simply wants to make money.[17] In the midst of this battle between a teenager's MTV-inspired whim, "male macho bullshit" (Buddy's projects) and "lost artsy generation crap" (Dawn's screenplay), Guy (Frank Whaley), a young studio assistant whom Buddy regards with ruthless contempt, begins an affair with Dawn and grows weary of Buddy's ill-treatment. Eventually, Guy goes to Buddy's house, ties and gags him, tortures him (without inflicting too much damage), and threatens him with a gun. Dawn appears, attempting to mollify Guy and clarifying, remorsefully, that Buddy's adage "You gotta give action to get action" has been realized in her affair with Buddy. We later hear a shot—presumably Buddy has paid for this final insult—and the scene fades from view, coming back up on the studio and a renewed relationship between him and Guy. Dawn is dead and with her *Real Life*. The implication of this somewhat startling conclusion seems clear: this Hollywood privileges the relationship of men, endorses "male macho bullshit" over art, and will not tolerate a woman's interference. She has to be done away with, and the ritual of doing so cements the homosocial bond.[18] This possibility is intimated in Guy's finding the key to Buddy's house under a statue of a fragmented torso of a female body—it holds the key.

Mamet's Hollywood isn't much different, although his sharks seem smaller, more frightened, less able to assert their will, less potent. Sexuality, then, is more than the vehicle of tired metaphors and old jokes in *Speed-the-Plow*; "buddy films" signify more than a popular film genre. As Gould and *his* buddy Fox joke in Act One—the play, after all, follows a kind of familiar "buddy" narrative—this prison film will not only make them money, it will also move them up into "the big league" (p. 22); it will afford them the opportunity "to kick some ass"; and, most important, it will allow these self-described "old whores" to get "out of the barrel" and become phallically empowered. That is, instead of living the punchline of an old joke about being trapped in a barrel and subjected to a pre-arranged anal violation ("It's your turn to be in the barrel tonight" is the laughline I know, as cowboys at a remote camp take their turns playing the receptacle behind the knothole), the prison film will allow Fox and Gould to impose their own brand of sexual-industrial power on others. "Up the ass with gun and camera" (p. 27), Fox remarks—up someone else's ass, in other words. No "imperial selves," Fox and Gould hope simply to regain their phallic potency, a more enduring restoration than one night alone with Karen can facilitate.

The script she promotes, conversely, is written by an Eastern "sissy," a "fruit"; thus, if Gould were to produce it instead of the buddy film, as he contemplates in the last act of *Speed-the-Plow*, it can only be from Fox's perspective because he "squat[s] to pee"—because he is either a "sissy" himself or an "old woman" (p. 92). After Gould regains his "senses," Fox warns Karen that if she ever returns to the movie lot, he will kill her, just as surely as she would have been complicitous in the murder of their manhood had Gould passed on the prison film. The phallic "players," recalling Altman's film to which I shall turn momentarily, are reunited at the end of Mamet's play, however, to push their script to the studios and assert themselves in (insert themselves into?) the industry with a renewed sense of mastery, while Karen is rudely escorted off the premises. Like Dawn in *Swimming with Sharks*, Karen and the threat she represents to phallocracy must be overcome. Although it is almost axiomatic that the real determinative power to make the movie resides elsewhere in plays like *Speed-the-Plow*—in anonymous and unseen producers, foreign investors, the grandsons of wealthy producers, and so on—Gould and Fox have nonetheless survived Karen's challenge and emerged as "men." Her momentary "seduction" of Gould, her suasion of him from his routine, is effectively stifled: phallocracy has survived for at least another day.

The Hollywood of *Speed-the-Plow* is also the scene of David Rabe's *Hurlyburly* (1985) and Arthur Kopit's *Road to Nirvana* (1990), originally entitled *Bone-the-Fish* (1989), which is, at least in part, a parody of Mamet.[19] All of these plays represent the Culture Industry at its most commercial, and Kopit's vulgar and scatological play is Baudrillardian both in its excess and in its treatment of the image as sexual object. Importantly, though, Kopit understands the relative powerlessness of producers like Gould and Fox, their positionality within a larger industrial network over which they exercise very little control. Hence, unlike Odets's Hollywood, a bastion of male supremacy and centralized power located within studio offices, Kopit's Hollywood is dominated by pop stars like Nirvana (Madonna, clearly) who possess the unique ability to turn themselves into the very image the public craves—and to induce the public to believe they can take intimate possession of the image.

In *Road to Nirvana*, Al Sereno, a sleazy, drug-dealing producer, and his girlfriend Lou have secured an option on a blockbuster filmscript: the biography of the reigning pop super-star, Nirvana, called

Moby Dick with the rock star playing Ahab and Melville's whale transformed into a phallus. All Al and Lou need is the technical expertise of Al's former partner Jerry, who has left Hollywood and embarked upon the less lucrative career of making educational films. Al and Lou, however, have to be certain about Jerry's commitment to this project and therefore demand his participation in increasingly severe rituals to test it. These include first making a small incision in his wrists, as both Al and Lou have previously done—shedding some blood for the partnership. Act One ends with an absurd extension of Al's predictions of the lengths other producers would go to make this film. A butler enters and places a serving dish in front of Jerry that, after uncovered, is seen to contain excrement. Jerry exclaims, "Holy Shit!" to which Al responds, "It's as close as we could get" (76)— "*pure* nun shit" obtained from a convent. This symbolic material, Al emphasizes, is more than a commodity: "I mean, one cannot *BUY* this stuff!" The Act One lights come down with Jerry, spoon in hand, contemplating his dilemma to Al and Lou's chorus, "One spoon for the kingdom! One spoon *or you're out*" (78). The lights fade to black.

Al and Lou take Jerry to Nirvana's mansion in Act Two and, after an appropriately dramatic delay, she is introduced by a radio disc jockey and enters to the music of one of her hits blaring out of a public address system. Nirvana performs for her visitors, effacing the line between public and private realms. The opening verse of her song, "Who I Am," promises the listener that "There's nothing you can't view," and the refrain seems particularly relevant to Kopit's (and Baudrillard's) conception of the image as sex-object, as always accessible in our postmodern Paradise:

> This is it! Who I am!
> I am everything you want me to be.
> This is it! Who I am!
> Come inside of me. (81)

Here Kopit echoes Baudrillard's thesis in *The Ecstasy of Communication* (1987) that images have indeed "*become our true sex objects*, the object of our desire" (35), alluding also to Gould's lecture to Karen on the function of the movie business:

> *Make the thing everyone made last year. Make that image people want to see.* That *is* what they, it's more than what they want. It is what they require. (74)

Nirvana dons a variety of disguises throughout the scene, ones that conceal her face especially, the only part of her body that is private. In performance, her made-up face and the rest of her body—especially her breasts tattooed with giant butterflies—belong to the public. But on her terms. In a *double entendre* Kopit included in *Bone-the Fish* but cut from *Nirvana*, Nirvana, then named Zalinka, demands to see Jerry's balls. Nervous and hoping to distract Zalinka, Jerry says, "Your tits are very nice. And so are your butterflies." She responds, "They're Monarchs." And indeed they are in Kopit's play: although we can "come inside" her image, the producers can't "fuck with" her or those she loves (91), as she warns them. She's got the monarchs, which also represents a kind of media imperialism or false Utopia that partially defines the postmodern condition. Lee in Shepard's play and movie, *True West* knows this Paradise: it's the "kinda place you wish you sorta' grew up in" and the "kinda place that sorta' kills ya' inside" (*Seven Plays* 12).

Al's promotion of the project and the rituals assuring Jerry's commitment continue full force in the second act of *Road to Nirvana*, culminating in Jerry's once again being asked, this time by Nirvana, to make a symbolic "sacrifice." After inspecting his "private parts," Nirvana, who has a surgeon on her house staff and an operating room under her mansion, demands that Jerry surrender his testicles to her as a sign of his loyalty. Frightened and appalled, Jerry runs to Al exclaiming, "She wants my balls," a price that even Al considers too dear. The loss of both testicles is too much, though Al has already made a similar gesture of commitment, so he negotiates a lesser, uh, price with Nirvana, as he proudly tells Jerry: "I knocked it down to one." The "choice of which—left or right—is yours" (116). Jerry is incredulous, a response which Al simply cannot understand: "Jerry, I swear, for a deal like this, a one-ball give-back isn't bad" (116). The play ends with Jerry entering the steamy operating room, moments later screaming in the distance, and Al and Lou wondering why God "smiles on some. . . but not on others" (124). Lou concludes that such is the "mystery" of life, and they snuggle contentedly knowing that Jerry has just clinched the deal for Moby Dick—Nirvana's great phallus, not Herman's white whale. The Baudrillardian "artificial paradise" that is America is now well within their reach.

Unlike Gould and Fox—and Buddy and Guy in *Swimming with Sharks*—Al and Jerry are not necessarily empowered by the end of *Road to Nirvana*; the homosocial bond, the friendship over which Al rhapsodizes in the concluding moments of the play, does not augur the return of a phallocratic regime in Hollywood. Rather, producers like Al Sereno and Jerry regain "paradise"—the term Al uses in Act One to describe the film project with Nirvana—as near or total castrati. There is no phallic victory or conquest; no charade of heterosexual conquest or localized power in an industry. Power resides in Nirvana's image—and in her Monarchs; paradise or nirvana in Kopit's Hollywood reduces sexual difference as it also finds its provenience in simulation or the image regarded as sexual partner and magical dispenser of pleasure.

It is against this background that I want to conclude by reading perhaps the most famous filmic representation of Hollywood since Billy Wilder's *Sunset Boulevard* (1950), Robert Altman's *The Player*, the screenplay of which presents virtually all of the patchs in the ideological quilt I have been piecing together: art versus mass culture, "feminine" seduction versus phallocratic regime, and simulation versus "reality." Central to such a reading is Altman's reinvention of one character in Michael Tolkin's unexceptional 1988 novel about the Culture Industry: June Gudmundsdöttir (Greta Scacchi), the eventual love interest of the film's protagonist, the young movie executive, Griffin Mill (Tim Robbins). In Tolkin's novel, June Mercator is an employee of the commercial art department of the Wells Fargo Banks; in Altman's film, June is a multi-media artist born in Iceland with a British accent. In the novel, June is introduced to Mill in an unmemorable telephone conversation; in the film, Mill, while talking with her on his cellular phone, first sees June by peeking in her window, where she is distanced from him behind a wrought-iron grill, window glass, and a blue light filter she uses in her art. June Gudmundsdöttir, in short, is calculated to play the exotic Other to Mill's anxious young executive: not a bestial or colonized Other, but an "alien" and "foreign" one, as Altman variously describes her, remote and very desirable (Smith and Jameson, 26).

She is also everything Mill and his lover at the beginning of the film Bonnie Sherow (Cynthia Stevenson), a story editor at the studio, are not. June's frustrated boyfriend, the unsuccessful screenwriter David Kahane, calls her the "Ice Queen" because of her emotional coolness; and later at Kahane's funeral her emotional iciness is conveyed by a white dress and pale blue scarf that contrast sharply with the predominantly black attire of other mourners (and with the steaming hot tub into which Bonnie earlier leads Mill and in which she initiates their sexual intimacy). Most important, June neither knows nor cares anything about film, which makes Altman's commentary about her so paradoxical: "[S]he's the ultimate movie character. She's the movies"

(Smith and Jameson, 26). But clearly she *isn't* the movies, particularly in her initial appearances on screen: she's art or, more literally, an artist. And Altman is, at least publically, critical of the avarice that he regards as "crushing" such artists and, more broadly, "our country. . . our culture." "That's what Hollywood is like" (28), he asserts, and at least on one level that's precisely what *The Player*, like all of the plays discussed above, is about: commodities crushing art. (Though in an elaborate, extremely ironic scene at the Los Angeles County Museum written for the film, Griffin Mill speaks exuberantly of "film art" as if the phrase were no longer an oxymoron. Here Cher appears in a dazzling red gown, the "hot opposite" of the cool blue "Ice Queen," and thus a continuation of the triangulation of Art-Commodity-female body seen in both *Swimming with Sharks* and *Speed-the-Plow*.)

Yet June is representative of contemporary culture in more ways than one in Altman's film, for his redaction of Tolkin's character seems unequivocally joined to two other declines: the credibility of his own jaundiced thesis about Western culture and the rule of Western phallocracy. That is to say, insofar as the former matter is concerned, while Altman regards his film as revealing something essential about Hollywood's inherent corruption, a bemused Paul Newman offered him a very different, remarkably *un*-intellectual, reading of *The Player*: "I know what this picture's about," Newman reportedly told Altman after a screening. "It's about getting to see the tits of the girl whose tits you don't care about seeing, and not getting to see the tits of the girl whose tits you want to see" (as qtd. in Smith and Jameson, 26). Altman's response to Newman, "You're absolutely right," confirms what every viewer finally realizes about the film: *The Player* itself, whatever its political pretensions or its director's putative critique, is little more in some frames than the striptease Roland Barthes dissects in *Mythologies*.

Appearing frequently in a diaphonous white undershirt under an open blouse that conceals her breasts and, at the same time, reveals their contours, June also represents woman "rendered divine again and thus controlled, reduced to the coolness of marble breasts" (François Roustand, as qtd. in *Seduction*, 23). The artist herself thus becomes a work of art to be gazed at, as Mill does upon first "meeting" her, before he becomes the subject of her art, captured visually behind scrims and bars of paint. Who controls whom, finally, in Altman's script? Who, ultimately, becomes the object of the gaze, who the privileged subject? June at first becomes the challenge to Mill that Baudrillard defines as "seduction": that "lightning flash" which melts the "polar circuits of meaning" (*Ecstasy* 58); that which causes one to deviate from *his* everyday routine (gendered pronoun totally intentional); that which poses a profound "challenge to the male to be the sex, to monopolize sex and sexual pleasure. . . a challenge to go to the limits of its hegemony" in a society in which phallocracy's power is in decline (*Seduction* 21). Later, though, June's iciness has been melted, and in the film's closing shots she is eight months pregnant waiting eagerly behind a picket fence and blooming flowers for Mill to return home from work. Her art, apparently, has been abandoned; her former boyfriend who meets Mill at a showing of Vittorio De Sica's *The Bicycle Thief* (1948) is dead and with him any attempt to make a film of the quality of De Sica's or those masterworks alluded to throughout; the improbable film script for *Habeas Corpus*, in which Bruce Willis saves Julia Roberts from the electric chair, is developed, produced, and has enhanced Mill's power base. Art loses; commodity wins; the feminine threat is subdued, this time by transforming her into another June—Mrs. Cleaver of *Leave It to Beaver*. And, although Altman regards this conclusion as overtly parodic of the "absolutely ludicrous" and conventional "Hollywood ending"—and although it minimizes the homosocial bond so evident in *Swimming with Sharks*, *Speed-the-Plow*, and *Road to Nirvana*—it also replicates the vanquishing of the feminine threat in the first two of these. Only this time, the threat is subdued not by mach intimidation or murder, but by the "normative heterosexual script," complete with the babies, picket fences, and flowers so often associated with it.

Altman's conclusion might also be read as an extension of Baudrillard's observation in *America* that, in the postmodern moment, the "latest fast-food outlet, the most banal suburb, the blandest of giant American cars or the most insignificant cartoon-strip majorette is more at the centre of the world than any of the cultural manifestations of old Europe" (28). For in what might be termed the "Revenge of the Colonized," not only in Baudrillard's postmodern culture but in popular American film *European* "high" culture is overwhelmed by American mass culture, just as Griffin Mill melts and conquers June in *The Player*, turning the European artist into an all-American mother. A similar conquest, albeit one that hardly resembles the pregnancy and nostalgic domesticity in Altman's film, occurs in the Bruce Willis hit *Diehard* (1988), in which a classically-educated and sophisticated German terrorist (Alan Rickman) is not only defeated and killed by a tough New York cop (Willis), but midst almost constant gunfire and explosion is relentlessly quizzed about Gary Cooper and John Wayne westerns. Staged on the specifically trans-national stage of a Japanese-owned building in downtown Los Angeles, Hans Gruber (Rickman), able to identify the handiwork of London tailors and speak several languages, meets his doom at nearly the same moment he fails his test on *High Noon*. Here, unlike in the "Hollywood plays" discussed above, John McLain's (Willis's) wife (Bonnie Bedelia) is truly a superfluous figure; as Eve Kosofsky Sedgwick and commentators on gay theatre like John Clum have pointed out, the woman is a minor, yet crucial, figure in facilitating a homosocial bond, in this case between Willis and the black L.A. police officer (Reginald VelJohnson) who finally saves his life. Not so in the Culture Industry. Griffin Mill wins over June, Buddy and Guy get rid of Dawn, Gould and Fox are free of Karen—and a couple of geldings find Nirvana.

These texts are all part of Baudrillard's America and of a twentieth-century genre of "Hollywood plays" or "Hollywood on Stage." Amidst the collapse of once stable binarisms (clearly both the image/reality and male/female oppositions are collapsed in Kopit's play, though the latter is restored in the others), in the fog of what Rabe's Eddie in *Hurlyburly* calls "TV thoughts," and in the imperialism of simulation and hype, image-viruses are at work effecting slight but certain mutations in our culture. Power exists in the image and in the void called a corporation, not in godlike producers or studio heads. Some of these mutations may even prove to be more than slight, but fatal, "ecstatic," or catastrophic, though it's impossible to predict these things. And what of the problem Bond and Shepard's Lee identify: what happens when, as Bond puts it, we are destroyed by the "iconology of perfection" that is the image, the stock-and-trade of Bobby Gould, Griffin Mill, Nirvana, and the other sharks swimming in the above discussion? For Bond, "Wants can have no Utopia—if you are in heaven you cannot have Utopia."[20] This statement does not mean that poverty and suffering do not exist in our world; rather, it suggests that a child here and in what was once called the Third World "starves to death . . . not because it has needs, and because no one comes with bread and water, but because it wants luxuries" (238). So do we all, if Mamet's Gould is correct, and they are all realized in the Culture Industry's production and diseemination of the image. But what price do we all pay to bask in its refulgence—or to become intimate with it? What is at stake in our access to it? Nothing much, if depictions of Hollywood on stage are at all accurate, just gender difference, phallocracy, the formation of subjectivity, and—most important—

resistance to a cultural imperialism whose domination may be growing more potent each day.

NOTES

1. All quotations from Horkheimer and Adorno's *Dialectic of Enlightenment,* trans. John Cumming (New York: Continuum, 1972), will be followed by page numbers in the text.

2. Theodor W. Adorno, "Culture Industry Reconsidered," *New German Critique* 6 (Fall 1975): 12.

3. George Abbott, "Foreword" to the Spewacks' *Boy Meets Girl* and *Spring Song* (New York: Dramatists Play Service, 1946), 3.

4. Andreas Huyssen, *After the Great Divide: Modernism, Mass Culture, Postmodernism* (Bloomington: Indiana University Press, 1986), 194. Huyssen's chapter "Mass Culture as Woman: Modernism's Other" will, in particular, undergo considerable revision here, as the high art/mass culture binarism, when recuperable at all in contemporary drama, is typically gendered in just the opposite way.

5. Robyn Wiegman, "Introduction: Mapping the Lesbian Postmodern," in *The Lesbian Postmodern,* ed. Laura Doan (New York: Columbia University Press, 1994), 8.

6. I am referring here to John Tomlinson, *Cultural Imperialism* (Baltimore: Johns Hopkins University Press, 1991); and to Fredric Jameson, *The Seeds of Time* (New York: Columbia University Press, 1994), esp. ch. 1. Tomlinson notes that "common to many critical discourses of cultural imperialism" is the claim that "capitalism is an *homogenising* cultural force. The perception here is that everywhere in the world is beginning to look and to feel the same. . . . I think the evidence of a general drift towards cultural convergence at certain levels is undeniable" (26). Jameson regards it a prinicipal antinomy of postmodernity that there exists "an unparalleled rate of change on all the levels of social life and an unparalleled standardization of everything—feelings along with consumer goods, language along with built space—that would seem incompatible with just such mutability." Baudrillard, as we shall see, takes the point even further into the space of gender.

7. Arthur Kroker, *Spasm: virtual reality, android music, electric flesh* (New York: St. Martin's 1993), 26.

8. Jean Baudrillard, *America,* trans. Chris Turner (London: Verso, 1988), 46–47. All other quotations from Baudrillard's works come from the Semiotext(e) editions and will be followed in the text by page numbers. The only exception is Baudrillard's *Seduction,* trans. Brian Singer (New York: St. Martin's 1990).

9. Sam Shepard, *Motel Chronicles* (San Francisco: City Lights, 1982), 81. All quotations from Shepard's works come from this and the following volumes: *Hawk Moon* (New York: PAJ Publications, 1981); *Seven Plays* (New York: Bantam, 1981); and *States of Shock, Far North, Silent Tongue* (New York: Vintage, 1993).

10. The term "ideological quilt" comes from Slavoj Zizek, *The Sublime Object of Ideology* (London: Verso, 1989), 87–89. According to Zizek, "Ideological space is made of non-bound, non-tied elements, 'floating signifiers,' whose very identity is 'open,'. . . The 'quilting' performs the totalization by means of which the free floating of ideological elements is halted, fixed—that is to say, by means of which they become parts of the structured network of meaning" (87).

11. C.W.E. Bigsby, *Modern American Drama, 1945–1990* (Cambridge: Cambridge University Press, 1992), 198.

12. David Mamet, *Edmond,* in *The Woods, Lakeboat, Edmond* (New York: Grove, 1987), 228.

13. Gavin Smith and Richard T. Jameson, "Robert Altman on *The Player,*" *Film Comment* 28 (May-June 1992): 29. All other observations from Altman come from this interview and will be followed by page numbers in the text.

14. David Mamet, *Speed-the-Plow* (New York: Grove, 1988), 1. All further quotations from *Speed-the-Plow* come from this edition and will be followed by page numbers in the text.

15. Howard Korder, *Search and Destroy* (New York: Grove, 1992), 50. All quotations from *Search and Destroy* come from this edition and will be followed in the text by page numbers. All quotations from the film version of Korder's play come from Martin Scorsese's production of *Search and Destroy,* dir. David Salle, Nu Image, 1995.

16. One prominent exception to the gendered dynamic of this convention occurs in the screenplay of Salle's *Search and Destroy,* which drastically—and interestingly—alters Korder's play. In the play, Martin seduces a secretary/amateur screenwriter named Marie, who helps him meet Dr. Waxling and is never seen again. In the film, she has a much larger role, and in its last sequence she and Martin have actually made—and profited by—her *Alien*-like script (called *Dead World* in the film). As in *Alien,* a creature explodes from a man's body—in Salle's film, as in the play, the monster looks like a "gangrene penis with a lobster claw"—and the film's heroine "hacks it off" with a radial saw (30). The film concludes by underscoring Martin and Marie's successful relationship, and with their securing the rights to produce Waxling's *Daniel Strong,* thereby both replicating and overcoming the images of emasculation that seem to accompany representations of contemporary Hollywood.

17. *Swimming with Sharks,* dir. George Huang, Keystone Productions, 1994.

18. This formulation, I realize, comes very close to Eve Kosofsky Sedgwick's in *Between Men: English Literature and Male Homosocial Desire* (New York: Columbia University Presss, 1985). For Sedgwick, the "institutionalized social relations" of a homosocial economy dictate that "the woman is barely present, no more than the conduit for firming up the patriarchy and guaranteeing the young man's place within a social order in which the most heavily invested relations are those between men" (222). I hope to show that, in depictions of Hollywood on the contemporary stage, the woman is perhaps *too* present, too serious a threat to this economy and therefore must be dealt with in some decisive manner.

19. *Bone-the-Fish* premiered in the Humana Festival of New American plays at the Actors Theatre of Louisville in March, 1989. I wish to thank Michael Bigelow Dixon of ATL and Arthur Kopit for a typescript of the play, from which I shall quote in the text. For a 1995–96 British production of *Road to Nirvana,* Kopit has revised the play slightly once again. All quotations from *Road to Nirvana* come from the 1991 Hill & Wang edition of the play, and page numbers follow quotations in the text.

20. Edward Bond, "Notes on Post-modernism," in *Two Post-modern Plays* (London: Methuen, 1990), 239. All further quotations from this essay will be followed in the text by page numbers.

WORKS CITED

Abbott, George. "Foreword." *Boy Meets Girl,* by Sam and Bella Spewack. New York: Dramatists Play Service, 1946. 3–4.

Adorno, Theodor W. "Culture Industry Reconsidered." *New German Critique* 6 (Fall 1975).

Altman, Robert, dir. *The Player.* Screenplay by Michael Tolkin. Avenue Pictures, 1992.

Baudrillard, Jean. *America.* Trans. Chris Turner. London: Verso, 1988.

———. *The Ecstasy of Communication.* Trans. Bernard and Caroline Schutze. New York: Semiotexthe, 1988.

———. *Seduction.* Trans. Brian Singer. New York: St. Martin's, 1990.

Bigsby, C.W.E. *Modern American Drama.* 1945–1990. Cambridge: Cambridge University Press, 1992.

Bond, Edward. *Two Post-modern Plays.* London: Methuen, 1990.

Horkheimer, Max, and Theodor W. Adorno. *Dialectic of Enlightenment.* Trans. John Cumming. New York: Continuum, 1972.

Huang, George, dir. *Swimming with Sharks.* Keystone Productions, 1994.

Huyssen, Andreas. *After the Great Divide: Modernism. Mass Culture. Postmodernism.* Bloomington: Indiana UP, 1986.

Jameson, Fredric. *The Seeds of Time.* New York: Columbia UP, 1994.

Kopit, Arthur. *Road to Nirvana.* New York: Hill & Wang, 1991.

Korder, Howard. *Search and Destroy.* New York: Grove, 1992.

Kroker, Arthur. *Spasm: virtual reality, android music. electric flesh.* New York: St. Martin's, 1993.

Mamet, David. *Speed-the-Plow.* New York: Grove, 1985.

———. *The Woods. Lakeboat, Edmond.* New York: Grove, 1987.

Odets, Clifford. *The Big Knife.* New York: Dramatists Play Service, 1949.

Rabe, David. *Hurlyburly.* New York: Grove, 1985.

Salle, David, dir. *Search and Destroy.* Martin Scorsese, prod. Nu Image, 1995.

Sedgwick, Eve Kosofsky. *Between Men: English Literature and Male Homosocial Desire.* New York: Columbia UP, 1985.

Shepard, Sam. *Hawk Moon.* New York: Performing Arts Journal Publications, 1981.

———. *Motel Chronicles.* San Francisco: City Lights Books, 1982.

———. *Seven Plays.* New York: Bantam, 1981.

———. *States of Shock. Far North. Silent Tongue: A Play and Two Screenplays.* New York: Vintage, 1993.

Smith, Gavin, and Richard T. Jameson. "Robert Altman on The Player." *Film Comment* 15 (Winter 1989): 205–25.

Tolkin, Michael. *The Player.* New York: Atlantic Monthly Press, 1988.

Tomlinson, John. *Cultural Imperialism.* Baltimore: Johns Hopkins UP, 1991.

Wiegman, Robyn. "Introduction: Mapping the Lesbian Postmodern." *The Lesbian Postmodern.* Ed. Laura Doan. New York: Columbia UP, 1994. 1–20.

Zizek, Slavoj. *The Sublime Object of Ideology.* London: Verso, 1989.

Staging Hollywood, Selling Out

Marcia Blumberg

Gould: we're in business to. . . . Make the thing everyone made last
year. Make that image people want to see.

(Mamet. *Speed-the-Plow:* 56)

Hollywood has treated gay issues and characters with both abject fear
and too much respect. The fear derives from Hollywood's sole
motivation for any decision: marketing.

(Rudnick. "Out in Hollywood," *The Nation:* 36)

The Roman Catholic Cardinal of Los Angeles recently categorized
the Hollywood movie industry as "an assault against the values held
by the vast majority of the people in American society."

(Black. *Hollywood Censored:* 1)

Superman II will probably rank as the top moneymaking film of all
time, a feat that could say as much about the American society of the
1980s as it does about contemporary filmmaking.

(*Magill's Cinema Annual* (1982) Stephen Hanson: 2371)

David: I don't believe all relationships are the same. I don't believe
this man woman thing is the only way to live. I don't think we have
to love only one person. . . . I think love needs to be redefined.

(Fraser. *Poor Super Man:* 132)

Macho males and superheroes frame the epigraphs that map the
trajectory of my analysis as I revisit the title, "Staging Hollywood,
Selling Out," to explore two issues: the Hollywood compulsion for
commodification and the representation of sexual diversity to resist,

what Michael Warner terms, "a heteronormative understanding of society" (xi). For David Mamet and Brad Fraser, who are playwrights and screen writers, staging Hollywood signifies the exposure of networks of power. Yet Mamet's *Speed-the-Plow* (1985) and Fraser's *Poor Super Man* (1994) foreground antithetical tendencies: Mamet perversely celebrates Hollywood's predatory machismo, and Fraser, a gay playwright, counters Hollywood icons and values to celebrate polymorphous perversity. Mindful of Douglas Crimp's belief that it is "more productive: not to 'out' supposedly closeted gay men and lesbians, but to 'out' enforcers of the closet . . . and to reveal the 'secret' of homophobia" (308), I also interrogate representations of misogyny and homophobia in *Speed-the-Plow* and *Poor Super Man*; while characters in *Speed-the-Plow* and other Mamet plays apparently valorize dynamics of discrimination, Fraser re-visions the superhero to contest norms and expose these practices notwithstanding their enactment in the play. Here I employ Adrienne Rich's notion of "re-vision: the act of looking back, seeing with fresh eyes, of entering an old text from a new critical direction" (1979, 35). While Rich considers that this process "is for women more than a chapter in cultural history: it is an act of survival," I extend her rubric to argue that *Poor Super Man* challenges both women and men to explore the emergence of new possibilities that not only interrogate the conventional reception of the popular intertext but also undermine traditional views of societal norms especially at this critical time of the AIDS pandemic.

"Staging Hollywood, Selling Out," first examines the theatre of superstardom, mass-appeal, and worship of the profit motive replete with dog-eat-dog tactics and impoverished values. Mamet dramatizes these strategies in *Speed-the-Plow*, which Ray Conlogue calls a "gag that the theatre world is playing on the film world and its twin gods, Cupid and Stupid"(3); besides, as William Henry asks, is the play, "an outcry against Hollywood or a cynical apologia from a man who, in real life, is finishing one Hollywood movie and about to start another?"(123). In fact, the Broadway casting of Madonna effected a sell out of the small Lincoln Theatre venue and a transfer to a large theatre, where crowds of fans outside the stage door attested to the marketing power of mega stardom. This choice also begs the question of spectators' primary intent: to see Madonna or engage with Mamet's play. In *Speed-the-Plow*, an exchange between Karen, the ditsy temporary secretary and the newly promoted Hollywood producer, Bobby Gould, lays out the bottom line:

KAREN: Is it a Good Film?

GOULD: It's a commodity. . . . I'm not an artist. . . . I'm a businessman. . . . Some people are elected, try to change the world, *this* job is *not that* job. (1995 41)

Frank Rich considers this play "'the most cynical and exciting yet' of the 'genre' of writing about Hollywood by embittered novelists and playwrights; [it] 'pitilessly implicates the society whose own fantasies about power and money keep the dream factory in business'"(qtd. in Lieberson 3). Mamet's dialogue reinforces the dichotomy between movies as a business and as an art form and stresses the imperative to maintain the status quo so that the business of Hollywood can succeed.

The play dramatizes the expediency of conservatism in Gould's eventual reversal of his promise to green light a project called "The Bridge: or, Radiation and the Half-life of Society. A Study of Decay"(23). Gould's apparent non-endorsement of his friend's film in which a white prisoner begs the black inmates to accept him or kill him rather than "rape his ass"(11) to avoid "degradation" (12), incites Fox's vicious attack:

"What the fuck's wrong with you . . . ?. . . . You're gonna buy a piece of shit . . . spend ten million dollars for a piece of *pussy*. . . . Are you getting *old*? What is this? *Menopause*?. . . you *fool*—your fucken' sissy film—you squat to pee. You old *woman*. . . . *Fuck* you, the Head of Production . . . fucken' *wimp*, cost me my, my, my . . . *fortune?* Not In This Life, Pal. . . . I'll take charge. (66–70)

This highly abridged citation from a terrifying and very lengthy exchange exposes the commoditization inherent in the disdain for the serious project in favour of another populist violent action movie and excruciatingly performs on Gould and on unwitting spectators the violence of misogyny and homophobia. Notwithstanding a blanket aversion to rape as a gross violation, Mamet specifies an act of anal sex, which is what homophobic individuals typically regard as the "despised" practice of homosexuality despite its inclusion in the pantheon of heterosexual acts. Fox pointedly hits out with the terms "sissy film" and "wimp." His egregious naming of Gould as an "old woman, experiencing menopause, who squats to pee" denigrates women and equates a feminized man with utter powerlessness, an object of abjection. This misogynistic, homophobic bent has appeared in other Mamet texts and impels me to resist Mametolatry and ask the playwright in his characters' words: "What the fuck's wrong with you?"(66) "I don't understand"(59). Is the appeal to macho males coterminous with the cult of superheroes? Do heterosexist structures validate these representations and how does that implicate society? Mamet's essay titled "Decay" perhaps aids our "understanding" of his position:

> When we look at our society today we see many problems—overcrowding, the risk of nuclear annihilation, the perversion of the work ethic, the disappearance of tradition, homosexuality, sexually transmitted diseases, divorce, the tenuousness of the economy. . . . [P]roblems of the world, AIDS, cancer, nuclear war, pollution, are finally no more solvable than the problems of a tree which has borne fruit; the apples are overripe and they are falling—what can be done?. . . . *Nothing* can be done and nothing needs to be done. . . . [A]ll societies function according to the rules of natural selection and those survive who serve the society's turn. (112–115)

Mamet employs the discourse of homophobia in equating immense global problems with homosexuality. His conviction about the insolubility of the AIDS pandemic, which requires, amongst many aspects, the aggressive engagement of better political will, more economic backing, and deeper awareness, again homophobically sanctions the demise of a disproportionately affected gay community; similarly, the allusion to overripe apples implies rot and "natural" expendability. Mamet's Darwinian approach accords individuals the status of passive observers while the strong vanquish the weak and those who are different and, by implication, less worthwhile; this dynamic horrifically stifles change and refuses the capacity for power networks in society to redistribute more equitably across race, gender, class, and sexual orientation.

In an essay, "A Playwright in Hollywood," Mamet asserts: "we Americans have always considered Hollywood, at best, a sinkhole of depraved venality" (1986, 71). In 1992 the Roman Catholic cardinal of Los Angeles requested the elimination of the present ratings system and the reinstituting of Lord's code, devised in 1930 by a Catholic priest, Father Daniel Lord:

> [The code] soon became the Bible of film production—[it] banned nudity, excessive violence, white slavery, illegal drugs, miscegenation, lustful kissing, suggestive postures, and profanity

from the screen . . . his code also held that films should promote the institutions of marriage and home, defend the fairness of government, and present religious institutions with reverence. . . . Lord argued [that] movies cut across all social, economic, political, and educational boundaries, attracting millions of people to its theaters every week. In order to protect the masses from the evil influence of the movies, they had to be censored. (Black 1)

While the Cardinal was unable to turn back the clock and institute these restrictions nevertheless the impetus to lay the blame for societal ills at Hollywood's door continues. In recent attacks on Hollywood Bob Dole censured the movie industry for undermining American values. While gratuitous violence merits resistance across the political spectrum, the Republicans' targeting of supposedly liberal values espoused in many films as, in their view, a potential catalyst for the breakdown of the nuclear family and the corruption of other American societal structures reinforces this misguided and desperate retreat into the prison house of rigid norms.

Hollywood, the media, and fans exposed fickleness and bigotry in their reaction to Rock Hudson. This once-beloved film star's AIDS-related death in 1985 was staged in "before and after" photographs intimating decline associated with deception and depravity. Richard Meyer argues that "homosexuality supplants HIV as the origin and etiology of Rock Hudson's illness. Closeted through all the years of his celebrity . . . [his] secret finally registers . . . on the surface of his body" (275). Such dangerous elision of people and practices exacerbates homophobia. Simon Watney also emphasizes the "practical impossibility of Hudson's 'coming out' as gay in the American film industry of the 1950s, when he was at the height of his fame, given the intensely homophobic atmosphere of McCarthyite values in Hollywood" (87). Twelve years into the AIDS pandemic Hollywood produced a mainstream movie with a gay protagonist, who challenges injustice and beats the system, as he bravely fights AIDS and dies. *Philadelphia* occupies a liminal position between the popular trial format and the representation of serious issues, one possible narrative of AIDS and its ramifications; while exposing many societal complexities that inhere around AIDS, some problems are imbricated in the very modes of representation employed in the movie. By way of example, fear of offense sentimentalizes the family unit and normalizes the protagonist and his lover's relationship, which is never physically affirmed. Gregg Bordowitz also questions the protagonist's construction as an "AIDS hero" and cautions against this representation, which he considers

> a close cousin of the AIDS villain or the AIDS victim of the early
> eighties. . . . I reject or resist the notion of the hero because it still sets
> up this specular relation of the PWA as other. . . . In the end, I still
> think the AIDS hero is a formulation that speaks to the uncertainty
> and fears of the uninfected. (1994, 106,7)

Bordowitz alerts viewers that the movie's apparently gay-positive milieu raises aspects reminiscent of the phenomenon of reverse racism; while other contradictions are evident in this "feel good/bad" movie, *Philadelphia* nevertheless marks a greater degree of awareness of marginalization when compared with the homophobia directed at Rock Hudson or spewing from the characters in Mamet's *Speed-the-Plow*.

In contrast to Mamet's play, Fraser's *Poor Super Man* operates as an interventionary vehicle that occasions my second exploration, "*Staging* Hollywood, Selling *Out*." From Jerry Siegel and Joe Shuster's initial conception of an eponymous villain in 1933, "The Reign of Superman" (Andrae, 1980, 92), to their recasting of the figure as an American hero, Superman bounded into the theatre of popular culture in the 1938 Action Comics and ricocheted generationally through four Hollywood movies (1978–1987). Selling the superhero as an American icon, Superman movies scored at the box office but earned few accolades. Vincent Canby mused, "one has either to be a Superman nut . . . or to check one's wits at the door" (261). Sequels III and IV petered out: "Is it a bird? Is it a plane? No, it's Supertrash. . . . Superman has run out of diesel and is now flying on cheap muscatel" (Reed). Reviewing *Superman II*, Howard Kissel analysed the self-adulation by Americans:

> One of the things Americans have worshipped most
> conscientiously . . . is themselves. These rites have been observed not
> in ads but in movie theaters, where the larger-than-life images
> fleeting on the screen have frequently been reflection of our exalted
> notions about ourselves as a nation . . . the crude version is
> Popeye . . . the more refined one is . . . Superman, not merely
> omniscient and omnipotent, but morally impeccable. (10)

Disturbing reiterations emerge amid the ever-expanding narrative through the unquestioned focus on heterosexual relationships and entrenched gender stereotypes, which reaffirm patriarchal structures and machismo. If Clark Kent is a performative guise to protect Superman, *Poor Super Man* depicts a reversal when a gay artist claims and later negates an affinity with Superman to perform "selling *out*."

Umberto Eco's analysis of Superman's performance of heroic powers and his defence of "Truth, Justice and the American Way" interrogates aspects of the superhero which are imbricated in Fraser's play:

> Superman *could* exercise good on a cosmic level, or a galactic level, and furnish us in the mean time with a definition that through fantastic amplification *could* clarify precise ethical lines everywhere. . . . In Superman we have a perfect example of civic consciousness, completely split from political consciousness. . . . The paradoxical waste of means . . . astound[s] the reader who sees Superman forever employed in parochial performances. (my emphasis, 1972, 22)

Written over two decades ago, Eco's ideological critique of limited individual good deeds and acts of charity versus a lacunae of group action, and by implication a preservation of the status quo, forms an important *caveat* for Fraser's *Poor Super Man*. Is Superman so ethically impoverished and collectively ineffectual that his death should be welcomed rather than mourned?

Poor Super Man presents complex interactions that mitigate against blanket denunciations, the surety of heroes, and an ongoing denial of societal issues; at the same time, the play interrogates the fixity of categories in discursive, performative, and societal domains. Fraser argues that the title signifies the "unrealistic role models" for boys as well as girls:

> [S]o many men have trouble being vulnerable or dealing with their feelings. . . . [T]hey are so afraid of failure. . . . [There is] a real potential in our society for self-hatred because 'men never live up to the expectations of the society.' (Stein, 1994, 1B)

In addition, the three words also problematize the glorification of brute strength and invincibility implied in Superman's epithet, Man of Steel, and admit the wretchedness of societal dynamics that support those attributes of masculinity. The titular format also stresses the impoverishment of a society that relies on superheroes whether in comics, movies, a present lived reality, or history.

Querying the *Poor Super Man* stage picture demands engagement with an unstable urban 1990s locale synonymous with fragmentation. The title and subtitle, "A Play with Captions," mark liminal spaces between the theatre and Superman comics and movies. Spectators require a simultaneous engagement with the stage, a raked wooden floor signifying a tenuous grounding for five characters, and the backdrop, panels intermittently overlaid with lettering. These captions flash like film subtitles in counterpoint with staged action or speech to situate scenes, emphasize issues, and highlight the continuum of negotiation between reality and wish-fulfilment, truth and lies, or euphemisms and personal desires. Two hundred shifts in spotlighting evoke the bombardment of urban living and these multiple sites foreground a short-lived present and signify past and future scenarios to stage both ruptures and connection.

Stage locales (an artist's studio and a bedroom) serve as a space for straight and gay coupling and a place of dying; yet, *Poor Super Man* refuses the apparent dichotomy of the straight/gay binary with its assumed privileged and devalued terms. Neither does the play invert the hierarchy even though a gay artist is the central character. Instead, Fraser's play enacts aspects of Eve Sedgwick's broadening of the term, queer, to explore the plethora of possibilities that comprise gender, sexuality, and other "identity-constituting and identity-fracturing discourses" (1993 9). The unfixity of relationships in ever-changing scenarios relentlessly challenges perceived heterosexist norms and inspires re-visionings. Speech acts mediated by the captions as well as the coupling of bodies express a desire to relate meaningfully and keep loneliness and alienation at bay. Poignant, witty evocations of loss, pain, intimacy, and renewal articulate the dynamics of a preoperative transsexual living with AIDS, who recasts the staged events in a new time-space where even Superman cannot prevail.

Structurally *Poor Super Man* comprises two triangular relationships: one constituted by sexual desire, another performing the love of friendship. In both sets of linkages the pivotal character is a gay artist, who pursues self-knowledge and a meaningful relationship to rekindle his creativity. David is also the main reference point for the intertext, naming himself Superman (88) and Clark Kent (98), boasting about his "X-ray vision" (131), and confessing his outsidership: "I don't know anyone who's like me. I'm a fucking alien" (153). Unlike Superman's unrequited love triangle (the inept Clark Kent loving Lois

Lane, who desires the never-to-be-attached hero), David's sexual relationships refuse societally constructed boundaries of normative heterosexuality. Countering accepted Superman lore, Mamet calls "the man of steel":

> the most vulnerable of beings. . . . His power is obtained at the expense of any possibility of personal pleasure. . . . *He cannot tell [Lois] his secret, for to do so would imperil his life.* . . . He can have adulation without intimacy, or he may long for intimacy with no hope of reciprocation. Superman comics are a fable, not of strength, but of disintegration. . . . Superman's personalities can be integrated . . . only in death. (1989, 177 8)

In Fraser's re-visioning of the conventional love triangle, which usually posits two men in pursuit of a woman, two men desire each other and Matt's wife, Violet, is the betrayed victim firmly entrenched in heterosexist assumptions. David and Matt's burgeoning relationship initiates the artist's creativity and Matt's new desires and depths of intimacy. If Matt's ingrained heterosexism heralds the return of the repressed and derails their relationship, two issues are pertinent: the practice of anal sex and Matt's potential outing by David's friend. While Matt succumbs to a homophobic fear of societal castigation, "You think I want people saying I'm a fucking queer. . . . I don't want to be a famous fag" (147, 158), Violet discovers in David's paintings a different Matt. Although her own sense of failure as a woman and a wife remain intact, her admission, "he loved you as much as I did," acknowledges difference and validates David's conviction that "love needs to be redefined" (132,3). Matt's attraction is soon overshadowed by an inability to situate himself outside rigid traditional structures and David's resolve "to find someone like me—instead of trying to create him" (176) involves cutting ties with Superman to take control and make his life anew.

The friendship triangle, which comprises a gay man, a gay-identified single woman, and a preoperative transsexual, occupies more stage time and significance than the love triangle.

Moreover, Fraser's juxtapositioning of this trio, all of whom are affected by AIDS, with the married couple, whose remoteness from the issues as well as the lived experience signifies heterosexual structures of society at large, theatricalises what Douglas Crimp terms "the incommensurability of experience . . . certain people are experiencing the AIDS crisis while the society as a whole doesn't appear to be

experiencing it at all" (qtd. in Caruth and Keenan 1991, 539). Here the
dichotomy between the outside and the inside appears stable yet the
seemingly impermeable border between the two groups, if it ever
existed, does so no longer as men, women, and children are testing
HIV+. Certainly the extent of loss in the gay community is inestimable
and the level of stigmatization increases when homophobic discourse
differentiates between those it targets as perpetrators and others that it
classes as victims.

David's feisty friend, Kryla, regrets being single and obsessively
searches for a "man." Work provides no compensation for the lack of
serious relationships, which leaves her bitter at David's interest in Matt.
Fraser's construction of Kryla as a cynical experienced woman and
Violet as a young naive betrayed wife problematically exposes the
always already oppressive positioning of women in patriarchal culture
and reinforces the pervasive entrapment of gender stereotyping. Kryla's
recognition of her role model, "Lois Lane is the reason I entered
journalism"(28), also emphasizes the intertextual *caveat.* Her opening
words, "if you're born with a cunt you're fucked"(12) are destined both
to be and not to be fulfilled since she never successfully connects with a
man but always feels that as a straight woman she is singled out for a
tough time. Kryla continually reminds everyone how much easier it is
for straight men as well as gay men and even argues that "dykes are
lucky" (56). The play appears to lock the women into negative
constructions associated with their depiction as complainers, losers, and
victims and confines both women's potential for transformation, which
Keyssar considers a central attribute of feminist theatre (xiii), to the
final moments and their break with past dynamics.

Yet the play invests transformative potential and a model of
compassion in the relationship between David and his roommate,
Shannon, a preoperative transsexual denied the fulfilment of her dream
of becoming a woman because of AIDS. Shannon's distress at the
impossibility of crossing this sex/gender border evokes David's
unconditional affirmation: "I love you no matter who you are" (79).
The intense bonding and camaraderie between David and Shannon
forms a focus and concretizes Michel Foucault's concept that

> A way of life can be shared among individuals of different age, status
> and social activity. It can yield intense relations not resembling those
> that are institutionalized. . . . [A] way of life can yield a culture and
> an ethics. To be "gay," I think, is not to identify with the

psychological traits and the visible masks of the homosexual, but to
try to define and develop a way of life. (1989, 207)

This dynamic of friendship, culminating in Shannon's confrontation
with AIDS, engages David in her philosophy of living and dying and
inspires self-awareness and courage. Their exchange before Shannon's
suicide tellingly reinvokes the intertext. David's attempt at dissuasion,
"I'll use forgotten Kryptonian technology to suck the virus out of your
body," elicits Shannon's reminder, "You're not Superman, David"
(166). In the concluding dialogue, David's refusal of Kryla's peace
offering, Action Comic no 500 celebrating Superman's rebirth,
reinforces his final word, "Goodbye" (179), a reiteration of all the
characters' *adieus* to a childlike innocence and their collective
relinquishing of their superhero.

This ending foregrounds the gap between the myth and the
moment, a time characterized by the imperative for actions that arise,
not from super heroic feats, but rather from greater conscientization.
Despite the violent juxtaposition between the comics, the movies, and
issues of life and death on stage and in society, the final caption,
"Beginning" (179), invests *Poor Super Man* with a measure of
affirmation and renewal. This final tableau vigorously counters reliance
on a powerful superhero to fix the world, and the play in its entirety
simultaneously demythologizes Superman and emphasizes the
imperatives of self-knowledge and empowerment. Moreover, *Poor
Super Man*, unlike *Speed-the-Plow*, refuses to replicate a Hollywood
staging and *sell* out by worshipping the gods of consumerism and
conservatism while acceding to the fixity of socially constructed norms;
instead, in performing the negotiation of complex and changing
relationships, it "*outs*" homophobia and sells "*out*."

WORKS CITED

Andrae, Thomas. "From Menace to Messiah: the Prehistory of the Superman in
   Science Fiction Literature." *Discourse:* 2 (Summer 1980): 84–112.
Black, Gregory D. *Hollywood Censored*. New York: Cambridge University
   Press, 1994.
Bordowitz, Gregg. "Boat Trip." *American Imago*. 51 (1994): 105–125.
Canby, Vincent. "Super Cast." *New York Times*. 15 Dec, 1978: C15.
Caruth, Cathy, and Thomas Keenan. "'The AIDS Crisis Is Not Over': A
   Conversation with Gregg Bordowitz, Douglas Crimp, and Laura Pinsky."
   American Imago 48:4 (1991): 539–556.

Conlogue, Ray. "Fascinated By Values of the American Tough Guy." *Globe and Mail.* 6 Oct., 1990: A3.

Crimp, Douglas. "Right On, Girlfriend!" *Fear of a Queer Planet: Queer Politics and Social Theory.* Ed. Michael Warner. Minneapolis: University of Minneapolis Press, 1994: 300–320.

Eco, Umberto. "Introduction to a Semiotics of Iconic Signs." David Osmond-Smith, trans. *Versus: Quaderni di Studi Semiotici* 2 (1972).

Foucault, Michel. "Friendship as a Way of Life." *Foucault Live: (Interviews, 1966–84).* Trans. John Johnston. Ed. Sylvere Lotringer. New York: Semiotext(e), 1989: 203–210.

Fraser, Brad. *Poor Super Man.* Edmonton: NeWest Press, 1995.

Hanson, Stephen L. "Superman II." *Magill's Cinema Annual.* (1982): 2371–9.

Henry III, William A. "Madonna Comes to Broadway." *Time Magazine.* 16 May, 1988: 122–23.

Keyssar, Helene. *Feminist Theatre.* New York: Grove Press, Inc., 1985.

Kissel, Howard. *Women's Wear Daily.* 4 June, 1981:10.

Lieberson, Jonathan. "The Prophet of Broadway." *New York Review of Books* 35:12 3–6.

Mamet, David. "A Playwright in Hollywood" and "Decay: Some Thoughts for Actors." *Writing in Restaurants.* London: Faber and Faber, 1986.

———. "Kryptonite: A Psychological Appreciation." *Some Freaks.* New York: Viking, 1989:175–180.

———. *Speed-the-Plow.* New York: Grove Press, 1985.

Meyer, Richard. "Rock Hudson's Body." *Inside/Out: Lesbian Theories, Gay Theories.* Ed. Diana Fuss. New York: Routledge, 1991: 258–288.

Reed, Rex. *New York Post.* 17 June, 1983.

Rich, Adrienne. "When We Dead Awaken: Writing as Re-vision." *On Lies, Secrets and Silence.* New York: W.W. Norton and Co., 1979: 33–49.

Rudnick, Paul. "Out in Hollywood." *The Nation.* 5 July, 1993: 36–38.

Sedgwick, Eve Kosofsky. *Tendencies.* Durham: Duke University Press, 1993.

Stein, Jerry. "'Poor Super Man': Controversial Play about Men and Love." *Post.* 25 April, 1994: 1B.

Warner, Michael. "Introduction." *Fear of a Queer Planet: Queer Politics and Social Theory.* Ed. Michael Warner. Minneapolis: University of Minneapolis Press, 1994: vii–xxix.

Watney, Simon. *Policing Desire: Pornography, AIDS and the Media.* London: Methuen,1987.

Sanctity, Seduction or Settling Scores Against the Swine in *Speed-the-Plow*?

Leslie Kane

"My experience in the theater is that most commercial people are idiots and thieves, and I can't imagine in the motion picture world where the stakes are so much higher in terms of financial rewards that human nature will be on vacation."

> David Mamet (qtd. in Jean Valley, *Rolling Stone,* 3 April 1980)

Gould: Money is not the important thing. . . . I piss on money.
Fox: I know that you do. I'll help you.

> *Speed-the-Plow*

As Michael Hinden has noted in his fine study, "'Intimate Voices': *Lakeboat* and Mamet's Quest for Community," Mamet "tends to see community as an idealized nexus of human relationships" that when nourished by intimacy has the potential to dignify "the enterprise of collective work" (38, 46). However, in "Film Is a Collaborative Business," the notorious *American Film Magazine* (1987) article in which Mamet "committed Hollywood's unspeakable sin: writing the truth about backlot politics" (Stayton 1988, 6), the playwright, and sometime screenwriter, describes the film business as anything but collective enterprise: "From a screenwriter's point of view, the correct rendering should be, 'Film is a collaborative business: bend over'" (1989, 134)[1], or as Charlie Fox quaintly phrases it in *Speed-the-Plow:* "Life in the movie business is like the, is like the beginning of a new love affair: it's full of surprises and you're constantly getting fucked" (29).[2]

In numerous interviews and essays Mamet has discussed his experiences in Hollywood, what he knows we know is "a sinkhole of depraved venality" (1987, 77), his love of screenwriting, his desire to control the creative process, and the sheer joy—"Man oh Manischevitz

what a joy—" of working on a project which was *not* a
"'collaboration'" (1989, 135).[3] But when recently queried about
whether "some personal malice [is] reflected in" the caustic, corrosive,
and comedic portrayal of corruption in *Speed-the-Plow*, Mamet
characteristically quipped, "Not nearly enough" (qtd. in Norman and
Rezek 56), noting that there was so much to put in the play that it could
have run "50 hours" (Goldstein 35). Even without Mamet's recent
confirmation of the depth of his disdain, critics like Richard Stayton,
who has cast Mamet in the role of "Hollywood assassin," have read
Speed-the-Plow as "a scathing indictment of the way that Hollywood
does business" (6). Fueling the fire, the playwright admits with little
effort to conceal his purpose, "I hope so. It's very dishy. A very, very
inside Hollywood play" (qtd. in Stayton 6). Wryly drawing out the
"inside" joke Mamet adds, "A lot of people have been spreading the
ugly rumor that it's a play about my relationship with Art Linson. . . .
[but] it's absolutely not actionable that in an early draft of the play the
main character was called 'Art Linson'" (qtd. in Stayton 6),
encouraging the perception that *Speed-the-Plow* was inspired by the
scurrilous manner in which Hollywood conducts business in general
and spurred by antagonism, in particular, among Mamet, producer Art
Linson, and director Brian De Palma during the months preceding the
filming of his script for *The Untouchables* (1988, 136).[4] This incident
validated the playwright's long-held view that people who work in
Hollywood, specifically but not exclusively producers are "very, very
cruel and also very, very cunning" (qtd. in Savran 142).

The scores that Mamet has settled in *Speed-the-Plow*, however,
have a long history, dating back to his writing the screenplay for his
work *Sexual Perversity in Chicago*. Not only was he paid "a minuscule
amount of money for the rights to the play and the screenplay," recalls
the playwright (qtd. in Cinch 47), but when the script was rejected by
RCA and replaced by another, Mamet, who apparently judged *About
Last Night* to be a perversion of the intention of the original play,
disassociated himself from the film. The debacle of *Sexual Perversity*
notwithstanding, Mamet has written more than a dozen screenplays,
among them *The Postman Always Rings Twice*, *The Verdict*, *Hoffa*, and
Bookworm, and directed three, acknowledging that in Hollywood, "the
city of the modern gold rush," he and other players "permit ourselves to
be treated like commodities in the hope that we may, one day, be
treated as *valuable* commodities" (1989, 139), despite what he views as
a incompatibility of vision. "[I]f it's not bad enough for them," Mamet
told interviewer David Savran, the work is denigrated as "too

theatrical." Not only is this term "used as a curse word," but "[a]lso as an irrefutable statement. What are you going to say"? 'It's not theatrical'?" (142). Thus, although the playwright contends that "anything I [he] might know about American capitalism is not going to be found in a play [of his] " (qtd. in Norman and Rezek 60), a strong argument can be made that what he does know about the movie business grounds *Speed-the-Plow* in personal, historical and cultural references.

We make a great mistake, however, in equating Mamet's comments and essays, such as "Film Is a Collaborative Business," however much they provide a gloss for his work, with the play itself, and in delimiting *Speed-the-Plow* a shallow, cynical hatchet job on Hollywood as innumerable critics have.[5] Frank Rich's review of the New York production of the play is representative. Observing that "Hell hath no fury like a screenwriter scorned . . . [leading to] the same scorched-earth policy toward Hollywood that Nathanael West first apotheosized in *The Day of the Locust*," Rich identifies *Speed-the-Plow* as possibly "the most cynical and exciting" of six decades of literary reaction to Hollywood (C17). Whereas Nathanael West, like F. Scott Fitzgerald in *The Last Tycoon*, used "Hollywood for his satire on an America in the process of moral implosion," *Speed-the-Plow*, "lack[ing] West's paranoia and anger, his apocalypticism, as it does Fitzgerald's sense of tragedy,. . . . is aestheticised," notes C.W.E. Bigsby; "it becomes a badly plotted script . . . shot through with irony" (228) whose "locusts are blood brothers to the petty crooks of *American Buffalo* and the hungry real-estate salesman of *Glengarry*— blood brothers slavering for messes and messes of pottage" (Cohn 1991, 168).[6]

In the absence of apocalypticism, our understanding of the play's dominant tropes of revelation, transformation, material and spiritual wealth and wisdom, and its triadic structure, however, is immeasurably enhanced by exploring the historical and cultural references that inform *Speed-the-Plow* and code it dramatically and ethnically "[a] very, very inside Hollywood play" (Mamet qtd. in Stayton 6), in ways that are implicit rather than explicit. In a plot rich in theology and practical lessons one naturally presumes that a critical motif in *Speed-the-Plow* is learning. And, as I will subsequently discuss, pedagogical relationships are integral to this play. Clearly the rise, profit, and prominence of Jews in the entertainment business, especially their development of and prominence in the motion picture industry, center Mamet's focus on duplicity, power and loyalty in Hollywood firmly on ethnic ground, connecting this play to other Mamet plays that similarly address ethical dilemmas posed by the temptation to affluence, the desire for acceptance, and the betrayal of self and Other.

"From its origins," notes Stephen J. Whitfield, "Hollywood has been stamped with a Jewish personality, but nobody was supposed to know about it" (324), a paradoxical fact given that the era of the 1930s through 1959s "marked the perihelion of the studio system, whose brilliance was due almost entirely to Jewish personalities" (327).[7] And, although the movie industry employed a "veritable army of talent both in front and behind the camera, many of whom were Jewish" (328), disassociated from the urban Jewish communities of New York and Chicago, Hollywood was established as a secularized environment, whose Jewish producers invented and projected gentile fantasies upon a gentile nation. This translated into an industry in which, "Jewish movie moguls kept the Jews out of the movies" (Mamet qtd. in Norman and Rezek 149).

It is against such a background of social success as fact and dilemma that Mamet situates *Speed-the-Plow*. Conflating myth and reality—the historical periods of the 1920s and the 1980s—Mamet sets personal experience against the background of cultural experience, focusing immediate attention upon the ethnicity of his characters Charlie Fox and Bobby Gould (whose surname is an assimilated form of Gold), whose Jewishness and link to a tradition of commerce is as apparent as Levene and Aaronow's in *Glengarry Glen Ross*. Fashioning a complex construct in which to examine ethnicity and cupidity, Mamet intensifies the ironic disparity between the 1920s when sagacious producers, like Harry Cohn and Samuel Goldwyn, energized by the knowledge that only the smartest survive, were Hollywood *machers*, big wheels, who commanded enormous authority and salaries, vigorously pursued their objectives, and "settled their biggest deals over all-night poker games" (Haver 73); and the 1980s, when Fox and Gould, their visibility and impact diminished and "their value system . . . impoverished" (Hudgins 218), flatter themselves with the illusion of their initiative and convince themselves and others of their importance in an industry in which omniscient conglomerates manage producers as effectively as do Mitch, Murray and Lemkin their employees in *Glengarry*. But if Goldwyn's motto was, "A producer shouldn't get ulcers; he should give them" (qtd. in Whitfield 1986, 328), at least in the Hollywood of the 1980s and 1990s producers maintain the illusion of power: "They would sell their mothers," W. H. Macy recently recalled.[8] Seeing and seizing opportunity in the 1920s,

Jewish movie moguls, by dint of their heritage, timing, and outsider status, came to dominate Hollywood (as they did the entertainment business), a fact that linked them inextricably then and now to the gold rush. Acknowledging the initiative and business acumen that drove Hollywood and confronting head on the lure and license of Tinseltown, Mamet's play simultaneously reveals the disparity between Charlie Fox's dream of affluence and the reality of its corruptibility.

Reading *Speed-the-Plow* as a "Dark View of Hollywood as a Heaven for the Virtueless" in which Fox and Gould, long-time friends fantasizing about how much money they can make, Frank Rich likens their "sub rosa power struggle" to "a warped, Pinteresque buddy movie" (17). Paralleling the three revue sketches of the first act of *Glengarry Glen Ross* employed to enhance self-esteem, promote personal agenda and contextualize past and present events, performance is crucial in *Speed-the-Plow,* giving Fox the opportunity to recount his story about Douggie Brown coming to his house with the screenplay "like out of some damn fairy tale" (10); Gould the opportunity to tell Karen how "[t]o *make* something, to *do* something, to be *part* of something. Money, art, a chance to Play at the Big Table . . ." (40); and Karen the opportunity to recite the story of the decay of civilization and the possibility of grace. The "other" story not directly related but subtly communicated is that everything has changed since Gould's title as Head of Production was put up on the door. Opportunities for aesthetic, sexual, emotional, personal, and professional betrayals are as numerous as all those fine folk who keep calling, "[g]uys" who want him to make "remakes of films haven't been made yet" (6).

Since his early episodic plays, Mamet has emerged as an ingenious storyteller, in part, he says, because writing for film taught him "*to stick to the plot and not to cheat*" (1987, 77). Notably, in *Speed-the-Plow* Mamet spins a number of stories whose focus is the possibility of change as well as the process of transformation: as newly promoted Head of the Production, Gould is empowered to make choices and effect change; Fox possesses the potential to alter his career, finances and the way others think of him; Karen, herself a catalytic character right out of "the Temporary Pool," the potential to promote change for the world and, we subsequently learn, for herself (78). Although "[a]ll plays are about decay," notes Mamet, "expos[ing] us to . . . the necessity of change" (1987, 111), significantly in *Speed-the-Plow* narrative depicting change defines structure and informs subject in richly imagined and varying forms: the novel, *The Bridge: or, Radiation and the Half-Life of Society. A Study of Decay* on impending apocalypse; the fairy tale, producer strikes it rich; the saga of cupidity in Hollywood revealed in a roman à clef—replete with references to Mamet's experience during the making of the film *The Untouchables*—the chronicle of treachery, the story of seduction, the fable of redemption, the plot of the Doug Brown buddy film. In addition to these stories, there are at least two other literary works, in-jokes as it were, that serve to gloss the play: Mamet's six-page prose piece, "The Bridge," published in *Granta* (1985) about a nameless protagonist haunted by nightmares of nuclear holocaust that bears considerable likeness to the novel of the same name; and *Edmond*, repackaged for another medium as the "Doug Brown buddy film," complete with the degradation, prison imagery, rape, homosocial relationship, "some girl. . . . Action, blood, a social theme . . ." (13). Cumulatively, they illumine the subject of power: its promotion, perception, and abuse.

Equating the power relationship in "The Subject and Power," with "agonism," Michel Foucault argues that all power relationships, whether consensual or coerced, are by their nature necessarily unstable (428). Expanding upon Foucault's interpretation of agonism and his triadic pedagogical structure, Pascale Hubert-Leibler, finding the student-teacher relationship "especially susceptible to disruption" in Mamet's plays where the potential for dominance is intrinsic to the pedagogical relationship, maintains that the Mametic student-teacher relationship is characterized by a juggling of roles (79–80). In *Speed-the-Plow*, however, Mamet is a magician of sorts: he tricks us into seeing Gould as wise teacher in his pedagogical relationships with students Fox and Karen whose motivation and method to advance their education in the movie industry differs to the extent of each one's skill and his profit, only to reveal that Gould is the naïve, "educated" by one and enlightened by the other. This inversion of our initial perception illustrates what Deborah R. Geis terms Mamet's "increasing preoccupation" with trick-playing that redoubles "our desire to watch ourselves being fooled" (65).[9] But, not only does Mamet show us "the trick 'from the back'" (Mamet 1985, 26), he shows it to us backwards, revealing it first in practice and then in theory.

To illustrate the trickery of the "People Business" (22) in practice, Mamet opens Act 1 of *Speed-the-Plow* with a play-within-a-play—a device he used with great success in *Glengarry*—entitled "Young America at WORK and PLAY" (31) in which "the play's the thing," wherein we catch the cunning and the craft, if not the conscience of the king. Pantomime, pageantry, patronage, masquerade, and performance are all. Newly anointed Head of Production, Gould easily assumes the role of king, while Fox, his Harlequin—or rather *badken*, a Jewish jester afforded the privilege of caustic humor and social criticism without reprisal—and Karen (his courtesan?), assume supporting roles. Gould is a natural, commanding that protocol be observed, that coffee be flowing, that appointments be changed, and bank holidays declared. From his elevated position, he opines, coaches, admonishes, persuades, stipulates policy and teaches Fox, who has crawled in his shadow and on whose back Gould has achieved the power to bestow on him the name of producer of his own commodity. Although they joke that their friendship since the mailroom offers Fox entrée, "somebody I [he] could *come* to . . ." (15), what we observe is that the property, not the person prevails; indeed, as Gould becomes more enamored of the Doug Brown film, Fox, who has proffered the expected obeisance and gratitude, finds Gould warming up to the reality of profits and prestige for himself:

> FOX: "I'm going to be rich and I can't believe it."
> GOULD: "Rich are you kidding me? We're going to have to hire someone just to figure out the *things* we want to buy . . ." (19)

And, as he did in *American Buffalo,* Mamet illustrates through a now familiar theatrical prop, the telephone—one that in *Oleanna* emerges as a third character—that Gould's power extends beyond his name on the door, but as his end of the conversation reveals, as did Donny's with the coin dealer, Gould, too, is in a supporting role to the head of the studio, Richard Ross. Despite his demonstrated dictatorial behavior, Gould's efforts to produce Ross in the flesh and within the hour, fail miserably, tarnishing his self-aggrandizing image. Although he secures an appointment as promised, he is bumped until the following morning, creating a race to keep their option, their partnership and their fairy tale viable. But, in the "People Business"—and by extension all power relationships—Mamet reveals that power shifts in direct proportion to the individual who dominates speech. Even with the shadow of doubt that Ross will return from New York to greenlight their project within the prescribed time hanging over their deal, what is evident in this playlet is that a compact exists between Fox and Gould whose consummation now translates into a apparently easy, raunchy, celebratory banter between partners, from which Fox, protected by this masquerade, gets in more than one cutting remark that belies the equality of their partnership, exposing their friendship, like their deal, as inherently fragile, and their discourse, as a steady stream of

ethnically coded vacuous phrases, that Cohn terms "monosyllables with
shards of education" (1992, 116). And to celebrate their good and near
great fortune Fox, "The Master of the Revels" as he is so dubbed by
Gould, breaks into song. Typical of Mamet's use of lyrics, it is one that
not only underscores *Speed-the-Plow's* central theme of loyalty, but
wonderfully renders ironic comment on it. But, when Gould turns
philosophical it's time for a lesson.

It is in the role of educator and sagacious advisor that Gould
dominates both speech and their relationship. Speaking from a position
of wisdom and experience and an elevated position of power, Gould's
speech in the guise of lesson linguistically reestablishes his dominance
and Fox's supporting role. We intuit the irony of Gould's prudent
advice to his friend literally and metaphorically "stepping up in class"
and out into the line of fire (26). "They're going to plot against you,
Charlie, like they plotted against me," Bob warns. "They're going to go
back to their Tribal Caves and say 'Chuck Fox, the *hack*'. . . . Let's go
steal his job . . ." (26). [10] Drawing upon his depth of knowledge gleaned
from a quarter century in the entertainment business and from personal
experience, Gould imparts words of wisdom and valuable survival
skills to Fox about to "Play at the Big Table" but ignorant of its rules
and terms. The basic wisdom in such a situation, advises Mamet in
"Things I Have Learned Playing Poker on the Hill" is to keep one's
"mouth shut and . . . eye on the action" (1987, 95), but when Fox
reveals his ignorance, Gould pounces on his error, turning it into an
opportunity for a lecture:

> GOULD: Char, Charlie: permit me to tell you: two things I've learned,
>   twenty-five years in the entertainment industry.
> FOX: What?
> GOULD: The two things which are always true.
> FOX: One:
> GOULD: The first one is: there is no net.
> FOX: Yeah . . .? (*Pause.*)
> GOULD: And I forgot the second one. (33)

Gould apparently forgets the second "truth," because the only truth of
any consequence in Hollywood is the operative concept: "gross."
However, while the corollary to Gould's first principle remains an
unspoken maxim, implicit in "there is no net" is the truism that Gould,
balancing on a high wire without a net is a less "*secure* whore" (26)
than he would have Fox, or us, believe, a point underscored by the fact

that "Jews—even more than most other moderns—generally work without a safety net of faith" (Whitfield 337). It is in the area of faith—or the glaring absence of it—that Gay Brewer finds Gould "a parodic, inverted Christ figure, savior son of the studio" whose "deific allusions" are heretical (52). Having come amazingly close to the archetypal depiction of Jew as satanic figure, Brewer, entirely but not alone in missing both the ethnic coding of Mamet's character and the play's intended satirizing of satire,[11] argues that "the non-existence of net profits constitute[s] the . . . godly beneficence and wisdom" in one who panders to "America's baseness" (53; 52).

And, indeed, pandering is one those things that Gould does best. Dismissing Fox ostensibly so that he can calculate what he stands to gross on the "Doug Brown: Buddy Film," inclusive of "the rentals, tie in, foreign, air, the. . . . the sequels" (20), prior to their power lunch at the Coventry, Gould turns his attention to another figure worthy of delight: Karen. In Fox's view "she falls between two stools," neither "[a] 'floozy'," on the one hand, nor "so *ambitious* she would schtup you [Gould] just to get ahead" (35). When Gould rephrases the characterization, Karen emerges as "neither, what, dumb, nor ambitious enough," a description clearly losing something in the translation, but not so much that either will pass up the opportunity to gamble on whether or not Gould can bed her for five hundred dollars (36).

Intent on squeezing the seduction in before lunch and winning his five-hundred bet with Fox, Gould performs the role of educator for the second time this morning. Contrasting sharply with a steady stream of advice delivered to Fox in an imperious manner earlier in the morning that highlights Gould's position and power as a man on whose *"coattails"* Fox has been "riding, several years" (63), Gould—his diction cleansed of vulgarity—adopts a more informal pedagogical attitude toward Karen, encouraging her to address him by his first name, patiently explaining the nature of her error in calling the Coventry to reserve a table for him without identifying him by name, and forgiving a clearly monumental mistake, given that his name not only opens doors but (in his dreams) gets movies made—the highest accolade one has in Hollywood. "Listen," he says, "there's nothing wrong with being naïve, with learning. . ." (39), he instructs her, revealing himself as a patient, supportive teacher, encouraging a dialectic, asking rhetorical questions and answering them in simple, often simplistic, sentences, explaining terminology and identifying personalities, and commending her on her observations. To put it bluntly, "To get to the body," notes Jack Kroll in his review of the play,

"Bobby has to deal with the head." (273). Finding what he believes to be an eager ingenue, Gould extends familiarity even further by encouraging Karen to sit down and by revealing a secret, that in the telling, is no longer one. Echoing Roma's line to Lingk, "Listen to what I'm going to tell you now" (1984, 51), Mamet exposes the pitch packaged in the promise that seductively suckers Karen—and us—into listening to the elusive articulation of illusion.

As he conveys the mysteries of the movie business in a steady stream of abstractions that intimate community and creativity, his words, "To *make* something, to *do* something, to be a *part* of something" (40) have the power of sharing some profound truth, when in reality both community and his contribution are elusive, if not illusory. Circumventing Karen's question on artistic quality that he cannot answer, Gould delivers an apologia that exonerates, exculpates, and vindicates his deeds and decisions, shifting the focus to that which enhances his commanding image of responsibility and delineates his job as one, " bullshit aside" (62) with sufficient status to charm the pants off her, quite literally. Like Roma's speech to Lingk, it is a brilliant piece of artifice, mocking Fox's observation, "It's only words, unless they're true" (71), intended to mask meaning and intent. Seeking a sign of her comprehension Gould inquires, "You *see*?" "You follow me?" "You get it?" (41–42), and remarkably Karen, apparently hanging on every word, responds to his muddled peroration and questions, "Of course" (41), proving herself, at the minimum an attentive student, and more likely, his equal at trading in equivocation and obfuscation.

With Karen's promise secured to complete a book report assignment on *The Bridge*—a screenplay that subsequently competes for his attention and allegiance with the "buddy" film proffered by Fox—to be delivered to his home later that evening with its clear implication of assignation, Gould, having scored twice on his first day as head of production, is heady with glee. In fact, with "a sweet silly smile on my [his] face" (41), Gould can barely contain his delight, insisting that Karen call Fox's secretary so that Fox get the message that Gould won the five hundred dollar bet in advance of their lunch, "confirming," as Ann C. Hall notes, "that he has neither principles nor good taste . . ."(154). "It's the old Jewish joy of the deal," jokes Mamet. "Besides, the people in Hollywood are so funny. It's a place full of gamblers, hucksters, and con artists, including me. We're all rug merchants" (qtd. in Christiansen 18). Blinded by his ego, Gould believes that he has beguiled the ingenue with a slick solicitation of sex in the guise of a lesson, but Fox, a rug merchant himself similarly seeking approbation, spots a scam: "What is she, a witch?" (69). On this point the playwright admits that "[t]he thing that really interested me about screenwriting was the withholding of information," namely "[a]t what point do you give the audience information about the characters?" (qtd. in Vallely 45); it is a technique he utilizes to great advantage in this play.

Her identity and objective cloaked in mystery, at least for the moment, Karen does her best work at night. In a transposition of the teacher/student dynamic dramatized earlier in the day in Gould's office, Karen guides Gould into an intercourse characterized by sacred rather than carnal knowledge, dominating their learned discussion in Act 2 in what Brewer terms "Gould's mock temptation" (54)—although I would argue more a mockery than mock—by quoting at length from *The Bridge*, which it appears she has not so much read as digested. Embracing the book instead of Gould Karen tells him:

> when I *read* it . . . I almost, I wanted to sit, I saw, I almost couldn't come to you, the *weight* of it . . . (*Pause.*) You know what I mean. He says that the radiation . . . *all* of it, the planes, the televisions, clocks, all of it *is to the one end*. To *change* us—-to, to *bring about a change*—-all radiation has been sent by God. To change us. Constantly. (48)

However when Karen succeeds in convincing Gould that he was "put here to make the stories people need to see. To make them less afraid" (59), Fox is prepared to lay one more story on Gould:

> FOX: Why did she come to see you? Cause you're the Baal Shem Tov? You stupid shit, I'm talking to you . . . Why does she come to you? 'Cause you're so good looking? She *wants* something from you. You're nothing to her but what you can *do* for her. (72) [12]

Persuaded to greenlight the radiation film and thereby bring a message of grace to the world, a book that he knows "Won't Make A Good Movie" and "won't Get The Asses In The Seats"(53), Gould has in his process of attempting to do good betrayed his friend in favor of Karen. The abrogation of his oral promise to promote Fox's buddy film, and further his career by naming him co-producer, however much his buddy film recycles yesterday's bilge, violates a trust (Levine 124). Therefore, when Karen subsequently says, "I think I'm being punished for my wickedness" (80), she is not far off the mark, because apparently empowered by the apocalyptic novel, from which she learns and believes that "radiation . . . *all* of it, the planes, the television, the clocks, all of it *is to one end*. To *change us*—to *bring about a change*" (48), Karen has attempted to induce change in a done deal, and profited by "the snatching away another's anticipated gain" through the perversion of the truth (Levine 124).

Each character in *Speed-the-Plow* is on the verge of change at the end of this play, just as they are at the beginning, and Fox's transformation in this act is most notably communicated in his commanding speech and actions. In fact, "change" rather than "currency" or "commerce" is the play's operative concept, and Gould's metamorphosis its arc. But on the verge of what he presumes to be profound change in his life, career and financial status, Fox is confronted with and conflicted by an age-old dilemma which he has attempted to resolve throughout the night—one that parallels and sharply contrasts with Gould's dark night of the soul—by engaging in a Talmudic argument with himself whether on the one hand he is worthy to be rich, and on the other, whether he can live with the guilt of being greedy that Sanford Pinsker characterizes as archetypal "Jewish conflict" and Mamet implies is Jewish guilt (13). Having resolved that it would not be a sign of *chutzpah* to remind Gould to promote Ross both on the commodity and the dynamic team of limitless potential that brought it to him, Gould presents Fox with a dilemma that he did not even include in his deliberations: namely, that Gould would renege on his promise to option the Douggie Brown film. Stunned at the betrayal, the immorality of his friend breaking an oral contract, Fox is furious with Gould and with himself for failing to heed Gould's advice to watch his back.

Seeing his fairy tale devolve into a horror story, he is deeply shaken, but adopting the pose of deference and confidence that barely masks his unmitigated rage—a mockery of his behavior in Act 1 in which a "crescendo of demented gratitude" barely masks his unmitigated rage (Kroll 82)—Fox attempts to assure Gould that his concern is for his welfare and that he bears him no animosity. But his words, "I'm not upset with you" belie both his emotional state—"I have to siddown"—and the truth that in the course of a single day he has seen his greatest dreams and worst fears realized (65). Sharply contrasting with Act 1, energized by a giddy Fox crowing, " . . . I'm gonna be rich" (21), Act 3 confronts him with a grim reality implicit in Gould's promotion of *The Bridge*, that not only is he going to be poor, but his name may not even be "a *punchline* in this town" (69). Suddenly, he understands that Gould's former assurance that "Ross, Ross, Ross isn't going to fuck me [Fox] out of this [deal] . . ." in no way protected him from Gould who *is* "going to fuck" him out of this (22).

Endeavoring to (re)gain Gould's attention—and so save the deal— Fox says, thrice repeating the phrase, "Now, listen to *me*. . . . now listen to *me* now. . . . listen to *me* now" (65, emphasis added), as if the mesmerizing power of his voice, of the phrase and of their friendship will serve as the "*wake*-up call" (69) Gould seems to have missed this morning, in an attempt to swing the pendulum in his direction, reestablishing the prominence of his influence and of his project before time runs out on his deal. And, the difference in his demeanor and discourse is most apparent in the substitution of arrogance for deference. Thus, instead of complimenting Gould to curry favor as he formerly did, he insults him; "I'm talking to you like some Eastern Fruit," Fox rants, exploding when Gould attempts to interrupt him; "Shut up," he says imperiously, "I'm not done speaking . . ." (66), recalling the now classic distinction between "*speaking* . . . as an idea" and "*talking*" that culminates the duologue between Aaronow and Moss in *Glengarry Glen Ross* (39).

Armed with reason, ridicule, threats, and humor, Charlie Fox, whose name implicitly conveys his enhanced sight and heightened survival skills, springs into action, barbs flying, attacking Gould where he lives: "*your* contract's shit" (66, emphasis added), he yells, threatening the head of production with the worst evils that can befall him:

> . . . you're going to become a laughingstock, and no one will *hire* you. Bob . . . You'll be "off the Sports List." *Why*? Because they will not understand why you did what you did. You follow me. . . ? That is the *worst* pariah. Your best *friend* won't hire you. *I* won't hire you. Because I won't hire you because I won't understand why you . . . tried to make a movie that no one will watch. Are you *insane*? What the fuck's *wrong* with you? . . ." Have you read this book? (66)

Punctuating his diatribe with interrogatories and ethnically coded reference to the "worst pariah"—who is evidently a pariah's pariah— Fox envisions a future of disaster for Gould and acclaim for himself alternating it with the present moment, which from his perspective spells disaster for them both.

Ultimately, Fox brings about a change in Gould—thereby saving his own life and career and that of his friend—by identifying Karen as "Some broad from the Temporary Pool. A Tight Pussy wrapped around Ambition" (78). While his vulgar job description is one that has engendered criticism of Mamet's presumed misogynistic portrait, Fox's rhetoric is effective, apparently touching a familiar and familial cord in Gould, whose unity with Fox is communicated linguistically. In fact, assuming a commanding diction Gould expels Karen from their space by cutting off *her* speech. "We're rather busy now," he says; "Mr. Fox will show you out," reordering the trinity of relationships, leaving Fox to wonder aloud, "That was a close one. Don't you think?" (80), and the audience to wonder how many times Gould has been so tempted before. Karen's confession that she was motivated by ambition and personal gain, critical to the shaping of Mamet's well-made play, equates all three as whores while judging some actions more or less moral than others. Ironically, in this world obviously devoid of personal conscience, Karen's admission of cupidity is counterpointed with Gould's insistent demand for honesty: "Without the bullshit. Just tell me. You're living in a World of Truth. Would you have of gone to bed with me, I didn't do your book." (*Pause.*) (77). What her negative response confirms is in that the "World of Truth"—better known to audiences as the world of illusion—where conscience, courtesy and kindness are conspicuous by their absence, in other words, in the "People Business"—that is, in the business of human interaction— people betray people (22).

Motivated by fear and his desire "to do good" (81), one that unifies him with other Mamet characters who are "trying to do good in a bad world" (Mosher qtd. in Kane 242), Gould became, in his words, "foolish"(81), fooled into thinking that a "different thing" was a better thing. "She told me I was a good man," Gould confesses to Fox. "How would *she* know?," the incredulous Fox demands. "You *are* a good man. Fuck *her*" (81, emphasis added), turning Gould's admittance of error in judgment as it pertains to theology and human relationships, as well as business, into a pedagogical opportunity. In place of his former heated censure and furiously funny condemnation of Gould, "you *wimp*, you *coward* . . . now you got the job, and now you're going to *run* all over everything, like something broke in the *shopping* bag, you *fool* . . ." (70), Fox responds with compassion and camaraderie, complying with Jewish ethical law which rejects reminding a repentant person of his misdeeds (Levine 203). "Well," he says, "so we learn a lesson" (82). Contrasting sharply with his former loquaciousness, Fox's few words connote what Lawrence Kushner has characterized as "the most powerful moments of teaching [that] occur, when the teacher has enough self-control to remain silent" (33), or in Fox's case's nearly silent. And, picking up directly from the dropped thread of his previous thought, Fox adds, "Because we joke about it, Bob, we joke about it, but it *is* a 'People Business,' what else is there . . . ?"(81).

NOTES

1. David Mamet's essay initially aroused a great deal of commentary for its candor about backlot politics in Hollywood, but its value lies in its analysis of the dissimilarity of experience of the "screenwriter-for-hire" and the first-time director of *House of Games.* Moreover, this essay establishes an important time-frame and Mamet's personal knowledge of the film industry.

2. The world premiere of *Speed-the-Plow* (New York: Grove, 1988), under the direction of Gregory Mosher, was in May 1988 at Lincoln Center at the Royale Theater in New York, and featured Joe Mantegna as Gould, Ron Silver as Fox and Madonna in the role of Karen. The London premiere, also directed by Mosher, opened in January 1989 at the Lyttelton Theatre at the National, featuring Colin Stinton, Alfred Molina, and Rebecca Pidgeon. Future references to this edition will be cited parenthetically in the text.

3. In this regard see *On Directing Film* (1991), based on a series of lectures delivered at Columbia University in the fall of 1987, and "A First Time-Time Film Director" (1989, 117–33).

4. Among those spreading the rumors was an apparently flattered Art Linson, who informed journalist William A. Henry that "Mamet had to get his material somewhere." Henry also notes in this article that Ned Tannen, head of production for Paramount Studios was apparently the other model.

5. For example, see Mel Gussow, "Mamet's Hollywood Is a School for Scoundrels," *New York Times* 15 May 1988, sec. 2: H5+; William A. Henry, III, "Madonna comes to Broadway," *Time 16 May 1988: 98–99;* Jonathan Lieberson, "The Prophet of Broadway," *New York Review* 21 July 1988: 3–6.

6. Cohn develops an luminous comparative study of linguistic strategies based largely on analysis of Anglo/American diction, discourse and influence in "Phrasal Energies."

7. Research on the lives of lives, behavior and discourse of Harry Cohn, Samuel Goldwyn, and Adolf Zukor reveals remarkable parallels to the characters that Mamet has drawn in *Speed-the-Plow.* See in particular Steven J. Whitfield's essay, "Our American Jewish Heritage: The Hollywood Version" which offers an worthy historical perspective and rich detailed portraits of Hollywood moguls (1986, 322–40).

The scholarship on Jewish movie moguls and prevalence and prominence of Jews in the American film industry is prodigious. Consider along with David Desser and Lester D. Friedman's *American Jewish Filmmakers,* Budd Schulberg's, *Movie Pictures: Memories of a Hollywood Prince,* Lester D. Friedman's *Hollywood's Image of the Jew,* Patricia Erens's *The Jew in American Cinema,* and Ronald Haver's *David O. Selznick's Hollywood.*

8. Macy, interview by author, 22 May 1992.

9. In "David Mamet and the Metadramatic Tradition: Seeing the 'Trick from the Back" Geis argues convincingly that "Mamet's works do not demand the breaking of the fourth wall to call attention to 'the trick from the back'. . . . Rather, Mamet foregrounds the existence of *devices* in his works. . . ." And, in such works as *The Shawl* (1985) and *Bobby Gould in Hell* (1989), for example, "metadrama turns to trickplaying—when the theater is a 'house of games' which we enter aware with an awareness of our desire of being fooled" (65). Notably, *House of Games* and *Speed-the-Plow* were written in the same year.

10. Mamet calls direct attention to ethnicity here through biblical allusion to the twelve tribes of Israel and to the perjorative criticism of Jews as "clannish."

11. The playwright told Minty Cinch that "One reason I wrote *Speed-the-Plow* is because of the traditional wisdom that you can't write a play about Hollywood because you can't satirise [sic] a satire. I found that I could, no problem" (49).

12. Typically dismissed as arcania, Mamet's Jewish references are rarely analyzed in great depth. My response to this omission in Mamet studies is the subject of my forthcoming book, *Weasels and Wisemen,* and therefore exceeds the limitation of the footnote mode.

WORKS CITED

Bigsby, C.W.E. *New American Drama, 1945–1990.* Cambridge: Cambridge UP, 1992.

Brewer, Gay. *David Mamet and Film: Illusion and Disillusion in a Wounded Land.* Jefferson, NC.: McFarland, 1995.

Christiansen, Richard. "The 'Plow' Boy." *Chicago Tribune* 19 Feb. 1989, sec. 13: 18–20.

Cinch, Minty. "Mamet Plots His Revenge." *Observer* [London] 22 Jan. 1989: 47+.

Cohn, Ruby. *New American Dramatists 1960—1990.* 2nd. ed. New York: St. Martin's, 1992.

———. "How Are Things Made Round?" Kane 109–121.

————. "Phrasal Energies in Harold Pinter and David Mamet." *Anglo-American Interplay in Recent Drama*. Cambridge: Cambridge UP, 1995. 58–93.

Foucault, Michel. "The Subject and Power." Ed. Brian Wallis. *Art and Modernism*. Boston: Godine, 1984. 417–432.

Geis, Deborah R. "David Mamet and the Metadramatic Tradition: Seeing 'The Trick from the Back.'" Kane 49–68.

Goldstein, Patrick. "David Mamet Plays His Directing Card." *Los Angeles Times* 11 Oct. 1987: Calendar 27.

Hall, Ann C. "Playing to Win: Sexual Politics in David Mamet's *House of Games* and *Speed-the-Plow*." Kane 137–160.

Haver, Ronald. *David O. Selznick's Hollywood*.

Hinden, Michael. "'Intimate Voices'": *Lakeboat* and Mamet's Quest for Community." Kane 33–48.

Hubert-Liebler, Pascale. "Dominance and Anguish: The Teacher-Student Relationship in the Plays of David Mamet." Kane 69–85.

Hudgins, Christopher C. "Comedy and Humor in the Plays of David Mamet." Kane 191–226.

Kane, Leslie. "Interview with Gregory Mosher." Kane 231–247.

Kroll, Jack. "The Terrors of Tinseltown." *Newsweek* 16 May 1988: 82–83.

Levine, Aaron. *Free Enterprise and Jewish Law: Aspects of Business Ethics*. Library of Jewish Law and Ethics. Vol. 13. New York: KTAV, Yeshiva UP, 1980.

Macy, William H. Personal Interview. 22 May 1992.

Mamet, David. "The Bridge." *Granta* 16 (Summer 1985): 167–173.

————. "Decay: Some Thoughts for Actors." New York: Viking-Penguin, 1986. 110–117.

————. "Film Is a Collaborative Business." *American Film Magazine* [1987]. *Some Freaks*. New York: Viking, 1989. 134–43.

————. "A First-Time Film Director." *Some Freaks*. 117–133.

————. *Glengarry Glen Ross*. New York: Grove, 1984.

————. "A Playwright in Hollywood." *Writing in Restaurants*. 75–79.

————. *Speed-the-Plow*. New York: Grove, 1988.

————. "Things I Have Learned Playing Poker on the Hill." *Writing in Restaurants*. 93–97.

Norman, Geoffrey and John Rezek. "Playboy Interview: David Mamet." *Playboy* Apr. 1995: 51+.

Rich, Frank. "Mamet's Dark View of Hollywood as a Haven for the Virtueless." Rev. of *Speed-the-Plow*, by David Mamet. *New York Times* 4 May 1988: C17.

Savran, David. "David Mamet." *In Their Own Words.* New York: Theatre Communications Group, 1988. 132–144.

Stayton, Richard. "A Mamet Metamorphosis?" *Los Angeles Examiner* 21 Oct. 1988, sec. weekend: 6–7.

Vallely, Jean. "David Mamet Makes a Play for Hollywood." *Rolling Stone,* 3 Apr. 1980: 44–45.

Whitfield, Stephen J. "Our American Jewish Heritage: The Hollywood Version." *American Jewish History* 75 (1986): 322–40.

So Dis Is Hollywood: Mamet in Hell

Toby Silverman Zinman

It seems that profitable self-loathing (the bread-and-butter or wine-and-wafer of the talkshow circuit) has replaced repentance and rehabilitation, so it is not surprising that anti-Hollywood movies (like *Annie Hall, Day of the Locust, Postcards from the Edge, Barton Fink, The Player, Get Shorty*) keep winning the movie industry's accolades. And it has been a long-standing practice in the theatre for serious playwrights—especially those who have been seduced by the big-money-beautiful-women blandishments of Hollywood—to write anti-Hollywood plays; consider the tradition from Clifford Odets's *The Big Knife* all the way through to Sam Shepard's *Angel City*, David Rabe's *Hurlyburly*, and Arthur Kopit's *Road to Nirvana*.

Bertolt Brecht never wrote a play about his odd relation to Hollywood (although Christopher Hampton's *Tales from Hollywood* complicates the matter by using Brecht as a central character), but he summed up his feelings about Hollywood in this amusing economic as well as economical poem from his 1940 series, "Hollywood Elegies":

> The village of Hollywood was planned
> according to the notion
> People in these parts have of heaven.
> In these parts
> They have come to the conclusion
> that God
> Requiring a heaven and a hell, didn't need to
> Plan two establishments but
> Just the one: heaven. It
> Serves the unprosperous, unsuccessful
> As hell.[1]

David Mamet's indictment of Hollywood—as well as his seduction by it—as well as his success in it—is both more extensive and more ornate than any of the other playwrights I have mentioned. He has both written and directed successful films (*The Verdict, The Postman Always Rings Twice, The Untouchables, House of Games, We're No Angels, Things Change, Hoffa, Homicide*), as well as filmed versions of various plays of his, including the less-than-successful translations from stage to screen of *Glengarry Glen Ross* and *Oleanna*).

His attitudes toward Hollywood on record are revealingly self-contradictory; for example, in 1986, he published "A Playwright in Hollywood" in *Writing in Restaurants*, in which he states, "Now we Americans have always considered Hollywood, at best, a sinkhole of depraved venality. And, of course, it is. It is not a Protective Monastery of Aesthetic Truth. It is a place where everything is incredibly expensive" (77). He explains his cheerfulness in the face of this expensive venality by how much he learned about making movies and how much fun he had doing it. A year later he expressed a similar view from quite a different angle in an interview with David Savran:

> Hollywood people are very, very cruel and also very, very cunning. One of the things that they will say to me and to other writers, if they don't understand something or if it's not bad enough for them, is, "It's very theatrical. It's too theatrical." That is used as a curse word. Also as an irrefutable statement. What are you going to say? "It's not theatrical"? I try to write the best I can for whatever medium I'm engaged in. We all know that we should stay away from Hollywood, but we don't. I try to do the best job I can, because in addition to my own love of the work, I'm getting paid for it as a working man. (Savran, 142)

A few years later, in his book, *On Directing Film* (Viking, NY, 1991), he reveals an extraordinarily high-minded view of screenwriting, seeing it as something more like art than the result of "treatments" and "meetings," which seem to be the way most Hollywood films are created. He talks about the "director as that Dionysian extension of the screenwriter . . . who would finish the authorship" and sees "the craft of directing as the joyful extension of screenwriting" (xv–xvi).

Thus, Mamet's anti-Hollywood plays seem complicated by pomposity and self-delusion, a love/hate, approach/avoidance problem if ever was one, and thus become the perfect expression of that prickly tradition of the American playwright in sin city.

Mamet's tourist in and chief desecrator of the ruins of American morality is a recurring character named Bobby Gould, the archetypal Hollywood producer in *Speed-the-Plow*, who appears in many of Mamet's dramas in various incarnations, but always with more or less the same name. It is also worth noting Mamet's increasing interest in locating America's moral wreckage within a religious framework; this is especially true since Mamet recently discovered his Judaism and has grown more and more vocal and assertive about what it is to be an American Jew . All these issues—Hollywood, the making of movies, religion, and trash ethics—merge in the recurring figure of Bobby Gould. If we follow him through six dramatic works, spanning two decades of Mamet's career, we find Mamet has written a gaudy and deeply outraged parody of Dante's *Divine Comedy*, a kind of Diabolical Comedy for our times, with Los Angeles, the City of Angels, as Inferno on earth.

Bobby Gould is Mamet's Dante figure, traveling through a spiritual terrain of crisis, doubt and confusion; like Dante's character called "Dante," Mamet's Bobby Gould is having a mid-life crisis of epic proportions, described by the famous opening lines of the *Inferno:*

Midway this way of life we're bound upon,
I woke to find myself in a dark wood,
Where the right road was wholly lost and gone.
(Sayers, 71)

He is surrounded by the same temptations: lust, pride and avarice (or, more interestingly put, self-indulgence, bestiality and fraud). Dante's journey through the inverted cone of hell is a salvific one; his exploration of self, guided by Virgil, the allegorical incarnation of Human Wisdom, allows him to delve deeper and deeper into the human capacity for sin, until finally he confronts the ultimate symbol of evil, the winged Satan trapped in his frozen lake, exiled at the furthestmost point from the warmth of God's love. It is Dante's capacity to learn to hate sin rather than sympathize with the tormented souls he meets that allows him to emerge with his soul intact, ready for the trek up the mountain of Purgatory to prepare for the beatific vision.

Dante the poet engineers Dante the character's story as a lesson in surviving the temptations of Dante's world, the specific and dangerous world of Florentine politics which had taken so great a toll on the poet's life as well as the general and dangerous world of human weakness; we feel that this perilous journey is undertaken for the highest stakes; we cannot fully appreciate *The Divine Comedy* if we do not acknowledge that it is not merely earthly life but the immortal life of the soul that is at risk.

In Mamet's plays we feel that something more than merely personal life is at stake; I make no claims for Mamet's theology, but rather that his work is informed by the secular equivalent of salvation, a deep belief in cultural rather than individual morality. For Bobby Gould the Dantean journey is inverted, since Mamet has him travel away from rather than toward deliverance, away from self-discovery toward self-delusion, away from redemption toward damnation, and damnation turns out to look a lot like earthly success. Thus purgatory is short-circuited and heaven and hell become one, in far more complex ways than Brecht's little poem suggests, although for Mamet, that merger is not a hostile takeover but a leveraged buyout, the result of a complete collapse of all opposition to immorality.

American Buffalo (1975), takes place in a junk shop run by Don, who has planned a stupid heist of a valuable buffalo-head nickel with the mean-spirited and violent Teach. This young Bobby (with no last name at this point) is Don's protege, who is eager to be guided through the store full of rubbish that is the American mise-en-scene. The American buffalo—coin and animal—is long gone, along with the delusive values of that "Home, Home on the Range." Plenty of discouraging words are heard here, and both Teach and Donny fail Bobby. His love and loyalty, well-laced with stupidity, are rewarded by violence and betrayal as the entire society founders, and there isn't a Beatrice in sight (not only is the cast all male, but the attitude toward women in this play's world is summed up by Teach, in one of the most memorable entrances written for the American stage: "Fuckin' Ruthie, fuckin' Ruthie, fuckin' Ruthie, fuckin' Ruthie, fuckin' Ruthie."). As Hersh Zeifman has pointed out, the literal as well as figurative ruthlessness of Mamet's world is, of course, the point.[2] So Bobby stumbles around this infernal junkshop with two would-be Virgils, neither one wise or trustworthy. The final exchange is a heartbreaking parody of repentance and forgiveness:

> DON: Bob
> BOB: What?
> DON: Get up. *Pause*
> BOB. I'm sorry.
> BOB: I fucked up.

DON: No. You did real good.
BOB: No.
DON: Yeah. You did real good.
Pause
BOB: Thank you.
DON: That's all right.
Pause
BOB: I'm sorry, Donny.
DON: That's all right.
(END OF PLAY)

It is interesting that in Mamet's most recent full-length play, *The Cryptogram* (1995), the husband who has abandoned wife, son and friend, the unseen but motivating evil force behind this play, corrupting and destroying, is named Robert, referred to by his wife as Bobby. Now Bobby has grown up into the betrayer of trust, and his young son is, in effect, sent upstairs to bed to kill himself with a German knife that turns out to be a purchased souvenir rather than a war memento. Like *American Buffalo's* mysterious pigsticker, the knife is the center of the action of this play; once again, life revolves around abandoned articles—torn blankets, borrowed books. Even more startling a connection is that the wife is named Donny. These names and character traits circulate in Mamet's work like the objects in a junkshop, turning up over and over again like a bad nickel.

The temptation to allegorical reading is huge in all of Mamet's drama; certainly Mamet's mise-en-scene is too literal and naturalistic to be "symbolic," which is to say it is neither allusive nor accretive through time—the way symbolism develops resonance and complexity—but, rather requires the elaborate parallel and simultaneous reading allegory demands. This essentially medieval motion of mind holds before us, simultaneously, analogous stories and corresponding universes (one the physical, one the metaphysical), giving us engaging plot on one level and, at the same time, socio-philosophic critique on another. Thus, just as Dante explores his moral cosmos and created an adventure story in the form of an epic poem to convey his vision, so Mamet explores his moral cosmos and creates apparently realistic play after apparently realistic play to convey his. In this way, the junkshop is both literal junkshop and allegorical America; *The Cryptogram's* comfortless living room, with a staircase leading up into the terrible darkness is both the place these people live and an allegorical representation of the forlorn and barren relation between this

mother and child. It is another desolate arena of betrayal, as stark as the
junkshop is cluttered. Like the concluding lines of *American Buffalo*,
the superficially plain and simple language of *The Cryptogram* seems
to have allegorical weight:

> JOHN: Are you dead?
> DONNY: What?
> JOHN: Are you dead? (*Pause.*)
> DONNY: Why do you say that?
> JOHN (*simultaneous with* "that"): I heard you calling.
> DONNY: Go back to bed, John.
> JOHN: I heard voices . . .
> DONNY: . . . you should go back to bed.
> JOHN . . . and I thought they were you. (*Pause.*)
> DONNY: It was me.
> JOHN: And so I said, " . . . there's someone troubled." And I walked
> around. Did you hear walking?
> DONNY: No.
> JOHN: . . . and so I went outside. I saw a candle. In the dark.
> DONNY: Where was this?
> JOHN: In my room. It was burning there. I said, "I'm perfectly alone."
> And I think I was saying it a long time. Cause I didn't have a
> pen. Did that ever happen to you?
> DONNY: I don't know, John.
> JOHN: So I came downstairs to write it down. I know that there *are*
> pens up there. But I don't want to look for them.
> (DONNY *goes to him and cradles him.*)
> Do you think that was right?
> DONNY: Shhh.
> JOHN: Do you think that I was right?
> DONNY: Go to bed.
> JOHN: Mother? (*Pause*)
> DONNY: What?
> JOHN: Do you think I was right.
> DONNY: I don't know, John. (75–76)

The Cryptogram manages to be both chillingly naturalistic (a story
of a deeply disturbed child and his incompetent and self-absorbed
mother) and, on its allegorical level, the story of Youth who/which is
sent to his/its death by Adulthood; along the way, as he climbs up, out
of childhood, he loses the blanket (Comfort), his father (Protection),

and leaves behind, below those he thought were the pillars of his life: Del (Trust) and his mother (Unconditional Love). The dark at the top of the stairs is, allegorically, Experience, the world of Adulthood which is, according to Mamet's vision, a world of cruelty and vile self-interest. The knife, the emblem of his father's false heroism, will, allegorically as well as realistically, become the instrument of the death of Innocence.

In *The Disappearance of the Jews* (1982, 1987), part of a trilogy of one-acts called *Three Jewish Plays*, Bobby (he still does not yet have a last name) is already in Hollywood, but has returned for a brief visit to his hometown, Mamet's hometown, Chicago; the reunion with his boyhood friend Joey in a hotel room reveals Joey's discontent and his longing for life as he imagines it was in a European shtetl. He pictures himself working at a forge and people saying, "There goes Reb Lewis, he's the strongest man in Lodz.... He once picked up an ox.... Or some fucking thing" (15 His indictment goes beyond his own life to the life of contemporary America:

> this shit is *dilute*... the doctors, teachers, everybody in the law, the writers all the time geschraiying, all those assholes, how they're lost... of course, they're lost. They should be studying *talmud*... we should be able to come to them and say, "What is the truth...?" And they should *tell* us." (14)

While Joey is longing for the lead in some machoized *Fiddler on the Roof*, Bobby, significantly, longs for Hollywood in the twenties, "Jesus, I know they had a good time there. Here you got, I mean, five smart Jew boys from Russia, this whole *industry*..." (18) His conversation reveals his marriage and family life in shambles and his spiritual life a sham. Near the end of the play, Bobby says, "God *damn* me.... *(pause)* D'you ever think we would live to be this old?" (25)

Sure enough, God damns him.

In *Bobby Gould in Hell* (1989) our guy wakes up in Hell. His diabolical Interrogator, irate at having his fishing trip delayed, attempts to find out whether Bobby Gould is A Bad Man—which seems to be defined, initially, as someone who mistreats women and lives for pleasure. Bobby disavows all wickedness and refuses to acknowledge any blameworthiness. After much annoying chitchat, Glenna, a woman he seduced, told he loved, and then never called, is brought to Hell to testify against him. She turns out to be so hilariously obdurate that she refuses to leave Hell until The Interrogator asks her "nicely." When

Satan finally comes up with his "last offer": "If you'll go home, I'll pardon all humanity," Glenna, Mamet's prototypical female, replies, "What am I . . . cattle? That you think you can trade on . . . trade, trade on my *emotions*?" (31)

This is not only not Beatrice, this isn't even Eve. Glenna tortures the Devil with newspeak and psychobabble:

> "Because, you know, these things in our life: we needn't be *ruled* by them. But our *Spirits* are a *closed system.* Y'understand? You can't act one way during the day and not expect it to . . . to . . . reflect on what transpires at night, to . . . to *express* itself in your . . . in your . . . nobody help me now . . . in your . . . in . . . what was I talking about? In your relationships" (33)

The Book the hellish bureaucracy consults—a record of his life—says he "treated her shoddily," but Bobby Gould stands his ground and refuses to admit he is a Bad Man. The Devil, disgusted with the entire proceedings, capitulates, and offers him the chance to return to life, with all the sorrows and cruelties of his past erased. But Bobby, like Glenna, applies the vile standards of the contemporary world to the offer: "You say, 'go back, I give you the Power to Do Good.' And I say, why would you do that?"

> INTERROGATOR: Call it an act of whimsy.
> BOB: Bullshit.
> INTERROGATOR: Well, pardon my French.
> BOB: No, Bullshit. Please: one thing I learned on the earth. If it looks Too Good to be True—it's not true. I go back and "Do Good" . . . what does it *cost* me?
> INTERROGATOR: Nothing.
> BOB: All right then, what's in it for you? (41–42)

This argument goes on and on until finally, in the middle of a sentence, Bobby loses his soul, becomes a Bad Man, and admits it, realizing that his evil was based on moral self-delusion—"whatever I did, I told myself it was the act of a Good Man."

The fundamental Dantean logic of the punishment's fitting the crime is ironically played out in Mamet. Dante's lost souls are condemned to torments of hell designed to underscore their sin and force them to repeat their error forever, and Dante's character "Dante" learns enough from his visit to Hell to right himself and achieve

Paradise. Bobby Gould visits Hell, comes to understand his wickedness, and is, like Dante, sent home, except Bobby Gould is condemned to return to Hollywood.

Speed-the-Plow begins with what sounds very much like a continuation of *Bobby Gould in Hell.* The opening line of this earlier play (1985) is Bobby Gould's: "When the gods would make us mad, they answer our prayers. . . . I'm in the midst of the wilderness." This Dantean opening works together with the play's ironic title: according to *The Home Book of Proverbs, Maxims and Familiar Phrases,* "God speed the plough" is an English proverb dating from the 15th c. when it meant, not, God hasten the plough, but God prosper the plough—that is, may your work go well and profitably. In later use it seems to be only an expletive phrase meaning, Good Luck. Bobby Gould's Hollywood plough is surely sped; not only is he back in Hollywood, he has been promoted: Gould tells his temporary secretary, "Hey, I prayed to be pure . . . I said God give me the job as Head of Production. Give me a platform to be "good," and I'll be good. They gave me the job, I'm here one day and *look* at me: a Big Fat Whore" (43).

The plot revolves around a temp secretary who tries to promote herself by promoting a high-minded End of the World film as opposed to a meaningless buddy-movie moneymaker. She champions a novel written by an "Eastern Sissy Writer," a long-winded, pretentious indictment of Western Civilization and its disintegration into literal trash; a choice bit is read aloud by Fox, Bobby Gould's longtime pal and partner in schlock: "The wind against the Plains, but a not a wind of change . . . a wind like that one which he'd been foretold, the rubbish of the world—swirling, swirling . . . two thousand years . . ." (24)

When Karen—the instant object of Bobby Gould's lust—challenges him "But why should it all be garbage?" Bobby Gould replies, "Why ? Why should nickels be bigger than dimes? That's the way it is." (29) Thus the garbage aesthetic is not only firmly established but clearly articulated. Bobby Gould confesses to her that he "prayed to be pure" that "the job corrupts." Although he flirts with the idea of the redemption of making an "artsey" film, he comes to his depraved senses when he realizes that Karen slept with him only to advance her career. His need for spiritual legitimacy ("I was *called* to my new job" [italics mine]) is overwhelmed by his need for power and money. In the catechism that ends the play, the two producers celebrate their prosperity in an exchange that harks back to *Bobby Gould in Hell:*

FOX: . . . And what *if* this fucken' "grace" exists? It's not for you.
You know that, Bob. You know that. You have a different thing.

GOULD: She told me I was a good man. . . .

FOX: I know what you wanted, Bob. You wanted to do good.

GOULD: Yes. (pause) Thank you. . . . I wanted to do Good . . . But I
became foolish

FOX: Well, so we learn a lesson. But we aren't here to "pine," Bob,
we aren't put here to *mope.* What are we here to do (pause) Bob?
After everything is said and done. What are we put on earth to
do?

GOULD: We're here to make a movie.

FOX: Whose name goes above the title?

GOULD: Fox and Gould

FOX: Then how bad can life be? (81–81)

The play answers Fox's question.

In "A Tradition of the Theater as Art" (in *Writing in Restaurants*),
Mamet passionately argues in essay form the same indictment he
creates dramatically in *Speed-the-Plow:*

> We live in an illiterate country. The mass media—the commercial
> theater included—pander to the low and the lowest of the low in the
> human experience. They, finally, debase us through the sheer weight
> of their mindlessness.

> Every reiteration of the idea that *nothing matters* debases the human
> spirit.

> Every reiteration of the idea that there is no drama in modern life,
> there is only dramatization, that there is no tragedy, there is only
> unexplained misfortune, debases us. . . .

> Who is going to speak up? Who is going to speak for the American
> spirit? For the human spirit? (21)

This impassioned rhetoric, filled with the earnest rhythms of a man
preaching to the converted, finds its dramatic expression in *Speed-the-
Plow*.

In *Homicide*, the main character is named Bobby Gold, a big-city
detective who is a crack hostage negotiator nicknamed, "The Orator."
In the course of doing his job, pursuing a killer, he becomes both

betrayer and betrayed; along the way, literally, he gets caught up in an apparently unrelated plot involving Zionist terrorists who force him to face his past rejection of his Jewishness (and thus the slight name change) and the anti-Semitic world he works in. In Bob Gold, "the talkin' man," Mamet seems to have created his most obvious surrogate; like Dante writing an epic poem about his surrogate's spiritual crisis, Mamet has made a movie about his—writing, directing and even going so far as to cast his father as an actor in it.

But once again, with still another dramatic chance for rehabilitation, Gold's journey is not salvific. Significantly, when a cop brings in a man who killed his wife and children with a deer rifle, the arresting officer says, "What'd you do, mistake them for a deer?" and Gold says, "Hey, all we got to do is *catch* 'em, we don't got to figure them out, thank God." (16) A few pages later, after the murderer attacks Gold, trying to get his gun, in order, he says, to kill himself, and he offers this, worthy of one of the *Inferno*'s damned: "Perhaps someday I could help *you* . . ." Gold: "Now. How could *you* help *me* . . . ?" The man replies, "Perhaps someday I could tell you the nature of Evil. . . . Would you like to know how to solve the problem of evil?" And Gold answers, "No, man, cause if I did, then I'd be out of a Job . . ." (20).

And so, we feel, would Mamet be. Mamet has made a career out of the inspection of America's spiritual trashheap, and like his Bobby Goulds, he knows that the most glamorous ruins and the most ruinous glamour is Hollywood. When Mamet was asked if he saw any likelihood of our society's extricating itself from the wreckage, he replied with an hilarious and savage postmodern inventory:

> It's like the weather. People get oppressed by the heat and humidity, it's got to rain before it's going to clear up. There are ebbs and flows in any civilization. Nothing lasts forever. We had a good time. We had Tennessee Williams. We had the hula hoop. We had the Edsel. All kinds of good stuff. The Constitution. To name but a few. Shelley Winters. Now you've got to pay the piper. Big deal. (Savran, 144)

Paying the piper: Dante knew all about that.

NOTES

1. I am indebted to Laurence Maslon for the discovery of this poem. His amusing essay (*American Theatre,* October, 1995) suggests that "legitimate theatre's ongoing siege of Hollywood" began in 1925 when Herman J. Mankiewicz sent a telegram from Hollywood to Ben Hecht in New York which

read, "Millions are to be grabbed out here and your only competition is idiots." (27)

    2. Actually, Zeifman's point is even richer, that the society of *American Buffalo* is both "ruthless and graceless."

WORKS CITED

Dante. *The Divine Comedy: Hell.* Trans. Dorothy L. Sayers. Baltimore: Penguin, 1949.

Mamet, David. *American Buffalo*. New York: Grove Weidenfeld, 1976.

———. *Bobby Gould in Hell.* New York: Samuel French, 1989.

———. *The Cryptogram.* New York: Vintage, 1995.

———. *The Disappearance of the Jews in Three Jewish Plays.* New York: Samuel French, 1982.

———. *Homicide.* New York: Grove Weidenfeld, 1992.

———. *On Directing Film.* Viking, 1991.

———. *Speed-the-Plow.* New York: Grove, 1988.

———. *Writing in Restaurants.* Penguin, 1986.

Savran, David. *In Their Own Words: Contemporary American Playwrights.* New York: Theatre Communications Group, 1988.

Stevenson, Burton. *The Home Book of Proverbs, Maxims and Familiar Phrases.* New York: Macmillan, 1959.

Zeifman, Hersh. "Phallus in Wonderland: Business and Machismo in *American Buffalo* and *Glengarry Glen Ross*" in Kane, Leslie, ed., *David Mamet: A Casebook* (New York and London: Garland, 1992) 123–35.

The Myth of Narcissus: Shepard's *True West* and Mamet's *Speed-the-Plow*

Katherine H. Burkman

It's a scientific fact. For every two years you live in California you lose two points off your I.Q. It's redundant to die in L.A.

Truman Capote

Sam Shepard's *True West* (1980) and David Mamet's *Speed-the-Plow* (1988) are twin plays about twins. Although the dramas appear to be very different on the surface, they duplicate each other both in terms of their plots and their protagonists. Such similarity only becomes troubling, however, because of a kind of duplicity that lurks in the duplicating process; the playwrights, who purport to offer a critique of Hollywood, offer instead a celebration of that which they critique. One may well wonder how two such gifted American playwrights as Shepard and Mamet managed to arrive at such sameness. What is the power of the Hollywood myth that mesmorizes those who would combat it? What evolution in our culture might account for the way cinema, which originally imitated theatre, has in the hands of two major American playwrights virtually swallowed it up?

I would suggest that the power of the Hollywood myth, the glamorous scenario envisioned by Lee in Shepard's *True West* that you can become an overnight star in an effortless burst of creativity, has its underpinnings in the myth of Narcissus and the narcissism that Christopher Lasch asserts underlies the American culture in general. Whether producers of scripts (the characters in *Speed-the-Plow* or writers of scripts (the characters in *True West*), the glamour of the movie world involves a narcissistic escape akin to that which the spectator experiences when viewing a film.[1]

A culture organized around mass consumption encourages narcissism—which we can define, for the moment, as a disposition to

see the world as a mirror, more particularly as a projection of one's
own fears and desires—not because it makes people grasping and
self-assertive but because it makes them weak and dependent. It
undermines their confidence in their capacity to understand and shape
the world and to provide for their own needs. (Lasch 33)

The lost and dependent Lee in *True West* assures his brother that he can
make his fantasies become reality, that he can become a film writer
with ease. "I could be just like you . . ." Lee informs his brother,
"Sittin' around dreamin' stuff up. Gettin' paid to dream. Ridin' back
and forth on the freeway just dreamin' my fool head off" (25). Lee's
brother Austin, who is in the business of turning out the movie scripts
that Lee aspires to write, knows the hollowness of such instant success,
but he in turn romanticizes his brother's life as an outlaw of the desert.[2]
In reality, about which neither brother has much sense, Lee is merely a
small time crook, who steals television sets. The fun in the play lies in
Shepard's critique of the West in its desert and Hollywood versions,
which involves exposing the twin nature of the brothers with their
interchangeable dreams.

    The encounter of the brothers in their mother's apartment is not the
encounter of doubles in which the protagonist must face in the Other a
darker aspect of a self:

> The most prominent symptom of the forms which the double takes is
> a powerful consciousness of guilt which forces the hero no longer to
> accept the responsibility for certain actions of his ego, but to place it
> upon another ego, a double, who is either personified by the devil
> himself or is created by making a diabolical pact. (Rank 76) [3]

The brothers are not Other to each other; there is no difference. Both
are living in illusion, for the desert that Lee's father inhabits is no more
"real" than the Hollywood that covers over some part of it. Visiting his
father in the desert, Lee has found it to be a wasteland for the drunk
who have lost their teeth, their bite: Austin tells Lee about how their
father lost his teeth one by one and then in a bout of drinking lost his
false teeth as well: "First he lost his real teeth, then he lost his false
teeth" (41). Taking out the false teeth on a drinking spree with his son,
his father, Austin tells Lee, dropped them in a doggie bag with some
Chop Suey.

We went back but we never did find it. (*pause*) Now that's a true
story. True to life. (42)

The double loss of real and false teeth becomes one of the play's
numerous metaphors for the lost nature of the "True West" in its
manifestations as either Hollywood or the desert that spawned this
horrific flower. Only loss is true, "true to life." Each brother senses his
own hollowness but idealizes the other in hopes of inhabiting a truer
self. The film script that Lee conjures up, in which two brothers are
involved in a pointless chase scene, neatly reflects and sums up Austin
and Lee's own plight. The brothers, Lee explains as he describes his
script idea, are in a desert and run out of gas:

> So they take off after each other straight into an endless black prairie.
> The sun is just comin' down and they can feel the night on their
> backs. What they don't know is that each one of 'em is afraid, see.
> Each one separately thinks that he's the only one that's afraid. And
> they keep ridin' like that straight into the night. Not knowing. And
> the one who's chasin' doesn't know where the other one is taking
> him. And the one who's being chased doesn't know where he's
> going. (27)

The brothers are like Narcissus sitting at the pool, in love with an
idealized image of himself that he fails to realize is just that, an image.
      As Austin and Lee struggle over who will get the keys to Austin's
car as if that will determine the "true" victory in their power conflict,
we begin to realize the "false" nature of the struggle (not true at all) as
they turn into each other: Lee struggles to write his script,
"Contemporary western. Based on a true story" (18), while Austin
steals toasters and prepares to leave for the desert. Each brother wishes
to be the other, each failing to realize that they are indistinguishable.
      At the outposts of the play's geography are Alaska, from which the
boys' mother returns only to depart when her sons won't "behave" and
the desert, where the boys seek a father who is as absent for them as
their mother is. Richard Gilman writes that the rootlessness of the West
is Shepard's natural setting as it is "almost the condition of life" in his
dramatic world.

> But at the same time the West, particularly California, is the place
> where, most acutely, visible success, gestures of self, personality,

fame are means, conscious or not, of making up for or disguising the lack of roots. (xxi)

What is most compelling in Shepard's drama is his projection of the myth of Hollywood as the other side of the bankrupt coin of the "true" West that Hollywood in turn tries to romanticize in its Westerns. When Austin informs his producer that his script is superior to his brother's, he defines the two Wests which are really one.

> He's [Lee] been camped out on the desert for three months. Talking to cactus. What's he know about what people wann' see on the screen! I drive on the freeway every day. I swallow the smog. I watch the news in color. I shop in the Safeway. I'm the one who's in touch! Not him! (35)

Not, may we say, either one!

In his twin version of *True West*, Mamet creates in *Speed-the-Plow* another appearance of difference that is an illusion. In Mamet's drama, the twin protagonists, Bobby Gould and Charlie Fox, have the opportunity to produce a buddy prison film with a star, a film that reflects them even as Lee's film reflects the brothers in *True West*. Buddies themselves, the two men laughingly envision themselves as whores who are about to become "rich" whores (31–32), producers who make vacuous films: Fox explains to Karen, a temporary secretary, that Gould "takes his coffee like he makes his movies: nothing in it. . . 'Cause he's an Old Whore" (31).

Like Shepard, Mamet sets up a false Other as Gould is seduced for a time by Karen, who wants him to produce a film with substance. Here Shepard's false opposition between Hollywood and the desert becomes a false opposition between West as Hollywood and East. Gould has been giving a "courtesy read" to a novel called "The Bridge: or Radiation and the Half-Life of Society, A Study of Decay" (29), a novel he explains that is "From the East. An Eastern Sissy Writer" (29). Karen's emotional report to Gould on the book he gives her to evaluate exposes both the book and her as ludicrous. The novel, she rhapsodizes, invites us to revel in the radiation that changes us. The author, she explains, "says that the radiation. . . *all* of it, the planes, the televisions, clocks, all of it *is to the one end*. To *change* us—to, to *bring about a change*—all radiation has been sent by God. To change us. Constantly" (64). As Clive Barnes notes, "Mamet never gives art an even break against mammon" (quoted in Hall 155).

The difference again, then, proves illusory as the seemingly innocent Karen, who promotes the Eastern novel and herself, is just another kind of whore, who sleeps with Gould to get him interested in the novel. Mamet never gives any serious credence to the novel as a work of any more substance than the buddy film the male whores agree to make. And Gould, whose flirtation with an "art" film turns out to be only a flirtation with Karen, returns to his "buddy" Gould from whom, it turns out, he is basically indistinguishable.

Like Shepard, Mamet offers an amusing and somewhat biting critique of Hollywood, exposing its myth as shallow, materialistic, and dehumanizing. But like Shepard again, Mamet plays fast and loose with his audience, proving that he and Shepard are buddies at heart, barely more distinguishable from each other than their protagonists, whom they seem so intent on exposing but whom they tend to celebrate at the same time. Stephen Watt, in his cogent analysis of *Speed-the-Plow* ("Representing Hollywood on Stage; Structural Allegories, Phallic 'Players,' and Colonized Consumers"), has quite rightly suggested that "Hollywood on stage is gendered in ways analogous to Hollywood on film," so that Karen's threat to Gould and Fox's masculinity must be removed if they are to get on with making the prison film that will empower them "to impose their own brand of rapine on others: 'up the ass with gun and camera'" (Watt 5). While Ann Hall believes that Karen disrupts and exposes "the male system as a house of cards" ("Playing to Win: Sexual Politics in David Mamet's *House of Games* and *Speed-the-Plow*" 138), and that the casting of Madonna in the role underlines the ambiguity of Karen as virgin/whore that the director sought (149), such ambiguity seems to be sadly missing in the script.

Indeed, the casting provides clues to the way the drama plays into the Hollywood myth it purports to critique. Karen/Madonna as sex object can't be taken seriously by either Gould or by the audience. An object can hardly disrupt—it can only titillate with a slight flutter. In her singing career Madonna refuses to be such an object, her very offering of herself as a sex object performed with irony and control that becomes a comment on the objectifying of women. As Karen, however, a character who seems to fight Hollywood sleaze, her offers of salvation are as vacuous as the text that she wishes Gould to embrace— "I know what it is to be bad. I've been bad, I know what it is to be lost, I know you're lost" (77). Given such blatant cliches, how can the audience not be relieved when the men throw her out? Because Karen/Madonna remains even more stereotyped than the men, she does not offer any actual disruption to the "buddies," who happily escape her influence.

Once again, there is no Other. Narcissus pays no attention to the nymph Echo, who pines away with love for him, but we hear her voice as distinct, at least in Ovid's version of the Narcissus myth. Reduced to an echo, she infuses that echo with her authentic experience.

> Meanwhile Narcissus, strayed from all his friends,
> and began to shout, "Is anybody here?"
> "Here," Echo answered, and the wondering boy
> Looked far around him and cried louder, "Come."
> "Come," she called after him. . . . (Ovid 96–97)

Since Echo manages, in the confines of her loved one's words, to make her own statements, it is not surprising to hear that even when she has long vanished from the forest, her voice remains with her bones:

> Far from her usual walks on hills and valleys,
> She's heard by all who call; her voice has life. (97)

Mamet, however, makes his character all body and no voice, a hollow echo of the aspirations of the men for power. Insuring that Karen will remain "temporary" by giving her more vacuous cliches to speak than he gives to the men, Mamet, in Brechtian terms, does not dismantle the ideology of the patriarchal texture of the Hollywood myth that the play depicts. Since the woman identifies with her oppressors and adopts their strategies and behaviors, she becomes their twin, not their double. Rather than the melodrama of the good girl versus the bad guys, Mamet rather gives us the melodrama of the bad guys, who are boyish and foolish, versus the worse woman.

Shepard indulges in a similar denigration of women by bringing on a character as mother in *True West* who is the very personification of absence. True, the men are for all intents and purposes orphans, in that their father is as absent as their mother, having become as childlike as they are. But the mother's treatment of her sons' murderous wrestling match as the bad behavior of children indicts her as part cause. "You boys shouldn't fight in the house," she exclaims as they begin their fight to the death. "Go outside and fight" (56). Perhaps if she had paid more attention to her sons, they might have had a chance to grow up. The disappointment of the mother and the rage of the brothers are all part of their narcissistic dilemma, their lack of ability to separate from one another.[4]

Somehow the culprit here is not the bad boys, who are again rather endearing, but the mother, who like Karen is permanently temporary and absolutely muddled. She has come back early from Alaska, she explains, partly because she missed her plants, whose death she nevertheless brushes off with, "Oh well, one less thing to take care of I guess" (54), and her big news is that Picasso is in town. Informed by her sons that Picasso is dead, her reply is: "No, he's not dead. He's visiting the museum. I read it on the bus. We have to go down there and see him" (55). Unlike Mamet's Karen, Shepard's Mom does stumble in her capacity of wise fool on one important truth. When her sons inform her they are off to the desert, though not the same desert that their father inhabits, she announces: "Well, you'll probably wind up on the same desert sooner or later" (53). What escapes her, however, is that she inhabits that desert, or rather, that the desert inhabits her.

Like Gould, Lee, essentially motherless, longs for a woman who will reflect him in some way:

LEE: Is it too late to call a woman? You know any women?
AUSTIN: I'm a married man.
LEE: I mean a local woman. . .
AUSTIN: How 'bout some toast?. . .
LEE: I don't need toast. I need a woman.
AUSTIN: A woman isn't the answer. Never was.
LEE: I'm not talkin' about permanent. I'm talkin' about temporary.
(44)

Shepard is no less aware than Mamet that his male characters treat women as temporaries—what is an idea in Shepard becomes a metaphor in Karen's position as "temporary"—but since the women are not just considered temporary by the men but are portrayed as vacuously temporary, the critique is undermined and the buddies' view of women is subtly reinforced.

Mamet has found the perfect actor for his rendition of the Hollywood myth on stage in Joe Mantegna, who revealed to Leslie Kane in an interview not only the secret of his successful acting of Mamet roles but also his unconscious collusion with Mamet in undoing some of the social critique that the plays might hold. The secret to playing his role in *Glengarry*, he notes, was "falling in love with the character as opposed to looking at him from the outside . . ." (Kane

256), as anti-Brechtian as one can get. He goes on to say that "In other words, all these attributes that perhaps to somebody else were sleazy or despicable, to me were all attributes. They were confidence, they were power, they were respect, they were compassion, caring" (256). Mamet, like Montegna, identifies with the Hollywood moguls' misogyny and self-hate, finally sentimentalizing male bonding and celebrating it even while he exposes its basis. He can't even let Gould go, resuscitating him in a 1989 play, *Bobby Gould in Hell*, in which Hollywood is now hell itself and he is accused of being "cruel without being interesting" (42), as if somehow being interesting would be a saving grace. For Mamet, Gould and Fox are entertaining clowns, and that is their saving grace.

Similarly, Shepard identifies with and romanticizes the brothers who fully understand their own failures as artists and human beings (AUSTIN: "There's nothin' real down here, Lee! Least of all me". . . LEE: "I'm livin' out there 'cause I can't make it here!" (49)). In Shepard's hands, however, the critique of a bankrupt Hollywood is undermined because he lovingly creates Peter Pan characters, who somewhat charmingly refuse to give up their childhood dreams. They are like Rabbit in Shepard's earlier play, *Angel City* (1976), who resists the crazed world of film but realizes he does not want to leave what has become a hell, and who ends up by becoming the film. Locked in a love/hate embrace at the play's conclusion, Austin and Lee are also like Narcissus at the pool, still worshipping an idealized image that they know is hollow but that they are incapable of rejecting as only an image. Ovid's description of Narcissus just after he rejects the insight that his image is himself could just as well be a description of Austin and Lee: "He spoke and half mad faced the self-made image" (99).

Finally, the myth of Hollywood on the Shepard and Mamet stage, despite all the playwrights' efforts to deconstruct and expose it as bankrupt, retains a glamorous potency, a potency that depends on a subtle misogyny and that is at its core deeply narcissistic. There is no real tension in the conflicts in these Hollywood dramas, no real contest between the self and Other, no confrontation of the self with a double that might provide subtext. While such lack of duality in plays that appear to explore the self in terms of an Other may be viewed as merely an illustration of postmodern insights about the lack of centering and identity, the flattening out of character would seem rather to mask the narcissistic trap that the playwrights seem to fall into as they critique a narcissistic culture.[5] Without conflict there is no integration, just a merging that leaves the characters empty. In *The Minimal Self*,

Christopher Lasch finds that the central concern of much contemporary art is just the kind of illusion of oneness that the plays project, one that provides "immediate relief from the burden of selfhood" (165).

> An inner agenda nevertheless underlies much of contemporary music, art, and literature, one that seeks to recapture a sense of psychic oneness without taking any account of the obstacles, psychic or material, that lie in the way of that oneness. (Lasch 165)

When Estragon complains in Beckett's *Waiting for Godot* that nothing happens, we know that nothing really has happened and that this happening is a profound experience in which the characters are more than buddies—they are friends. But Shepard and Mamet, despite their wry humor in pointing out the bankruptcy of the myth of the west, fail to see their complicity in its celebration. They are like Shepard's Austin, who accuses Lee of scripting a melodrama not worth the writing, but who aspires to live that melodrama himself. They are like Narcissus at the pool, who has seen that what he worships is only an idealized image of himself, but who rejects that knowledge. The myth of Hollywood on stage, then, is the story of one, Narcissus, who thinks he is two, and Mamet's and Shepard's treatment of that myth on stage is the story of two who are really one.

NOTES

1. "The ego's desire for a stress-free state results in a narcissism that shuts out the anxiety-generating external world and in extreme cases leads to suicide" (Slethaug 13).

2. Alice Miller explains the relationship of the myth of Narcissus to narcissistic disturbance in her book, *The Drama of the Gifted Child*.

> The legend of Narcissus actually tells us the tragedy of the narcissistic disturbance. Narcissus sees his reflection in the water and falls in love with his own beautiful face, of which his mother was surely proud. The nymph Echo answers the young man's calls because she is in love with his beauty, just as their mothers are with our patients. Echo's answering calls deceive Narcissus. His reflection deceives him as well, since it shows only his perfect, wonderful side and not his other parts. His back view, for instance, and his shadow remain hidden from him; they do not belong to and are cut off from his beloved reflection. (49)

Miller further explains that his passion for his false self prevents Narcissus from loving himself (50).

3. The term double is a slippery one and Rank's is an early definition. Gordon E. Slethaug in *The Play of the Double in Postmodern American Fiction* discusses postmodern definitions (Derrida and Foucault's). By viewing reality as a construct of language, these thinkers have a more linguistic view of the figure, "instead of treating the double as a separate person or separate aspect of a personality" (25).

4. "We cathect an object narcissistically, according to Kohut (1971), when we experience it not as the center of its own activity but as a part of ourselves. If the object does not behave as we expect or wish, we may at times be immeasurably disappointed or offended, almost as if an arm ceased to obey us or a function that we take for granted (such as memory) lets us down. This sudden loss of control may also lead to an intense narcissistic rage" (Miller 31)

5. In his book, *Shattered Selves,* James M. Glass offers a critique of the celebration of some postmodernists of a decentering that he finds frightening. Suggesting that several object-relations theorists "offer a critique of postmodernism's celebration of multiplicity," Glass adds: "It should be noted , however, that object-relations theory with its clinical backdrop, its empirical foundation in the experience of the self, and its concept of, if not a unitary, at least a cohesive self moves against several arguments in postmodernism" (49).

WORKS CITED

Gilman, Richard. "Introduction." *Sam Shepard: Seven Plays.* New York: Bantam, 1981: xi–xxvii.

Glass, James M. *Shattered Selves: Multiple Personality in a Postmodern World.* Ithaca and London: Cornell University Press, 1993.

Hall, Ann C. "Playing to Win: Sexual Politics in David Mamet's *House of Games* and *Speed-the-Plow.*" *David Mamet: A Casebook.* Ed. Leslie Kane. Vol. 12, Casebooks on Modern Dramatists. New York: Garland Publishing, 1992: 137–160.

Kane, Leslie. "Interview with Joe Mantegna." *David Mamet: A Casebook.* Ed. Leslie Kane. New York and London: Garland Publishing, 1992: 249–269.

Lasch, Christopher: *The Minimal Self: Psychic Survival in Troubled Times.* New York: W. W. Norton, 1984

Mamet, David. *Speed-the-Plow.* New York: Grove Press, 1985.

———. *Bobby Gould in Hell. Oh, Hell!: Two One-Act Plays.* New York: Samuel French, 1991: 5–45.

Miller, Alice. *The Drama of the Gifted Child: The Search for the True Self.* New York: Basic Books, 1981.

Ovid. *The Metamorphoses.* Trans. Horace Gregory. New York: The Viking Press, 1958.

Rank, Otto. *The Double: A Psychoanalytic Study.* Trans. and Ed. Harry Tucker, Jr. New York: New American Library, 1971.

Slethaug, Gordon E. *The Play of the Double in Postmodern American Fiction.* Carbondale and Edwardsville: Southern Illinois University Press, 1993.

Watt, Stephen. "Representing Hollywood on Stage: Structural Allegories, Phallic 'Players,' and Colonized Consumers." Unpublished paper given at M/MLA, 1994.

Shepard, Sam. *Angel City. Angel City & Other Plays.* New York: Urizen Books, 1976: 5–54.

———. *True West. Sam Shepard: Seven Plays.* New York: Bantam, 1981: 1– 59.

Alienation Effects and Exteriorized Subjectivity in *Angel City* and *The Bostonians*

RJ LaVelle

Man is the measure of all things . . . —Protagoras

I begin with the quote above because it offers us two competing readings to focus and organize the analysis of the Sam Shepard's *Angel City* and Henry James's *The Bostonians*. The one most common describes the unity of a centered self as being the thing that gives all others order. Man is the valued term. ***Man*** is the measure of all things. The other reverses this traditional reading and serves up an emptied center and a dispersed subjectivity, with measure more important than Man. Man is ***the measure of all things***. To quote from Tom Cohen's *Anti-Mimesis from Plato to Hitchcock*:

> Protagoras, whose famous dictum on the *metron*—that is "Man is the measure of all things. . . . ," often cited as a founding text (however contradictorily) of relativism, humanism, and pragmatism—may be read as a *performative* text in which the category of "man (*anthropos*)" is decentered, dismantled, and dissolved by a term, measure, which inscribes this non-subject in an activity of sheer semiosis and differencing. . . . (Cohen 92)

I do not propose to trace where this leads Cohen, but intend instead to use this observation, along with others about language and subjectivity gleaned from modern theory, as a starting point around which several binary oppositions, such as public and private, center and margin, interior and exterior, may be marshaled and then disposed of, hoping that they might lead to answers about the growth of modern media of communication. What might the two texts say about the relationship between subjectivity and this exteriorized space of measure populated and defined by things? Henry James' *The Bostonians* and Sam Shepard's play *Angel City*, each rich in spatial imagination, are situated on either side of the blossoming of the media age, and each, in its own way, offers a meditation on public and private discourse, interior and exterior, and their interpenetration.

I will begin in the "post-modern" and work my way back to the "modern." *Angel City* presents a nightmarish, yet comic Hollywood in which "character" as we normally conceive of it ceases to exist and, instead, becomes a shifting field of pop-culture discourse woven together in a quasi-expressionistic fury. I use the term quasi-expressionistic to foreground the fact that without traditionally constructed characters, no interior landscape can be made explicit. With a lack of the centered self that somehow marks and masks the conglomeration of interior, unconscious desires, that particular project is impossible. Yet the play remains "expressionistic" if we take the very construction of the texture of the weave and what might lie behind the fabric as the subject to be expressed. This "weave" expresses the total economy of the Hollywood dream-machine in which character is woven together, unraveled, and shuttled back into the original structure. The "disaster" or the "miracle" that the Hollywood producer needs to save his film, and for which he hires Rabbit Brown, is as all consuming machine that configures all possibility.

So far presented, this play might seem like yet another cliché-ridden critique of the film industry serving up a tired exposé of its evils, but read according to the logic of the play, this is perhaps where its brilliance lies. In a world where pop culture largely governs the possibility of expression, the most savage critique is a quotation that exposes the system from within. However, rather than venture into an explanation that might reveal a nostalgia for the centered subject that such critiques of Hollywood have as their basis, I will instead explore some theoretical insights that might reveal the beauty and terror of the "disaster" and/or "miracle" of which the play speaks. Using very liberal interpretations of thoughts put forth in Nietzsche's *The Birth of Tragedy* and Walter Benjamin's "The Work of Art in the Age of Mechanical Reproduction," joined with Voloshinov's philosophy of language, I will attempt to explain the alienation effects that Shepard achieves and their relationship with post-modern subjectivity.

In the stage directions for the play, Shepard writes:

> The term "character" could be thought of in a different way when working on this play. Instead of the idea of a "whole character" with logical motives behind his behavior which the actor submerges himself into, he should consider instead a fractured whole with bits and pieces flying off the central theme. In other words, more in terms of collage construction, of jazz improvisation. (6)

These directions and their relation to the segments of controlled chaos are essential to an understanding of the play. Each character's mesmerized, disjointed discourse reveals itself to be nothing more than the discourses of the movies. The dreams they dream and the desires they have are built by the dream-factory for which they work. Lanx dreams of being a famous prize fighter who then sells his life story to a major studio. Tympani dreams of having a nostalgia-laden movie version of a diner that focuses on narcissistic images: "Everyone's face is reflected in (chrome) stools" (33).

Wheeler also speaks of a film event that will show the audience to themselves, "penetrating every layer of their dark subconscious," and that act will "create mass hypnosis" (15). Yet if very nature of the interior desires of the on-stage characters is produced by the already existent "mass hypnosis" of Hollywood, what is revealed is already evident; the "subconscious" is structured by the films themselves. Playing off the clichéd nature of the dreams, and the desire to uncover, to reveal the "inner nature" of the film audience sets up a dynamic by which what creates "the mass hypnosis" is the very revelation that it is "mass hypnosis." The power of the film event for which Wheeler wishes is that it sweeps away the illusion of a centered subject with interior and individual desires and reveals that interior as always already inhabited by language and other media of communication.

In his article on *Angel City*, Leonard Wilcox writes that "dialogue advertises its quoted and clichéd nature . . . the play presents itself as a compilation of borrowings." His observation, linked with Voloshinov's Marxist linguistics, are perhaps a perfect tool with which to reflect on the "post-modern" condition, or more generally upon the illusion of the unified, centered subject. I emphasize the more general nature of this state of affairs so as not to suggest that Hollywood has somehow "colonized" a once virgin interiority in which we were able to express our original individual desires. A quick look at *Don Quixote* will prove that exteriorized subjectivity has been with us for quite a while. I take up *The Bostonians* in this essay precisely because it is not a post-modern text and will help to avoid containing the effects of a mediated

subjectivity to the comfortable realm of the "post-modern," while also
allowing the examination of changes in modes of mediation.

Voloshinov's Marxist linguistics state that the interior is, and
always has been a social space. He first destroys individualistic
subjectivistic linguistics that have drawn a distinction between "that
inner something which is *expressible*, and its *outward objectification*
for others" (Voloshinov 282). The following is worth quoting at length:

> The experiential, expressible element and its outward objectification
> are created, as we know, out of one and the same material. After all,
> there is no such thing as experience outside of embodiment in signs.
> Consequently, the very notion of a fundamental, qualitative
> difference between the inner and outer element is invalid to begin
> with. Furthermore, the location of the organizing and formative
> center is not within (i.e. not in the material of inner signs) but outside.
> It is not experience that organizes expression, but the other way
> around—*expression organizes experience*. (283)

It follows that language, art, and popular culture, among other things,
are the modes of expression that organize experience from without. I
again call attention to Protagoras and the metron: "Man is *the measure
of all things*." To objections that this would leave everyone completely
devoid of agency, Voloshinov grounds communication and language in
use, in the *instance* of the utterance thrown across as a bridge between
addresser and addressee. "Even if a word is not entirely his,
constituting, as it were, the border zone between himself and his
addressee—still, it does in part belong to him" (284) The generative
nature of linguistic phenomena is expressed textually in the fact that the
characters whose dreams are structured by Hollywood also participate
in making those dreams, they are both acting on and affected by the
dream-machine they service. This dynamic can be seen as a feedback
loop with the constant exchange and mutation of exterior signs that
move from outside to inside, and then back again. The idea of a
centered subject, an individual interior that serves as an origin of
experience, is merely an illusion.

Once again, I stress that Voloshinov's theory does not just describe
a postmodern subjectivity, and here, I would like to digress into
Nietzsche's *The Birth of Tragedy*. In this work Nietzsche writes of
music and the collapse of the *principium individuationis* and the
Dionysian terror and ecstasy when one "glimpses into the innermost
depths of man" (Nietzsche 36). This view is fearsome for there is

nothing there to see. This, he believes, is the thrust of Attic Tragedy. Nietzsche explicates with a story. When King Midas traps the wise Silenus and asks what is best and most desirous for man, Silenus responds:

> Oh, wretched ephemeral race, children of chance and misery, why do you compel me to tell you what it would be most expedient for you not to hear? What is best of all is utterly beyond your reach: not to be born, not to be, to be nothing. but the second best for you is—to die soon. (42)

The Greeks responded to this terror of the nothingness of existence with the Apollonian, the impulse toward beauty and the *principium individuationis*. They erected the idea of the individual over the framework of nothingness. Yet, the Dionysian void is constantly evoked and, at the same time, veiled in Attic Tragedy. The Apollonian is dominant in Greek culture, but in Tragedy there are moments when the Dionysian breaks through the framework that attempts to cover it, and the *principium individuationis* falls apart.

Angel City presents a similar collapse of the *principium individuationis* and exposes the shifting sands upon which our illusorily centered subjects exist. Shepard even gives us insight into the very composition of those sands. Wilcox writes:

> Yet, if Shepard's textualized surfaces enter directly and exuberantly into popular myth and idiom, they have darker implications. For they cast doubt on the existence of any reality that might precede or transcend the pervasive coding of popular culture. (67)

I agree with Wilcox here, yet I disagree with the implicit thrust of his statement. With the "darker implications," he seems to be saying we would be much better off without the pernicious influence of pop-culture and film. I believe, however, that this "pervasive coding of pop-culture" is revolutionary and perhaps beautiful in that it so obviously reveals, in the performative text of Shepard's play, how our subjectivity is always already mediated. The power of film is that it reveals that mediation so much more effectively than other forms of ideological inculcation because film spectatorship is much more bounded and guided by the medium of presentation.

In "The Work of Art in the Age of Mechanical Reproduction" Walter Benjamin gives an early explanation of the power of film. The following passage is a peripheral part of that rich essay, but offers a vivid explanation of the challenge that new modes of communication and art present to the "consciousness" formed under the domination of other modes of exterior, material expression.[1] The conflict that Benjamin points to will be seen more clearly in *The Bostonians*, situated as it is during the flowering of the newspaper age in America. Benjamin cites Duhamel, who still maintains the distinction of an inner experience and an outer expression, and struggles with film, a medium that makes the illusion of "individuality" more difficult to maintain.

> The painting invites to spectator to contemplation; before it the spectator can abandon himself to his associations. Before a movie frame he cannot do so. No sooner has his eye grasped a scene than it is already changed. It cannot be arrested. Duhamel, who detests the film and knows nothing of its significance, though something of its structure, notes this circumstance as follows: "I can no longer think what I want to think. My thoughts have been replaced by moving images." (Benjamin 238)

Duhamel, I argue, could not think freely in the first instance, it only became much more obvious when he was watching a film. His attitude in front of a painting is also bounded by ideology; what he thinks, the associations that he can make, are socially determined, but the structure of the spectatorship of a painting is illusorily "individualized," veiling its boundedness in the social sphere. Again I quote Voloshinov:

> Thus the personality of the speaker, taken from within, so to speak, turns out to be wholly a product of social interrelations. Not only its outward expression but also its inner experience are social territory. Consequently, the whole route between inner experience (the "expressible") and its outward objectification (the "utterance") lies entirely across social territory (Voloshinov 289).

It follows that changes in the modes of expression will change "inner experience."

Towards the beginning of *Angel City* Rabbit Brown makes a remarkably similar observation on the nature and power of film:

> I've smelled something down here ... Making me daydream at night ... the vision of a celluloid tape with a series of moving images telling a story to millions. Millions anywhere. Millions seen and

unseen. Millions seeing the same story without ever knowing each other. Without even having to be together. Effecting their dreams and actions. Replacing their books. Replacing their families. Replacing religion, politics, art, conversation. Replacing their minds. And I ask myself, how can I stay immune? How can I keep my distance from a machine like that. (Shepard 13)

According to Benjamin and Voloshinov, he cannot. The exterior signs gradually invade and re-order the subjective interior. Rabbit's response is to come south to Hollywood to participate in the feedback loop that will allow him some agency in the system.

One of the alienation effects of film that the play carries out arises from the tension inherent in the competing discourses that structure subjectivity. That is to say, Hollywood is not the only source of material discourse that goes into the mixture. It does, however, make that mixture more volatile, as the "real" of people's lives does not correspond with the "real" of the movies. The contrast serves to make the content of both the personal social world and the mass mediated world more readily apparent as being constructed from without. If Hollywood has such a power to invade and reorganize, then the "original" contents must be similarly imbued. Again the play makes these tensions evident. Miss Scoons enters a trance and states:

I look at the screen and I am the screen. I'm not me. I don't know who I am. I look at the movie and I am the movie. I am the star. I am the star in the movie. For days I am the star and I'm not me. I look at my life when I come down. I hate my life when I come down. I hate my life for not being a movie. (21)

Yet the spectator realizes while watching the play that a huge chunk of the "character" presented upon the stage is precisely part of a movie. Miss Scoons's dilemma is a crisis of a subjectivity that has no originary center, yet cannot be fully and totally embodied in one, and only one system of exterior material signs. Film identification is a moment of danger which reveals the emptied center—"I'm not me. I don't know who I am"—but film discourse is not the only discourse that composes "consciousness"—"I hate my life for not being a movie."

Perhaps this is the overarching alienation effect of the play; it points out that the center is empty, presents how we are constructed from the outside, in part, by film, but also points out that this source conflicts with other spheres of influence in our lives. With this made evident we must eventually leave the theater and negotiate with and act upon the various sites of discourse that form our subjectivity. We are the movie and we are not the movie at one and the same time. This I believe is the chief A-effect of film, curiously activated, or made obvious, in the theater. The collapse of the *principium individuationis* becomes the signal and the chance to effect revolutionary change.

I complete my analysis of *Angel City* with the many-layered spectatorship ending the play, and as the readers of this essay and the spectators of the play, file out of the theater they can take what the play has taught them about subjective selves, and travel backward to examine how another text, *The Bostonians*, deals with the issues brought up. At the end of *Angel City* the theater audience contemplates the stage turned into a double screen. Wheeler and Rabbit have turned into slimy green monsters in a scifi horror disaster film that Lanx and Miss Scoons sit watching, "eating imaginary popcorn." Afterwards they comment upon it with inane dialogue from what Wilcox terms "a 1950's 'juvenile delinquent' film" (Wilcox 72). In an attempt to resist the reality that they have become "captured in celluloid and (will) never get out," Wheeler tears open one of the medicine bundles that Rabbit arrives with earlier in the play (52). It signifies the West, the "Looks-Within" place, the center or origin. Rabbit had earlier told Wheeler:

> It's a very dangerous medicine bundle. In fact it's the only authentic
> bundle I've got. The rest are imitations. . . . There's a warning written
> on the outside of it saying that if it's ever opened a terrible force will
> be let loose in the world. (42)

When he rips open the "Looks-Within" place, "a slow, steady stream of green liquid, the color of their faces, oozes from it onto the stage" (53). What is inside is revealed to be what was outside. This realization is the "terrible force . . . let loose in the world." The center has become the exterior and the exterior the center.

The Bostonians also has a powerful topographical imagination, mapping the relationship between inside and outside, liminality, and the construction of subjectivity. These different facets concentrate in the term "place." Both Henry James and Sam Shepard present powerful meditations on place as myth and as the ground in which subjectivity is planted. Shepard's land is the mythical American West and its relationship to an equally mythical Hollywood. James sets up a binary opposition between the North and South on the very first page, but what at first seems to be a clearly sketched division, metaphorically representing two different moral attitudes or traditions, blurs, and almost hopelessly complicates the links between personal and political, individual and public, inside and ousted, and the stances taken toward the domination of others. Looking at metaphorical centers and margins and their relationship to place and the struggle over Verena will help focus this complexity.

Place is important because it serves as the ground upon which the subjectivities of the "individual" characters are constructed. In much the same way as the films of Hollywood serve as the external material in Shepard's play, place provides the external material in *The Bostonians*. But *The Bostonians*, unlike *Angel City*, is a work whose characters are presented as "individuals." Returning to Voloshinov, however, we find that even a thing like "individualism" is a function of social milieu or place.

> Individualism is a special ideological form of the "we-experience" of the bourgeois class. . . . The individualistic type of experience derives from a steadfast and confident social orientation. Individualistic confidence in oneself, one's sense of personal value, is drawn not from within, not from the depths of one's personality, but from the outside world. It is the ideological interpretation of one's social recognizance and tenability by rights, and the objective security and tenability provided by the whole social order, of one's individual livelihood. (288)

It follows that, in order to analyze the existence of a viable individual, the "place" in which one performs "individuality" must be examined. But, in the novel North and South have ceased to function as an effective ground. Basil Ransom's South has been destroyed and is going through real and metaphorical reconstruction. His "center," which is organized from without by his "place," is gone; his desire for Verena is at once to thwart Olive (the northern reconstruction; "He, too, had a private vision of reform, but the first principle of it was to reform the reformers" (James 16). and to rebuild the South along his own lines. Olive Chancellor, on the other hand, is so thoroughly grounded in her milieu that she cannot exist outside of it. She is, however, forced to try, as the slow evolution that puritanism undergoes, transforming into transcendentalism and embracing a progressive politics, necessitates a move from inside (a life of the soul and God) to outside (a utopian politics). Verena is Olive's attempt to make that move.

Examining place in its various permutations makes these desires apparent. Rather than presenting us with two well-defined "places" (North and South) the novel perhaps gives us five, the mythical North and South which no longer function, the "real" North and South, and what remains in the middle, a new ground in which neither Olive nor Ransom have their feet firmly placed, but in which Verena is completely at home.[2] The interplay among these various grounds is a rich window that looks out onto the confused landscape of the novel.

The mythical North and South are possibly the easiest to map as they are still implanted in the readers' minds. They are still powerful, but are almost immediately emptied out and contrasted with the real. The North, represented by Boston, calls forth the high moral purpose of the New England puritan tradition and its evolution that gives birth to transcendentalism. It was the seat of the Abolition movement and the cradle of the *new ideas* so often referred to in the book. On the first page, I draw your attention to the first paragraph. Miss Luna states, "She is very honest, is Olive Chancellor; she is full of rectitude. Nobody tells fibs in Boston; . . ." (James 1). Olive is fully made a part of the city and it and she serve as the location of moral integrity. Her individuality is grounded in a "steadfast and confident social orientation." Her house on Charles Street and her access to the Beacon Street elite attest to this—"the Chancellors belonged to the bourgeoisie—the oldest and the best" (30). This fact animates her desire to escape the small circle in which she runs, to effect change on a wider scale, to import her "center" into the public sphere. "The most secret, the most sacred hope of her nature was that she might some day have such a chance, that she might be a martyr and die for something" (10).

Ransom, in contrast, has had the chance to die for something; "he was an offshoot of the old slave-holding oligarchy which, within (Olive's) own vivid remembrance, had plunged the country into blood and tears" (9). This war has devastated the "real" South and has left its myth as just a memory.

> The State of Mississippi seemed to him the state of despair; so he surrendered the remains of his patrimony to his mother and sisters, and, at nearly thirty years of age, alighted for the first time in New York, in the costume of his province, with fifty dollars in his pocket and a gnawing hunger in his heart. (10)

He is driven from his destroyed center.

A short while into the initial conversation between Miss Luna and Basil Ransom, the text engages and disengages these mythical places and stresses their contrasts to the "real." It signals the games it is playing with the various landscapes. Miss Luna refers to Boston as an "unprevaricating city," disdaining its strict relationship to the truth. Ransom reacts to her disdain by replying "I pretend not to prevaricate," to which she responds, "Dear me, what's the good of being a Southerner" (1)? Already, not one page into the narrative, the machinery of the mythical North and South have been engaged and will shape the way the reader receives the text. The North is related to truth, moral seriousness, and progressive politics, while the South is left *pretending* "not to prevaricate," left only with its charm-stained and guilty past of slavery and civil war.

Yet even at the outset, Miss Luna's playful tone indicates the ironical attitude she takes toward the myth of the city. She is fully aware of the Northern myth and at once acknowledges and mocks its veracity. The narrator also plays similar games with the Southern myth.

> (T)he reader is . . . entreated not to forget that (Ransom) prolonged his consonants and swallowed his vowels, that he was guilty of elisions and interpolations which were equally unexpected, and that his discourse was pervaded by something sultry and vast, something almost African in its rich basking tone, something that suggested the teeming expanse of the cotton-field. (2–3)

I think I need not insist this is the realm of the mythical. The text mobilizes a series of cultural, economic, sexual, and political constructions that form a constellation of impressions around that oh-so-strange word, "the South." The vocabulary is nearly comical and touches on all four aspects I've mentioned. "Prolonged," "guilty," "sultry and vast," "almost African in its rich basking tone," "the teeming expanse of the cotton-field." This short sentence expresses the entire myth of the South—exotic, sexy, other, dangerous, and culpable.

The myth, however, is invoked and at the same time undermined. Before this digression, Ransom asks Miss Luna if he might be appropriately dressed for dinner with Miss Chancellor. She replies in a bantering manner, "Are you ever different from this?" As if to point out the game that is being played with mythical landscapes and cultures, Ransom responds with yet another myth, but this one is dislodged from the North/South dynamic. "Oh yes, when I dine out I usually carry a six-shooter and a bowie knife" (3). Curiously he uses the frontier myth, the myth of the west, to point out and respond to the others. They all are revealed to be cultural constructions—with certain relationships to the actual of course—that guide and distort readings of the happenings in the novel.

To summarize, James's narrator points out the errors of reading within the contours of the mythical landscapes. The centers are emptied out at the outset and frustrate the desire to draw a simple binary opposition in which Olive represents the progressive forces of liberation and Ransom represents the retrograde forces of oppression. The framework revealed, while invoking the myths, supports a "real" North and South, both somewhat devastated and in which both Ransom and Olive are out of place or ineffectual. The centers of their worlds can no longer function.

Olive's is nothing but a center with no access to the margins. Ransom remarks that "he had never seen an interior that was so much an interior as (Olive's) queer corridor-shaped drawing room" (13). Olive's problem is that she has no access to the outside—she admits several times, "I can't speak" (32). Her interior corridor connects with nothing. Her desire is to exist effectually at the margins, to communicate, to infect other centers with her own, and she needs Verena to do this. She wishes to publicize her private discourse.

Ransom's center has been destroyed by the war. He is driven from his mythical land and must reside in a type of non-space filled with people in transition, immigrants stranded at the mouth of a river. (Of course, New York has its own traditions and its own elite, yet they are shown in a much more carefree light than the Boston elite.) In short, New York seems to represent a place in the constant process of creating itself. It is at once a center and a border. Ransom's desire can be seen as an attempt to regain or recreate a center, to privatize public communication. Is New York the fifth place in the novel? Perhaps.

New York may better be expressed metaphorically as one of the many liminal places in the novel, borders that, in any theory exploring inside and outside, are essential to the construction of the interior. Among these liminal places is the mythical West and what it may represent. We recall that Verena, the object of the struggle between Olive and Ransom, makes her first appearance in Boston after a speaking tour in St. Louis. If we view the mythical North and South as the competing, although devastated, metaphorical centers of the novel, St. Louis is surely the most liminal. Situated on a river and the staging ground for the communication of the West and the East, the new and the old, its association with Verena's character and talents seems natural. She is a master of public discourse, but has no private center. Her often repeated phrase "it's not me" is an apt description of this being of total transition, of liminality with no center and no margin. She is pure transmission, exchange.

The various minor characters' obsession with the press and the popular media of communication also expresses this fifth space. What matters most to them is not what the media communicate, but that they simply do so. Transmission is favored over what is transmitted. These characters, although comically presented, represent the germination of the idea that the outside holds primacy over the inside, something fully present a century later in *Angel City*. The views of Mr. Pardon are particularly illustrative. When Olive asks him if he cares greatly about the emancipation of women, "(t)he question appeared to strike the young man as abrupt and irrelevant" (121). Earlier the narrator states, "All things, with him, referred themselves to print, and print meant simply infinite reporting . . ." (117). The idea that one might care about what is reported is alien to him. Or again, "He regarded the mission of mankind upon the earth as a perpetual evolution of telegrams; everything to him was very much the same . . ." (117). Mr. Tarrant feels similarly. "Human existence to him, indeed, was a huge publicity, in which the only fault was that it was sometimes not sufficiently effective." (96). Verena, as I said earlier, is the consummate representative of this mode of being.

What is interesting is that the desire to reconstruct or revitalize their centers infects both Olive and Ransom with this fifth space. Their centers being no longer viable, they are in the process of being re-ordered and re-oriented from the outside. Ransom finds the energy to complete his conquest of Verena after he successfully places an article. And Olive, in her desire to maintain the control over Verena that is slowly slipping away, must thrust her into the public sphere and promote her like those whose wishes she had earlier disdained. In the desire to frantically reconstruct or revitalize centers, the myths of which are known to be fallacious, the margins hold sway.

To conclude, reading and contrasting the ways in which these two texts use the interplay between center and margin, inside and outside, offers valuable insights into the nature of subjectivity. Starting with the postmodern, in which all centers consist of what is found outside, and moving back to the modern, in which previously functioning centers that served to ground individuality futilely struggle to maintain their integrity, the two texts reveal the masked ideological nature of individuality, the exterior construction of subjectivity, and its relationship to changing modes of discourse. In "The Work of Art in the Age of Mechanical Reproduction," Walter Benjamin writes of the relationship of modes of production and what they bring to bear on subjectivity and perception:

> During long periods of history, the mode of human sense perception changes with humanity's entire mode of existence. The manner in which human sense perception is organized, the medium in which it is accomplished, is determined not only by nature but by historical circumstances as well. (Benjamin 222)

Technological transformations in discourse lead to a displacement of subjectivities formed under different technological means. The revolution in the reproducibility of art—moving from copying with a stylus, to founding or stamping, to woodcuts, to print, to lithography, to photography, to film—has changed the exterior *pragma* or "things" with which the interior subjectivity is organized and mobilized. Setting two texts against each other, each with a different relationship to history and mass media, exposes the functioning of this process of re-ordering. Using this contrast as an alienation effect that helps dislodge ideological "individuality," helps remove it from the "place" in which it seems natural and makes sense, the texts state that *man* is not the measure of all things, but rather that "Man is *the measure of all things . . .*"

NOTES

1. According to Voloshinov consciousness is a fiction "(o)utside embodiment in some particular material (the material of gesture, inner word outcry) ." (Voloshinov 289)

2. Europe can also be considered one of the places in the novel, but it figures less prominently in *The Bostonians* than in other James novels.

WORKS CITED

Benjamin, Walter. "The Work of Art in the Age of Mechanical Reproduction." in *Illuminations.* Trans. Harry Zohn. New York: Schocken Books, 1969.

Cohen, Tom. *Anti-Mimesis from Plato to Hitchcock.* Cambridge: Cambridge UP, 1994.

James, Henry. *The Bostonians*. Oxford: Oxford UP, 1992.

Nietzsche, Friedrich. *The Birth of Tragedy.* Trans. Walter Kaufmann. New York: Vintage, 1967.

Shepard, Sam. *Angel City, Curse of the Starving Class and Other Plays.* New York: Urizen Books, 1981.

Voloshinov, V. N. "Social Interaction and the Bridge of Words." in *Contemporary Critical Theory.* ed. Dan Latimer. New York: Harcourt Brace Jovanovich, 1989.

Wilcox, Leonard. "West's *The Day of the Locust* and Shepard's *Angel City:* Refiguring L.A. Noir." *Modern Drama.* 36:1 (1993) 61–75.

"It's Symbolic!"—Arthur Kopit's Revised *Road to Nirvana* and Its Portrayal of Hollywood and Society

Todd M. Lidh

Rarely on the stage do words, actions or even characters mean one thing anymore. Unlike in the morality plays of the medieval and Early Modern periods where Prudence, Vice, Anger and Love physically inhabited the stage, modern plays are rife with conscious metaphor, double meaning and social commentary. Arthur Kopit, in his 1989 play *Road to Nirvana*,[1] turns back the theatrical clock to this earlier time while turning the tables on fellow playwrights, audiences, critics and the theater world itself. Kopit creates a world in which ethical systems exist which are contrary to the expected, characters use the word "fuck" as if it were necessary for proper syntax and grammar, and metaphors revert to their literal ancestry. In his scathing portrayal of Hollywood and the "business" that it does, Kopit places on the stage a play which many might find offensive, even pornographic, but which at least, as Kopit states "is not a boring play." A humorous understatement, this comment by Kopit sets the stage for an analysis of a work which creates characters both lovable and loathsome who exist in a world which appears remarkably familiar yet horrifyingly foreign. But Kopit's play, similar to works produced in Hollywood, is not without its revisions, changes and alterations. As Kopit himself wrote in an earlier play, *End of the World*, "I do very careful work, I'm sure you've heard" (7). In fact, Kopit does do careful work, and for a December 1995 production of *Road to Nirvana* in Edinburgh, Kopit returned to the play to see if there was any room for improvement and enhancement. I had the opportunity to talk with Kopit at great length just after he made, as he termed it, "a slight change" to the script.[2] During that conversation and in subsequent ones, he discussed the process of composition and revision, his ideas regarding the production and staging of the play, reaction to the play across the country and throughout the world as well as his own interpretation of the play's success. In addition, Kopit made available to me a facsimile copy of his revision to the opening of Act II which I have incorporated into this essay.

Even this was not the first revision Kopit made to this play— perhaps the most apparent being that the play's original title was *Bone- the-Fish*, first performed at and commissioned by the Actors Theatre of Louisville's 13th Annual Humana Festival. For obvious reasons, numerous critics—both literary and theatre—have commented on the parallels of Kopit's play to David Mamet's *Speed-the-Plow* which opened just a year prior.[3] Both plays address the topic of Hollywood movie-making, focusing on the interaction of two movie producers— Bob Gould and Charles Fox in Mamet's, Al and Jerry in Kopit's. Even Kopit acknowledges the Mamet play as a catalyst to his own: "Four or five days after [seeing the play] I was filled with rage ... I was filled with rage at David for casting Madonna; I thought he'd sold out." While some critics have seen Kopit's play as a "slavish, envious," even "nasty" (Rich C 1), Kopit saw it as a chance to address a fundamental question provoked by *Speed-the-Plow* but not answered by it: "Are there really no standards whatsoever for anything that has to do with excellence?" His answer was *Road to Nirvana*, a play guided by two overarching principles: nothing written should be just for shock value, and the concept of good taste must be abandoned in order to be true to his characters, the ones which provide a much-more detailed and memorable answer to Kopit's question.

Al, a one-time-studio-exec-turned-independent-film-maker (per- haps by choice, perhaps not), is arguably the protagonist, although Kopit defines the word in the strictest of terms: "in the world of the play, Al's the hero, the protagonist; he knows what he wants and he goes and gets it." Al lives with Lou (short for Louise), who at the beginning of the play "is on the chaise in a bikini, bottom only" (7). In Kopit's mind, "this was the only calculated image. . . . I needed to let the audience know: 'hold on to your seatbelts; anything can happen.' In that world, the world of the play, she would never have been wearing a top." At the start of the play, Al and Lou await the arrival of Jerry, a former colleague and friend of Al. Jerry had been fired by Al years before but still works tangentially in the industry producing educational films for high schools and colleges. Throughout the first act, the three are served sporadically by Ramón, a Spanish-speaking house servant who essentially contributes nothing verbally but, according to Kopit, "is the only sane person . . . poor guy, he thinks this *is* America." The fifth and final character listed in the play's *dramatis personae* is Nirvana, an enigmatic presence who does not make her appearance until Act II. Essentially, however, the play revolves around her and her life story—a word-for-word rewriting of *Moby Dick* with her name substituted for Ahab's.[4]

Al has invited Jerry to his "modest L.A. bungalow" (7) to enlist his aid and willingness to sacrifice for "the deal to end all deals" (42). Kopit's attack begins with this line and all of its implications, and the concept of sacrifice is the basis for his inverting and literalizing of standard metaphors often associated with Hollywood—cutting your wrists, eating shit, even giving up a testicle. What was Kopit's goal with this scenario? "I knew that I was going to take a 'normal,' moral, kind of square guy who had values, some sort of moral values . . . and by the end of the story [have him] give up one, maybe both of his testicles and believe he's done a good thing." As the play progresses, Al, Lou and eventually Nirvana make seemingly ludicrous requests of Jerry who, after understandable hesitation and even outrage, eventually accedes and even presses forward passionately. Toward the end of the play and echoing an earlier proclamation by Al, Jerry says, "Here's the point: if two [balls] is what it takes to make you know that I'm with you, come what may, for better or for worse, two it is . . . This film is going to make fuckin' HISTORY! And I am going to be part of it . . . And no one's going to fuckin' stop me" (123). With that, Jerry goes offstage with Nirvana, his presence noted only once more with a stage direction: *A scream can be heard from the steam room.* The stage direction which follows indicates that both Al and Lou wince, and it is only to be expected that the audience would as well.

The play's entire focus centers on the concept of making "the deal," the one which will assure money, success and fortune. Kopit felt strongly, however, that this could not be a play about money: "If it were just about money, if Jerry was to go through everything he goes through, it would have to be about more than just money. It need to be more—it needed to be about immortality." This characterization of people who spend their lives pursuing such an elusive goal does not originate with Kopit; rather, he simply pulls from his own personal experience in the Hollywood movie industry from the early 1960s through today. "I remember my fringe producers," he says, "the guys on the outside; the scramble to get in; the need to make the deal or you were done for; that desperation." Al's proposal to Jerry—selling to a major studio the rights to Nirvana's life story, whether or not it "holds up to scrutiny" (62) as Jerry questions early on—smacks of just that

type of desperation with Al's most emotional appeal resulting in his
outburst: "I want to make my fuckin' MARK! I wanna put my fuckin'
footprint down *in the sands of TIME*! That's what I want" (68).

Jerry eventually does everything that Al and Lou ask of him: he
literally cuts his wrists to show his loyalty [the literal metaphor taken
from Al's "You know how many people in this town would cut their
wrists for this?" (50)]; he also agrees to eat a spoonful of shit at the
close of Act I to demonstrate even more forcefully his dependability in
the crunch [taken from Al's earlier question to Lou: "Am I shitting
him?" (44)]. Without eating this one spoon, Jerry is out—in the world
of the play, it is all or nothing. Finally, he commits himself wholly to
the project, completely abandoning his earlier reservation about the
laughableness of Nirvana's life story and forgoing his own personal
moral code; by the end of the play, Al, Lou and Nirvana have brought
Jerry around to thinking only of the money, power, fame, even
immortality that this movie deal will give him—sacrifice be damned.
His role model for this line of thinking? Al, who has already given up
one of his balls just to get the option on Nirvana's story and had given
the other one up "years ago in a deal that sounded kinda good at the
time" (118). For Al, and eventually for Jerry as well, the **symbolism** of
the act is infinitely more important than the physical consequences; one
need look no further than the play itself where, no fewer than seven
times, Al uses the phrase "It's symbolic" as a line of argument to
convince Jerry.

It could be argued that Kopit's entire play can be described by the
same two words: it's symbolic. As Kopit himself says, "Everything in
this play is symbolic of something. Al and Jerry aren't doing all this for
the money; to them, even the money is just symbolic of the power and
fame." Kopit's characters resist simple one-to-one parallels with
anything in the real world; rather, they each serve to symbolize multiple
elements of society at large—drugs, sex, power, business, even love
and friendship—and Kopit sees the play as a whole as symbolic of the
state of theatre at the time he wrote it: "Mamet is a *really* good writer,
and he got more praise for his play than he should have. . . . I thought
either I don't know anything, or they don't know anything. He
should've gotten taken to task for it. . . . He wrote a wonderful play
called *Edmund* that got slammed; it shouldn't have gotten slammed, it's
a brilliant play. . . . Is this now a totally relativistic society? If so, how
can you teach? It's a disservice to playwrights." Kopit felt the only way
to express his anger and answer his questions was to write *Road to
Nirvana*.

Strictly based on its characters, setting and plot, Kopit's play could be considered merely a play which represents the evils of Hollywood on the stage, beginning with the aforementioned fringe director/producer character, stereotypical on one level but rooted in true-to-life on another. But more important both to the play and to Kopit himself is the examination of the "pop star" character represented by Nirvana. Kopit's driving question behind the formation of this character was, "What makes someone who has no particular talent such a huge celebrity?" And, what does the existence of a such person say about the society which accepts and even revels in her celebrity?

Kopit believes that Madonna, the original inspiration for the character of Nirvana, exemplifies someone who is "a star by virtue of being a star. She's a star because of her talent for self-promotion." There is a stage direction at the beginning of Act II to reveal this element of Nirvana's character: *A woman is standing in the shadows, surveying the area. One can sense power in this woman, just from the way she stands. It's NIRVANA, making sure everything is in order.* Kopit decided that this one direction might not be sufficient to demonstrate Nirvana's "power" to a theater audience, so, for the 1995 production of the play in Edinburgh, he again revised this opening segment to include Nirvana's brief exchange with a new character, Neil (later changed to Trevor), one of her studio staff, in which she strongly dictates the modification of an already-released pop single. As the original version stands, Nirvana does not speak until just before Al, Jerry and Lou arrive for their final movie-rights negotiations. The previously quoted stage direction is the only indication given of Nirvana's nature and strength of character.

Kopit's revision explicitly stages what he was looking to demonstrate simply through his original short direction. The change begins abruptly with *Nirvana scowls. Something about the song seems to displease her* (Kopit II–1). Nirvana calls to Neil (who only "appears" over a P.A. system but is named in the text) and proceeds to curse at him over a) not being available immediately when she calls, b) not carrying the intercom with him to the bathroom, c) not knowing which song was just playing on the radio—her number one song, of course—and d) choosing the wrong track of a song she requested. Nirvana has decided to change the version of her song, already released, and when Neil points out this fact to her, she responds:

I am not remixing anything, Neil. I simply wish to locate the take we should've used, so I can let my band of geniuses hear how it ought to sound, so when I do it live, I won't have to worry about putting the entire fuckin' audience to sleep, and me along with them. (II–3)

Kopit felt that the original opening was not active enough, at least not from the perspective of Nirvana: "Instead of having her just listening to the song, passively . . . I wanted the audience to see that this is a real person who really can deal . . . she's much more dangerous . . . and she's in control." Nirvana is a singer, yes, but more importantly, she is a shrewd businesswoman: "She's all of these things; she's sane and insane." Kopit also wanted to show that Nirvana controls not only her actions but also her career and perhaps even those who appear to control her, namely Al and Lou. He says, "As peculiar as she is, she has to be able to handle the business; that's how she would stay there on top because she keeps everyone else off balance. [The question is] to what degree is she aware of her peculiarities?" Indeed, Nirvana has had enormous success, with her current release holding the number one spot on the music charts for fourteen weeks. What Kopit intended for his change to demonstrate is the paradoxical nature of her character: at one moment, she is completely dominating, totally in control; the next moment, one is hard-pressed to tell even if she is aware of what is going on around her. As the original script ran, the latter perception was the strongest and more likely to be believed, but the revision, as Kopit indicates, is much truer to life: "Anything that grounds her, that makes it feel that this is real and not conceptual is good. I wanted people to see that she's not in any way cartoon-like, that she's not theoretical." Did Kopit's change work for this recent production? In Kopit's own words, "It was far and away the best production of the play I've seen. . . . For the first time, I had no apologies for the play. It was just right."

Just how does this change affect the rest of the play? Immediately, Nirvana becomes more of character to be reckoned with, not merely a curiosity. Kopit comments, "It gives her drive, a darkness, a volatility. It gives the second act an edge but still keeps it comic." As the second act progresses, Nirvana's moments of awareness become more pronounced—her direct questions to Jerry: "You ever worked in features?" and "Why'd you leave" (87)—while her periods of vacuousness become more suspicious: "Before Lou came I was really very deeply fucked up. (*To Lou*) Would you say that's right?" (96). In a fundamental way, however, this revision by Kopit alters the power paradigm among the characters. If Nirvana remains as she is in the original version, she can easily be seen as nothing more than a drugged-up pawn of Al and Lou who has little to no power over what they do to her and her life. After the revision, her strong statements and precise characterizations of everyone (including herself) seem less petulant and accidental. While it may have always appeared that Nirvana had some sort of mind and exerted a form of dominance over Al and Lou, it is only in the revised version that the audience sees that mind working on her behalf.

This revision must also reflect Kopit's belief of the true nature of this type of "star": someone who has enough sense to make it to the top of a profession and enough savvy to stay there. The original Nirvana demonstrates few of these qualities, and an audience might find it difficult to believe that such a person could actually be a star, one whose life story (real or imagined) could be worth such sacrifice on Jerry's part; however, it is not uncommon for real pop stars such as Madonna or Cher (the two stars Kopit cites the most frequently in reference to his character) to have a kind of charismatic power over those who work for them. Both have been at the top of their profession for years, making millions and millions of dollars. While Kopit feels that neither has any tremendous talent, he cannot deny their success; the strength of character and depth of their drive are elements Kopit felt he had to get across to his audience, and the alteration he makes does just that. In addition, he also wanted to tap into the lifestyle these stars can lead; the change "was an attempt to deal with [Nirvana's] self-indulgence. If she wants to do anything, she can, and it's accepted."[5]

What does this new Nirvana indicate about society at large? Kopit wrote the play not strictly about Hollywood, but about the business that Hollywood **does**. In fact, this business is not unlike most businesses; it simply tends to be more public (as is Hollywood's nature).[6] To begin, Hollywood exists only in America, and a society which places such an emphasis on materialism and superficiality must have icons for those qualities. When this play is done in other countries—such as Sweden, Germany, Mexico and soon to be done in China (translated into Chinese)—Kopit explains that "it's seen as a play about business, not about Hollywood." While the concept of Hollywood is certainly well-known throughout the world, the cultural basis for it is not. Thus the character of Nirvana, despite her Buddhist name, is grounded in the American society from which she is created, and the revised Nirvana is a stronger iteration of this relationship between popular culture and popular icons. This relationship is not unlike the debate as to whether history creates great people or great people create history. Kopit's revision of and addition to Nirvana creates the same question: does popular culture create such popular celebrities or do popular celebrities create popular culture? A weaker Nirvana—more passive and acted on as opposed to aggressive and acting—negates this relationship and the interchange between these two agencies; Kopit's more sharply defined Nirvana fully embodies the question itself, providing greater complexity and more accurately expressing one of Kopit's overriding questions when composing the play: "what makes a star a star?"

Thus, the revised Nirvana casts a different pallor over Kopit's assessment of society at large. In his first version of the play, Nirvana is shown to be, for the most part, a gullible, malleable girl who has little control over what is happening to her. While she has control in some areas, she is subject to Al and Lou's dispensing of drugs, and this casts some doubt as to whether she is actually in control of anything. In this interpretation, one can certainly pity Nirvana for being at the mercy of ruthless Hollywood business people and an always-demanding public, one she only shows "her *public* face" because her real face is "the most private part of her entire body" (85). Society, then, becomes part of what Kopit accuses in his attack, placing much of the blame for the production of such a pitiable character on the shoulders of fans and others who will give to the producers of her life story "roughly anything from . . . Fort Knox to King Solomon's Mine" (67). As Al says early on in his pitch to Jerry, "I have hold of the hottest fucking property since the invention of film itself" (53).

The second Nirvana, however, is not quite so easy to place. In Act I, Al gives a telling description of Nirvana:

> She's a fuckin' ditz-head. I mean, she's a sweetheart, please don't get me wrong. It's just that little specks of white dusty stuff have channeled, through the years, from one nostril to the other, and back through here, and down into here, and up into here, and here. Bong her on the head, she resonates. (63)

While this may seem true of the first version of Nirvana, the revised Nirvana appears to be much better grounded, not a "ditz-head" at all. An audience would find it much more likely that she has led Al and Lou to believe this of her because it keeps them from taking even greater advantage of her: they do what she wants because they believe she is too simple to take advantage of them—a savvy Nirvana may know exactly what she is doing all along. For example, an exchange between Al and Jerry in Act I has a completely different connotation when read with Kopit's revision in mind:

JERRY: She's like a great fuckin' performer. This doesn't compute.
AL: In what way?
JERRY: She's in complete control up there. Every single moment.
    Absolute command. Knows exactly what she's doing!
AL: Right. That's *onstage.*
JERRY: So?
AL: Onstage, she's in a world she can handle.
(65–66)

To borrow license from Kopit himself, Nirvana, in a literal sense, is always onstage, and if what Al says at this point in Act I is true, Nirvana is and has been in control of her situation all along; however, an audience would find it difficult to believe this of a Nirvana whom they do not see take such control. Kopit's revision shows a woman who understands her work, has command of her career and generally seems to be aware of what is going on around her. In this case, society cannot be accused of contributing to the moral and physical downfall of a person; rather, society can only be blamed for creating and allowing to continue **an environment** which both creates and fosters such a person. The life Nirvana leads is one which many might envy, but Kopit demonstrates that even while maintaining some control over what happens to her, Nirvana still is living a life filled with pain, betrayal and fear. Kopit also questions a society which has as its "stars" people like Nirvana. Again, while she may be able to sing, she has no great talent which would otherwise distinguish her from the majority of people. Rather, her success can be attributed almost completely to her determination and shrewdness, demonstrated most clearly in the revised text, which have put her where she is—at the absolute top of her profession and at the pinnacle of celebrity.

What of the world Kopit creates in the play, especially considering this fundamental change to (or at least clarification of) Nirvana's character? The scathing representations on the stage actually lend a certain literalness to the "symbolism" contained by the play. Just as the metaphors take on their literal nature, the symbols in the play— character and plot—seem to take on a absurd realism. Thus Nirvana the character becomes, in the metaphoric world of the play, more of the goddess she believes she once was.[7] Each of the other characters can more easily be seen as subject to her control than in Kopit's earlier version. But, as the symbols themselves become more literal—both inside the world of the play and outside of it—so, too, do the questions initially asked of characters in the play which then become questions asked of Kopit's audience: "What price glory? What would anyone do for the 'brass ring?' And what exactly is the brass?" While the actions of Al, Jerry, Lou and Nirvana may seem horrifying, repulsive and even highly improbable to some theater-goers, Kopit places his characters in the world of Hollywood—a world of sex, drugs, power, money and, most importantly, make-believe—so how unbelievable are their actions ultimately? And, then, just how unbelievable is Kopit's assessment of society as reflected by these characters—not just as characters themselves, but as products of society at large?

Kopit states that he never set out for this play to become a commercial success: "you can't write a play like this and hope that you're going to make a fortune." Instead, he wanted a play out in the theater world that did not apologize for itself; that challenged its directors, actors and audiences alike; and that remained true to its principles. In this sense, *Road to Nirvana* more completely separates itself from the play which sparked its composition, *Speed-the-Plow*. While Mamet's play, with Madonna in tow, may have been a remarkable success on Broadway, Kopit's play rails against the type of "selling out" which Kopit himself believes occurred. Likewise, and perhaps more importantly, Kopit states, "I felt that too many plays were worried . . . too many writers, theatres were worried about their audiences' reaction; they didn't want to offend anyone. So I thought, well, fuck it. If it offends, great." Through his revision of the beginning of Act II, Kopit presents these goals and criteria even more clearly than in his original version. While his addition alters the character of Nirvana, it does so more in the sense of strengthening original intent rather than creating something completely different. Thus, for an audience, Kopit's driving concept behind this play and his desire to create characters both shocking and real become even more emphatic and, hopefully, more successful; and his portrayal of society, through the metaphor of Hollywood, becomes that much more complete.

NOTES

1. Arthur L. Kopit. *Road to Nirvana.* NY: Noonday, 1991. All quotations from the play are taken from this text unless otherwise noted. 1989 is used because that is the year that the original version of the play, entitled *Bone-the-Fish*, first appeared.

2. Quotations from Kopit are taken from interviews conducted on 7 and 8 November 1995 and 11 August 1996.

3. Kopit states, "The title was changed because I didn't want to overemphasize the Mamet connection."

4. Nirvana's other change is to make literal the latter half of the phrase "Moby Dick" and have, as part of her life story, her character riding a whale-sized penis across the open sea. As Lou comments in Act I, "A cock's more interesting" (64).

5. Case in point: in the original *Bone-the-Fish*, Nirvana first appears onstage dressed in a dog suit and remains so until after Jerry has "mock" copulated with her and growled to show his satisfaction.

6. Kopit tells the story of a gentleman who saw the play when it was produced at Houston's Alley Theatre in 1990: "A businessman came up to me and said, 'Mr. Kopit, loved your play. Now, I don't know anything about Hollywood, but I tell you, that's what it's like in my business, down at the office.'" One hopes this is not literally accurate.

7. Nirvana believes she is "the reincarnation of Hopsepsut, Nefertiti's sister, concubine of Amenhotep and rightful ruler of the Eighteenth Dynasty" according to Lou. "It's why so many of my fans believe they can see a divine and timeless spirit inside of me" adds Nirvana (96).

WORKS CITED

Kopit, Arthur L. *End of the World*. NY: Hill and Wang, 1984.

——. *Road to Nirvana*. New York: Noonday, 1991.

——. *Road to Nirvana*. Facsimile to author. 7 November 1995.

——. Telephone interviews. 7 and 8 November 1995 and 11 August 1996.

Rich, Frank. "Art Imitates Art (and Artists), and the Cost Sounds Excruciating." *The New York Times*. 8 March 1991: C1.

"The Devil Answers":
Drury Pifer's *Strindberg in Hollywood*

William Kerwin

Midway through Drury Pifer's 1993 play, the dramatist of the play's title tragically complains, "Why always money, money, money! What ever is food for the soul cannot make money." Never during this farcical treatment of the clash between European theater and American movies does the moral gap become any less absolute. Pifer's play is not about—as political candidates might say—New Ideas. He presents a very old thought, and the play's effect comes through its winking reprise of satirical presentations of Hollywood.

Pifer's writing career has crossed both generic and oceanic boundaries: he has written fiction, two dozen plays (Pifer helped found the Berkeley Stage Company), and a well-received memoir of an American childhood in South Africa. That autobiography, *Innocents in Africa*, has been praised by critics (including Doris Lessing) for its depth of feeling and poetic detail. Pifer also drew upon South African politics for the 1992 play *African Tourist*, a tale of political torture that was, strangely enough, billed as a comedy. That play, like *Strindberg in America*, premiered at Washington's Woolly Mammoth Theater; both also were nominated for the Helen Hayes/Charles MacArthur Award for Outstanding New Play (Pifer, cover).

Strindberg in America's opening scene lets an audience know that moral lines will not be blurred, and that Hollywood's conventional arrangements only thinly conceal moral, cultural, aesthetic and metaphysical fraud. The character Strindberg, speaking German, prologue-like introduces Pifer's production, offering three titles: *Strindberg in Hollywood*, *Strindberg im Amerika*, or *Inferno*. Everything rich becomes shallow, in a vision of movies as Culture Lite; Otis De Marko, the movie's slick producer, even rewrites Strindberg's *The Dance of Death* as *The Dance of Life*. Strindberg's initial plan to use Hollywood to save his family, and to inspire America in the process, has no chance.

So what is to be gained from this American morality play? In the medieval tradition the struggling sinner learns to strip himself of spirit-killing vanity, and probably Pifer wants to do a bit of such corrosive healing. But the primary catalyst here is not fear but humor, and the play delights in spinning absurdist jokes out of its programmatic conception of a cultural wasteland.

Pifer has his European and American characters present a dialogue about language, offering us two visions of the word which, though spoofs of our real-life options, remind us of the power of our choices, as writers or as consumers. "Has this director of yours not told you that words rescue the disorder of existence from nature?," Strindberg asks a young actress. Her verdict on the script (which, as she tells him, is not for a play but a movie): "Too many words." Car crashes and Arnold Schwarzenegger are added to the script. The director argues: "Augie, you can't set the whole movie in a living room. You've got to get the characters out in the real world. On the freeway." To this "Augie" replies in true Strindberg style: "A family is more dangerous than any freeway. The freeway is where you relax and meditate. At home is where the real destruction takes place." Words vs. Action becomes Play vs. Movie, and ultimately Europe vs. America, and Pifer doesn't care if we see it coming. All around are signs of comic inferno: the play takes place on Taco Bell Drive, and the nearby hospital is called Spencer Tracy General. Hollywood's defense of entertainment as its primary purpose involves the rejection of thought, as we can see in this dialogue between playwright and producer:

> AUGUST: Mr. De Marko, you are the beginner and I am the master. I have written fifty-eight plays. I have written on chemistry, philosophy, alchemy, philology—
> OTIS: Augie, you're in America, okay? We're the people who invented happiness. Philology is for unhappy people.
> AUGUST: We are Swedish. We are unhappy people.
> OTIS: We are an upbeat people. We invented pantyhose. We invented violence that doesn't disturb the viewer. We invented Snow White.
> AUGUST: The Germans invented Snow White.
> OTIS: This is where she made her career.

None of this quipping gives us new ideas, but it sums up an old one pretty well. Pifer plays the hedgehog, reminding us how it is an attitude toward language that creates commercialism as much as the other way around. *Strindberg in Hollywood* means language in America, and the play holds up its mirror to twentieth-century therapy-as-profit-making:

> OTIS: Listen, if we're talking midlife crisis, listen, no problem. I can factor that in.
>
> AUGUST: A midlife crisis? A man undergoes the dark night of the soul. He faces madness and ruin, and you call it a midlife crisis! Can't you see that when you shrink your language you shrink yourself right along with it?

Hollywood/America/Hell has no room for such notions, and Pifer's decision to keep the Strindbergs in nineteenth-century dress despite the Hollywood setting escalates the clash even further. The play is filled with jokes for the learned, echoing Strindberg's plays, Yeats's poetry, and other touchstones of the world we have lost. Please, Pifer seems to be asking us, Take pleasure in the old.

But, as the play reminds us, "this is no country for old poets." Where the morality play usually ended with the death of the seeker, and his painful reunion with God, *Strindberg in Hollywood* ends with the signed contract, a bonanza deal for the Strindberg family. Strindberg muses, just before he accepts the deal he has fought against so long, "I ask god a question and the devil answers." He signs for four million dollars. Life is hell.

WORKS CITED

Pifer, Drury. *Strindberg in Hollywood*. Ashland, OR: Oregon Shakespeare Festival Scripts, 1996.

The Last Tycoon: Elia Kazan's and Harold Pinter's Unsentimental Hollywood Romance*

Christopher C. Hudgins

Early in the first chapter of *The Last Tycoon*, F. Scott Fitzgerald writes these lines for his narrator, Cecilia: "You can take Hollywood for granted like I did, or you can dismiss it with the contempt which we reserve for what we don't understand. It can be understood, too, but only dimly and in flashes. Not half a dozen men have ever been able to keep the whole equation of pictures in their heads. And perhaps the closest a woman can come . . . is to try to understand one of those men" (Fitzgerald 3).[1]

Despite its casual if historically accurate sexism, the proposition seems reasonable: get to know an industry by fathoming the depths of one of its most knowledgeable captains. But this aesthetic plan, which remains at the core of Harold Pinter's adaptation, disturbed many reviewers of Elia Kazan's 1977 film. Some thought the film ineffectual in its portrayal of Hollywood and moving in its portrayal of Monroe Stahr and his failed love, while others argued that exactly the reverse was the case. Not surprisingly, the minority of reviewers who were clever or subtle enough to praise the film found its double focus on the Hollywood industry and on the personal life of Monroe Stahr to be unified, of a piece, suggesting that both elements were effectively developed and at least clearly related.[2]

---

*Editor's Note: One of the twentieth century's major dramatists, Harold Pinter is also a highly successful screenwriter. While not a stage play, Pinter's film script of *The Last Tycoon* attempts to analyze the Hollywood mystique, and it is powerful drama. After examining copies of the screenplay, Hudgins reveals the author's complex relationship of movie culture to American life.

In arguing that the film is actually a beautifully unified work of art, I will primarily rely on the published version of Pinter's screenplay and on my transcription of the film, though several other scripts provide interesting insights. The Harold Pinter Archive at the British Library includes four different drafts of the screenplay, while the American Film Institute's Mayer Collection holds two copies of the script, one bearing revisions labeled 10/30/75, evidently notations made during production.[3]

The Harold Pinter Archive also includes an undated five-page letter to producer Sam Spiegel in which Pinter summarizes his "random thoughts" after re-reading the novel "in complete ignorance of what you have in mind for the movie" (Box 32). In section one he comments that the staying power of the novel is due to Fitzgerald's romanticism: "He saw life and lived it with a disregard of sordid reality or banal explanations. Everything he created was touched by this same penchant for life as a fleeting, mysterious, occasionally lyric experience. The past, what it was like and how it touched the present, is the keystone of his work." In section seven, Pinter notes that "All there was to the sentimental side of the man's nature was a longing for the past, an unexplained attachment to his dead wife, who remains nebulous, a common first draft failing." And he suggests that the script should not go beyond the six chapters which Edmund Wilson includes in his edition: "since the novel is unfinished," he writes, "one owes it to Fitzgerald to try to stay within the limits he indicated, which I believe to be a romantic love story about a complex and meaningful man" (section 4).[4]

Pinter clearly admires Irving Thalberg, Fitzgerald's model for Stahr, calling him a "pope of pop art," "probably the most dedicated of the movie makers. . . . He was more than a showman. He knew the influence films had upon the public, and for that reason felt a responsibility toward his work that is virtually non-existent today" (section 4). But he also recognizes his flaws, writing in a note file dated 1 January 1994 (Box 32), apparently to himself, "The whole thing to do with dream and reality. For Stahr, making films is reality—or are films themselves reality? All aspects of reality outside of film activity don't seem to mean very much to Stahr. Since his dead wife was an important ingredient to this activity, to what extent is she real?" (7).

Centering on how unrealistic Stahr is in his perceptions of women, how romantic, Pinter goes on to suggest that in his marriage Stahr has not known a real woman, only a film star: "The assumption that they were happily married must therefore be a false assumption" (7). He adds, "Kathleen is real, but because real, elusive. (Reality being elusive whether it's actual or fabricated!). But the fabricated reality of films is a much easier one to master and control. Actual facts are clearly far more slippery. Kathleen is both concrete and slippery," and she "has him in thrall." In sum, Pinter remarks "Stahr is a man of aspiration and dream but of appreciable limitation. Reality impinges upon him in the shape of Kathleen. Reality obtrudes into the world of Hollywood, or begins to. The Hollywood world has enormous influence upon the world, while remaining in many respects isolated from it" (9).

In these notes, Pinter centers on two elements that unify the personal and the social/industry aspects of the script he later completed. As we've seen, he labels Stahr a dreamer in both arenas, though such dreaming *can* have positive as well as negative connotations; he also suggests that Stahr wants to "master and control" his reality, implying that such a wish for dominance extends both to the industry and to Kathleen. Mastering and controlling this industry through imaginative talent is at least partially admirable, but attempting to extend such mastery into the private world is fraught with peril, ethically and pragmatically in this instance. It doesn't work with Kathleen, on one level because Stahr is jousting with a phantom, his illusion of what the woman is; on a second level, his attempt to "keep" Kathleen, not to lose her, doesn't work because of Stahr's own failure of will, because of his inability, outside the world of industry, to make hard, brave decisions.

Understanding Stahr in love, and in work, is difficult because the character's complexity is so subtly evoked through unmediated action in the film. In the Edmund Wilson edition, the last Fitzgerald note is "ACTION IS CHARACTER" (163), which eerily echoes Pinter's own comments and practice. Since his first film, *The Servant* (Losey, 1963), Pinter has typically eliminated most first-person narration, a practice he continues even in his most recent script for *Lolita* (unpublished, unproduced, 1995). He said about *Accident* (Losey, 1967) that he'd hoped to provide "Just a level, intense look at people, at things. As though if you look at them hard enough they will give up their secrets. Not that they will, for however much you see and guess at there is always something more" (Esslin 228). In another interview, Pinter says "Let the action speak for itself"; one needs to avoid "sentimentality"— instead, simply "look at it as hard as possible" (Ciment 21).

Avoiding sentimentality, looking hard, recognizing that there is always more than what appears in characters' actions, these are difficult tasks for the artist, presenting difficult interpretive problems for an audience. Still, in films based on Pinter's scripts, subtle indicators of a range of valid interpretive responses usually comment on such actions. In *The Last Tycoon*, some of these clearly are Kazan's, but in many instances such indexes of interpretive response—montage, broader structural or echoing techniques, images that garner meaning through repetition—are in the script. Kazan, as a matter of fact, says that he was "reverential" toward Pinter's script, not toward Fitzgerald's unfinished novel (Silver and Corliss 43).

With more leisure for considered response than the reviewers, a good many critics still fail to read these indexes of intended response (Hans Robert Jauss's term) very well with regard to the film's depiction of Hollywood and the power struggle going on there in the thirties.[5] *The Last Tycoon*'s portrayal of Hollywood is actually fully but subtly developed. With occasional comic or even satiric tone, Kazan and Pinter succinctly evoke both the glories and the absurdities of the industry, the potential aesthetic triumphs and the difficulties one must overcome to achieve those triumphs given the system and the very human nature of those who inhabit it.

The opening scenes of *The Last Tycoon* begin to evoke the nature of the industry and its art, as well as Stahr's masterful, powerful role within it; they also serve as a structural subtext for the love plot to come. First showing us a variety of the industry's product and then the process behind the creation of that product, the film describes Stahr's relationship with every aspect of that process. We see him interacting with an almost Dickensian variety of writers, actors, and directors, and we also see his work within the overarching structure of the Board of Directors and the omni-present but never visible money men in New York. By measuring Monroe Stahr (Robert De Niro) against Pat Brady (Robert Mitchum playing a character based on Louis B. Mayer), these early scenes establish Stahr's aesthetic and managerial superiority and also prepare us to recognize Brady's resentment of his success and his passionate wish to destroy Stahr as soon as any opportunity presents itself. In short, the film depicts an industry in transition, at the beginning of the takeover of the money men, who continue, by and large, to triumph over those like Stahr who attempt to blend a commercial product with heart-felt aesthetic concerns.

The two screenings that open the film center our attention on female betrayal and on the mystery of women for men. A tenor emoting on the soundtrack, we first see in close up, black and white, a woman's face in front of a man's face, their embrace and her seemingly sincere kiss as she excuses herself. As the staff exchange obvious signals, a car pulls up, machine gun fire rings out, the man falls, and we cut to a shot of a mirror reflecting the woman's touching up her lipstick, apparently unconcerned. The camera cuts back to the man's head on the floor, a round, overturned table rolling back and forth in front of his face. In voiceover, we hear a man's voice saying "The end is too gory. Cut one roll of the table," and then we cut to the screening room, shot in color, as Monroe Stahr adds that the signal is too obvious, killing the surprise, that it should be cut (1/1 and 2).[6]

A beach scene from *Dark Moonlight* follows, again in black and white, with no soundtrack this time, a man in a tuxedo pouring champagne, alone on the beach, as a woman walks away from him toward the sea. In voice over, Stahr says "No, no, don't go to him at all. Stay on her. You don't need him. Stay on her all the way down to the edge of the sea. She's the one we're interested in" (194/3). This scene again demonstrates Stahr's sharp aesthetic judgment and the deference with which the others treat him. Like the gangster sequence, it also evokes the mystery of the feminine for the male. The shot suggests that the woman is leaving this paragon of male sophistication, and we wonder why, perhaps puzzling at the subtle connection of the two scenes showing women in very different circumstances leaving men behind. Clear echoes of this scene's beach imagery structurally link it to both of Kathleen's scenes with Stahr at his Malibu house.

One of the early scripts in the Pinter Archive includes a third screening scene showing the hero getting his girl at the last minute even though she is on the brink of marrying another man (Box 30). Cutting from bride and father waiting in a church vestibule, the camera shows us a rumpled man asleep in the alley. Lifting his hat, he says "Come on," and runs with his lady past limousines to drive off in a scruffy two-seater, her veils flying, romantically blissful. Had this scene made the final cut, it would have also ironically commented on Stahr's romanticism and its sources.

The cuts between the black and white "product" and the color scenes in the screening room shot, in combination with the voiceover, emphasize for us the difference between the illusion of film and the reality of the process of making it. That's doubly ironic, of course, given the film within the film structure. The voiceovers subtly suggest that reality and illusion can indeed overlap, the one influencing the other. Stahr's line about being interested in the woman, not the man, captures his own version of reality, which colors the way he wants his pictures, while also pointing toward his fascination, indeed obsession, with a certain type of woman, or at least his vision of what women should be.

This motif of betrayal and feminine mystery and ambiguity from the male "eye" continues as the film cuts away from the next color scenes with the old studio guide (John Carradine) to another black and white sequence, a scene with Didi (Jeanne Moreau) in a negligee making polite conversation on the phone with her absent husband about their child and how much she misses him as Rodriguez (Tony Curtis), bare chested, comes into the shot. When she hangs up, Didi rejects Rodriguez's advances, and he asks if she wants him to go. She at first tells him yes, but as he embraces her from behind, she turns, sensuously returning his embrace, her nails palpitating the flesh of his back, changing her "yes" to "no." In this instance, we are surprised, almost shocked, when we cut to a color shot of the crew who have been shooting this sequence.

Expecting another cut to the screening room, we are even more emphatically made aware of the process of manufacturing a movie, startled at the sudden shift from this slightly different illusion to the "reality" of the frame film. The scene also prepares us to recognize the similarities in Stahr's relationship with Kathleen, who has betrayed her fiancé with him and who gives him a series of ambiguous responses about how she regards their relationship, about what she really wants. The most specific echoing is the image of the embrace, which parallels in a variety of ways Stahr's forceful, commanding caressing of Kathleen's body in their second scene at the beach house. And finally, the scene continues to characterize Stahr, for he is in the background, here, seemingly omni-present throughout the studio, observing his director, Ridingwood (Dana Andrews), failing his task and his star (195–7/8–13).

The sequence in the Board of Directors dining room includes two other revealing commentaries on Stahr's relationship to his product. As we absorb the vision of Hollywood apart, distanced from the culture of the thirties, the luxury of the table, the fastidious dress of diners, Popolos (Tige Andrews) suggests to Stahr that they make *Manon* with a happy ending. Stahr replies, "It's been making money without a happy ending for a century and a half" (212/42). The line captures his balance, his recognition of the conditions of his industry; a profit is usually required, but he uses that logic here to justify an aesthetic end. And the idea for a *Manon* film carries subtextual implications for the "real" love story that's just beginning to develop. Of the two operas based on the Abbé Prevost novel, *Manon Lescaut*, Puccini's is the more relevant. Noted for his realism, Puccini's central interest in most of his mature work is the psychology of his heroines, who are madly in love, guilty about it and destroyed in the end. In *Manon*, though, a young man from a good family destroys his life for a courtesan. If the audience catches it, the allusion is ominous for Stahr's infatuation with Kathleen, who does have something of the courtesan about her, as we'll see.

During this same scene, Brady asks about the South American picture, which Stahr says is a go. Brady here takes the risk of criticizing the budget, but Stahr counters with his comment that "It's a quality picture," adding "It's time we made a picture that isn't meant to make money. Pat Brady's always saying at Academy dinners that we have a certain duty to the public. Okay. It's a good thing for the company to slip in a picture that'll lose money. Write it off as good will" (213–214/42). Again, the balance of Stahr's perspective, almost neoclassical, is the point; he advocates aesthetic responsibility, but he's also cognizant of a long-term financial advantage, the good will that such a picture can produce to the company's profit. As Stahr leaves the dining room before most of the board, moderate, not a glutton, without taking a drink, Brady's response is "Boy...," ironically labeling his immaturity relative to the much younger Stahr.

Another of these subtly revealing and unifying screening sequences, relatively late in the film, is perhaps the most significant in both its characterization of Stahr and in its subtextually labeling how we may understand the film as a whole. A rough cut of the nightclub scene that concludes the Didi/Rodriguez movie, the sequence follows Stahr's reading the letter from Kathleen telling him that she is to be married and the scene where Cecilia is so distraught with Stahr's ignoring her once more. Black and white, it opens as Didi and Rodriguez act out their characters' nostalgically repeating the opening gambits for their affair; but we discover that she has decided to leave him and return to her husband. As Rodriguez, the bar owner, plays the piano, Didi, now revealed as his singer, breathes these lyrics: "You have the choice / Brown sugar or white / You have the choice . . . / Love's dear delay / Love's dread delight." *She* breaks off and walks away, saying "I owe it to him. I must go to him." And then sings once more, "You had the choice today / But you would never say / No, you would never say" (105). Rodriguez tells her that he'll never forget her; Didi at first agrees, but when the heart-broken bar-keep bitterly tells her to remember him to her husband, who will never know, her as he has, she lashes out, telling Rodriguez that she's lied, that she'll forget him by tonight. In the film, she goes around the corner, leans against a wall, and sobs; as melodramatic music mounts, Rodriguez looks up from his piano, apparently having heard her. We cut to Stahr, in color, watching.

As Brady and one of his yes men mouth platitudes about French girls having depth, Stahr criticizes a line of dialogue from the scene and demands that it be re-shot, despite the $50,000 cost to do so. Though he's complimented the make-up and hair people, Stahr is clearly in an extremely bad state of mind; as he leaves Brady is impotently disgruntled. This screening room sequence continues to characterize Stahr as concerned about aesthetic quality, but here there is no justification or rationalization about the bottom line, and his judgement is called into question for the first time. The line he objects to is "Nor I you," Didi's response to Rodriguez that she won't forget him. Though the line is believable given her French-accented, non-native English, Stahr, like Rodriguez, has just had his hopes dashed by Kathleen's letter. He allows his personal despair to interfere with his professional judgement, and lashes out at Boxley (Donald Pleasence), the British writer who has written the scene, and at his Board, with none of his usual self-confident good humor.

Brady files Stahr's behavior as one more affront in the mounting number that accrue to provoke his final attack. The scene subtextually labels Stahr's situation since like these two fictional characters, he has tried to replay his earlier relationship with his dead wife with Kathleen. Didi's song also labels his later failure at relationship, foreshadowing the scene to follow, his second visit to the Malibu house with Kathleen. As we'll see, Stahr *will* have "had the choice" of trying to convince her to marry him, but he will put it off, frightened, the song suggests, by "Love's dread delight." The line subtly implies the ambivalence Stahr feels at the idea of loving someone who is not the perfect woman of his fictive imaginings, someone who does not adore his world of film and the power he wields.

This scene also labels Kathleen's previous behavior and that to come. Like Didi, and like Christine Linde in *A Doll's House*, Kathleen at first feels obligated to break off the relationship as forcefully as possible in a perhaps misguided attempt to be kind to the person rejected for reasons of duty. Didi says she owes a return to her husband; Kathleen says much the same thing about her fiancé. But Stahr concentrates on Didi's tearful remorse around that corner, emblematically centering on this aspect of the fiction's suggestion, hoping that Kathleen's letter revealing her *intentions* to marry may be similarly ambivalent and revocable. Unfortunately, even tragically, he has not paid attention to the need for forceful choice, the need to *say* what he seeks in his personal life with the same immediacy and decision he typically manages in his professional life.

The unifying connection, here, between the social, Hollywood plot and the personal, love plot is clear. Before this first major lapse on Stahr's part, roughly three-fourths of the way through the script, the film fully captures the nature of the industry in Stahr's relationship with his writers, with his actors, with his directors and with his staff. That relationship is typically portrayed as efficient and beneficent, both productive and caring whenever possible. As a whole, the portrait continues to emphasize the contrast and confusion between illusion and reality. Stahr's relationship with the Board, and with New York, of course, changes radically, mirroring both what happened historically to the industry and the source in Stahr's personal heartbreak for his own loss of professional control.

The scene with an old studio guide conducting a group of college girls through the studio follows the introductory screening room sequence. Here we see a miniature of the industry's relation to its public, its patrons' willing suspension of disbelief and their adulation of ever-so-distant, romantic stars. As the slightly comic but sympathetic old man takes off his hat, he guides the college girls into Minna Davis's dressing room. He claims contact with the mighty in telling them that he himself made the call to Mr. Stahr to announce his wife's final illness.[7] Photographs of Davis over his shoulder prepare us for the cut to a large painting, framed with elaborate lights, as if capturing her in a make-up mirror, an angelic image. That prepares us to recognize Kathleen's striking resemblance to this idealized portrait—not too difficult, since it's a painting of Ingrid Boulting with shorter blonde hair.[8] Manipulated by the industry-sponsored tour, the college girls' adulation of both Minna Davis and Stahr provides one of many comments on how Hollywood figures replace royalty in the American consciousness given its need for emblems of a life beyond the petty reality of day-to-day existence.

Once more foregrounding the illusion/reality motif, on a huge soundstage, the guide describes how Hollywood creates an earthquake scene. You rock the camera, he says, his old, thin body swaying back and forth, and then, repeating the gesture, more impressively describes rocking the room and throwing in a lot of dust. A girl suggests the addition of flying bricks, to which he jovially agrees. After the Didi and Rodriguez shoot, a sequence of cuts between Brady's office and Stahr's office leads up to the "real" earthquake at night. We see Brady's secretary feeling ill, in retrospect queasy from the pre-tremor, and then we see a chandelier swaying in Brady's office, a crack appearing in the ceiling of Stahr's office, panic in Brady's office. In one of my favorite touches, probably Kazan's, Brady abandons his daughter, seeking shelter himself under the frame of his office door, almost instinctively cunning, self-serving, and emotionally distant from even Cecilia (Theresa Russell). Cuts back and forth to the exterior, to the failed power plant, lights flashing on and off, and so on, establish the devastation outside the office.

The filmmakers walk a fine line here. They make this earthquake much less "corny" than any film utilizing the techniques the guide describes, but they also use those slightly melodramatic power station shots, sirens in the background, the frantic concern for Stahr's safety, and so on to emphasize the trauma of the event. Emblematically, the scenes which follow mark the major ground shift in Stahr's life, but within the context, still, of the illusory. For as Stahr hastens out into the back lots, taking control, aware of every nuance of his studio's property, we focus on a water tower's leaking a waterfall, then on the resulting flood. We see a minuscule village and palm trees swept away, meshing the illusion of the studio's stock in trade with the "reality" of this event. And finally, Stahr sees two women clinging to one another, riding the head of "Siva" down the flood.

Stahr's first response in the film is to remark, "Christ, we need that head next week" (25, 26). The script's identification of the head with "Siva," though, is typical of Pinter's use of images as subtextual labels. As Michael Millgate points out in his insightful essay on the novel, this scene is crucial in its making clear the relevance of Hollywood for Fitzgerald's vision of experience. Even with the ordinary and fake materials of the illusion factory in the foreground, the scene is "very nearly a miracle." In the novel, Fitzgerald writes that the head of the goddess "meandered earnestly on its way, stopping sometimes to waddle and bump in the shallows with the other debris of the tide." A worker tells Stahr, "We ought to let 'em drift out to the waste pipe, . . . but DeMille needs that head next week" (25). And then a vision of Stahr's dead wife climbs down from the floating head of the goddess. Millgate observes that this scene captures "The essential quality of experience for [Fitzgerald,] . . . the continual queerness and the occasional miracle of it, no less [a miracle] . . . for occurring always amidst commonplaces, vulgarity, and a good deal of evil" (297). He concludes that this "controlled and particularized realization of the miracle—the often absurd miracle—at the heart of ordinary experience" is the "essential achievement of Fitzgerald's mature fiction" (298).

Pinter's script captures that "queerness of experience" with arresting, evocative forcefulness. Stahr, already established as a man at the peak of his powers, a legend, but alone, isolated, suddenly has a woman float into his life, radically altering his fate, moving the ground he stands on, for all the world like that knock on the door one sunny morning in Pinter's adaptation of *The Trial*. In this film, we see a gorgeous closeup of Kathleen atop that goddess head, full blown, and cut back and forth between her and Stahr's absorbed stare. When we cut to the aftermath, Stahr dismissing his servant in his mansion, he takes a pill for his heart and begins to read those scripts. But he has entered a bedroom glaringly white to discover his dead wife, alluring, removing her cape, saying "I've come back." Boulting plays Minna Davis in this scene with the same hair we've seen in her earlier dressing room portrait. We cut to the "real" masculine bedroom, Stahr interrupting his lonely work, as he does recurringly from this point, calling on his staff to find the girl's phone number. The scene suggests both the unfruitful nostalgia that initially provokes Stahr's obsession and the illusory nature of his vision of this woman.

The use of Siva, often spelled "Shiva," underlines what a two-edged sword such miracles of queerness can be. Most simply, Shiva is the Destroyer, but gradually "it came to be felt that Shiva destroyed in order to make room for new creation. . . . By a further development . . . Shiva stands for life itself, tremendous vitality," and becomes associated with "the illusion-creating power that has produced the beautiful and terrible phenomenal world" (Noss 280–5). Even if we do not bring to the film such detailed metaphoric association, the image of the goddess, and of Kathleen's descent into the floodwaters, suggests that Stahr has a chance for a new, more vital life, but that he also may be destroyed.[9]

Several evocative scenes with his writers flesh out the portrait of Stahr as the titan of his industry. For example, when young Wylie White (Peter Strauss) chases Stahr down in the streets outside the writers' quarters, we see the bustle of cowboys, horses, Indians who greet Stahr, and a wagon of chorus girls passing by that distract Wylie. The scene comically blends the illusory with the "real" as the two discuss Wylie's latest script, a crane in the background lifting the head of the goddess across the sky. Wylie has discovered this sunny morning that two other writers, his friends, have been assigned to the same script he's been working on and is politely complaining to Stahr about it. Stahr's response, first is that he's sorry: "What can we do? That's the system" (215/44).

When Wylie points out that Stahr has invented the system, the producer, not unkindly, responds that the problem is "You've distorted the girl. By distorting the girl you've distorted the story." In the midst of several other rapid-fire business conversations, he adds that he's not interested in Wylie's fantasies. As he signs some papers a secretary has driven up to him on Wylie's back, asserting their relative positions, he tells the young writer: "You've given her a secret life. She doesn't have a secret life. You've made her a melancholic. She is not a melancholic." What's important is the way Stahr sees the girl, who "stands for health, vitality, love. You've made her a whore" (216/45). Wylie asks: "So how do you want the girl?"; Stahr replies, "Perfect." "Gee," says Wylie, echoing Brady's immature "Boy," at the Board's luncheon. Once more, Stahr's aesthetic concerns are responsibly linked to the bottom line, his assigning multiple writers to the same task in the interest of efficiency.

In the novel, the implications of this linkage of aestheticism with business emerge more explicitly in a conversation Stahr has with Boxley. There, Fitzgerald has the older writer complaining that the industry's system of mass production is all wrong. Stahr replies: "That's the condition. . . . There's always some lousy condition." He uses an example of making a picture about Rubens: "Our condition is that we have to take people's own favorite folklore and dress it up and give it back to them. Anything beyond that is sugar" (105), and he encourages Boxley to "give us some sugar."

At his best, Stahr struggles within the limitations of the financial conditions of the system to give the public something more than just mass production entertainment, and goes out of his way to try to help his writers do just that. In his scene with Wylie, Stahr teaches the youngster what he wants aesthetically. The problem is that Stahr wants that product to be based on *his* imagination, his wish to see the girl as the exemplum of healthy love. At times, Stahr's imagination is aesthetically shallow, completely the opposite of his insistence on making *Manon* with its unhappy ending. That Stahr wants the girl perfect also comments on his problems with perceiving Kathleen. Despite the fact that Stahr cannot see beyond his "scripting," we can see that there is much of the melancholic about Kathleen, a little of the whore, and certainly a "secret life," at first beyond his ken.

The film's Boxley scene accomplishes a similar dual purpose. The meeting with the three writers in Stahr's office follows Stahr's lonely trip up the stairs to his bedroom after his first failed meeting with Kathleen. In response to Boxley's complaint that he cannot work with the "hacks" Stahr has saddled him with, Stahr acts out a scenario to demonstrate how to capture the interest of an audience without the kind of stilted "talk" Boxley himself has written. The producer's story of a woman's coming into a room, emptying her purse, repacking it but leaving a nickel on the table, allows De Niro to work brilliant business to Pleasence's rapt attention: he mimics the woman's beginning to burn a pair of black gloves just as her phone rings; as suspense creates a captivating illusion without even the trappings of a shoot or set, Stahr speaks into the phone, in slight falsetto, "'I've never owned a pair of black gloves in my life," hangs up, and goes back to burning those gloves in the fireplace. Suddenly, he says, we notice another man in the room, watching the girl. He stops, Boxley wants to know what happens next, and Stahr replies "I don't know. I was just making pictures" (229/65).

The scene is the most effective in the film at suggesting the brilliant talent behind Stahr's extremely early success. He has the audience in his office (and us) on the edge of their seats with the mystery of the scene, with its suspense. We want to know who the girl is, why she's burning those gloves, what horrible crime she's covering up, and who that mysterious man is. Along with Boxley, we want to know "What was the nickel for?" Stahr has one of the other writers reply that the "The nickel was for the movies." When Boxley laughingly asks "What do you pay me for? I don't understand the damn stuff" (229/65), Stahr replies, "Yes you do. Or you wouldn't have asked about the nickel."

Again, Stahr is trying to help his staff to do good work. Though perhaps paternalistic, he's still trying to get the best he can from a "distinguished English writer" who has more to offer than he's been able to tap as yet. The scene also provides an echoing label for our better understanding of the film's conclusion, where Stahr repeats these lines as we watch Kathleen burning his letter in its distinctive blue envelope rather than the black gloves. Echoing this scene, Stahr's once more saying that he doesn't know what happens, that he was just making pictures, suggests that he has desperately wanted to believe that he could control his life, script it as he wished with the characters playing the roles he dictates, as creatures of vitality and health and virtue, should he desire it. Kazan comments that "I was just making pictures" at the film's conclusion is "full of self-scorn. . . . I think that's the best line in the picture. . . . It says, in effect, 'That's what I've done all my life, and I've got such a habit of looking at things as though they were pictures, and in my own life it's become that'" (Silver and Corliss 43).

The producer's similarly encouraging scene with the admittedly difficult Didi on the set, warmly reassuring her about both her aging appearance and her talent (218–20/46), is prepared for by the hilarious scene in his busy office with Rodriguez, who's come to Stahr for advice about his impotence (!) once neither doctors nor cat houses have been able to help (207–9/39–40). The film adds several wonderfully comic bits to the script to emphasize that Stahr's kindness has somehow managed to alleviate the problem. Though we don't hear the specific advice, when Stahr and Rodriguez emerge into his outer office, Stahr cuts off Rodriguez's thanks with "Just play the part the way I said." We see Rodriguez, all grins, running gleefully across the lawn, vaulting into his convertible BMW roadster, and peeling away, tires squalling. Later we see him and his remarkably plain wife at the writer's ball, both positively aglow.

This scene once more comments on the illusion/reality theme as Rodriguez wonders how he can appear in a love scene when he can't make it with his own wife, whom he adores. Stahr's response, on one level a cover story for the office to hide the subject of their real discussion, also implies that Rodriguez should play real life just as he would a part. Though the scene reinforces Stahr's beneficent kindness, it also suggests that at least a part of the reason for that kindness for his actors is to improve his product. The cumulative picture of Hollywood that emerges is that actors can indeed be prima donnas who must have their nurse maids to perform well. Cumulatively, too, the scene adds another element to the film's death and aging subtext, a typical Pinter motif. The dead if beloved actress Minna Davis, the fading Didi, the impotent Rodriguez in despair at his loss of vitality, the comic/absurd death of the editor in the screening room, and, above all, Stahr's emblematic heart disease and implied early death at the film's conclusion, all subtly imply that the choice of action "today" that Didi's song refers to is of great importance.

Stahr is too complex a hero always to be kind, even self-interestedly so. A streak of cruelty emerges both in his treatment of Didi's director, Red Ridingwood (Dana Andrews), and in his treatment of the Board. The film succinctly summarizes thirties Hollywood's directing system as Stahr dismisses Red from the picture. Like the writers, most directors were interchangeable, piece workers as far as the studios were concerned. Kazan economically suggests just what a slouch Ridingwood is, though, as he shows us the director lounging about, not communicating with the actors until an assistant lets him know that Stahr is on the set, more concerned with getting through the shooting schedule than with the quality of what he captures on film (8, 51–2). Stahr pulls him off the set, and, as the director gripes about his difficult leading lady, tells him that he just can't handle her, that another director is already on the set. Retrieving Ridingwood's coat from a waiting car, he reiterates, "You haven't touched what she's able to do." We see the pleasing results of Stahr's decision later in the rough cut screening, a remarkable contrast to Didi's attitudinizing in her first scene with Rodriguez.

The Last Tycoon's portrait of the Board and its relationship to the money people in New York amounts to a detailed examination of the central condition that constrains Stahr, within which he maneuvers brilliantly until his crisis, his earthquake. The first scene in Pat Brady's office, which follows the screening room sequences, begins with a voiceover as Stahr wearily lies down on his couch in his own modern office. Brady says "I love him," referring to Stahr. We cut to Brady pouring a drink, the first thing we see him do, in front of a tiger skin rug. After a shot of clearly expensive carved wooden lions on a shelf, Brady in his next breath complains to New York lawyer Fleishacker (Ray Milland) that New York has forgotten him, primarily because he has so loyally and generously supported Stahr. Fleishacker tries to reassure him, but Brady tells him he wants to see the recognition, pounding his desk, "I want to see it on this table. I want to feel it" (198–9/15). His own huge portrait glowering over the office and its wild animal decor suggests the savage egotism that drives Brady, despite that pose of loyal support.

The imagery repeated in the "leather" room that Stahr later ridicules at Brady's home during his meeting with Brimmer (Jack Nicholson), the animal skins are also in the foreground as Cecilia later discovers the nude secretary in her father's office closet (250–52/102). Brady's frequent drinking and the fact that his office contains no books, unlike Stahr's bookshelf-lined, tasteful, less grandiose quarters, furthers our unsympathetic response, as does that selfish disregard for his daughter during the earthquake sequence. Just before Cecilia's discovery of her father's peccadillo, he utters the real feeling subtextually and imagistically implied in his first scene: "It's Stahr! That goddamn little Vine Street Jesus! He's in my hair night and day. . . . He sits like a goddamn priest or rabbi and says what he'll do and what he won't do. I'm half crazy" (251/102).

The opening scene with Brady also begins to capture his basic dislike for the medium, his hatred of both writers and actors; Fleishacker, representing "New York's" sensibilities, echoes him. As

Brady sees his daughter pull up outside with Wylie, he says "Did you see that bastard touch my daughter?" and replies to the lawyer's question that "He's a goddamned writer"(199/15). The lawyer responds: "I was looking in at the writers' building this morning. I watched them for fifteen minutes and there were two of them didn't write a line." When Cecilia comes in and gives her father a warm hug, before he's introduced Fleishacker asks if she's an actress, perhaps a label for Brady's typical behavior with starlets. Brady proudly comments: "She's too intelligent to be an actress. She'll be graduating next June from Bennington with honors" (200/17). The line suggests both Brady's real opinion of the people who work for him and implicitly that of the Board and of New York, again in marked contrast to Stahr's attitudes.

As we've seen, the Board luncheon scene accentuates the group's concern for the bottom line, exclusively. Fleishacker and Brady exchange meaningful glances in this scene and several others, suggesting their collusion. Brady is purposeful in his bringing up the budget for the South American picture, of course, to foreground it for New York's representative, but at this point Stahr's success has made him too powerful to be vulnerable. Stahr appeals to the Marcus (Morgan Farley), clearly held in some awe by the rest, who backs him up as the one responsible for the company's huge profits, as the person to whom the company owes it all. That irritates both Brady and Fleishacker, but they can do nothing at this point. Emblematically, Morse is a very old man who now leaves the table, carried in the arms of his muscular servant, the victim of an unnamed disease. The scene implies that Stahr may soon be in trouble, his support on thin ice, the old ways fading.

The Last Tycoon's sympathy is clearly with its namesake and against the Board and its alliance, through Brady, with the New York money men, for the sequences involving the Board include the broadest comedy in the film. Other than Marcus, undercut in different ways, the Board members are painted, perhaps even caricatured, as shallow, uncultured, uninteresting and uneducated. That's particularly evident in Popolos (Tige Andrews), the Greek who constantly wails on about both the glories of the American system and his opinion that all communists are "fairies," and in the pathetic yes-man Eastwick and his reiterated "There are other aspects, of course."[10] The film's conclusion, as the Board fires Stahr, makes clear that this pathetic group readily follows Brady's lead, who in turn has sucked up to New York and its fear of the consequences of Stahr's mishandling the writer's representative,

Brimmer, the communist, a threat to Popolos' vision of the American way of life, the bottom line.

This evocative portrait of the conflict within the industry during a time of transition and change for the United States in general is very specifically related to Stahr's failure in his personal life, as we've suggested. After his sighting of Kathleen, Stahr constantly interrupts his business day for her, providing ammunition for Brady's and Fleishacker's hostile off-screen reports to New York. He takes a call at the Board luncheon about the girl's phone number, he calls Edna, whom he mistakes for Kathleen, from the set of Didi's film, and he refuses to talk to Brady about an "urgent call" from New York as he rushes off to meet her, Brady ominously watching from his window. Given Brady's informing Stahr that he's with Fleishacker and its timing, that call Stahr brazenly, heatedly refuses with "Not now!" (222/54) is almost certainly about the South American quality picture.

After meeting Kathleen, Stahr basically ignores his company table at the Writer's Ball when he discovers her there, another of those queer coincidences, and leaves in ardent pursuit. With mounting disregard for his best professional interests, he ignores an impressive list of callers at his home after his first idyllic night with Kathleen, including one from his chief supporter, Marcus. Soon after his discovery of Kathleen's letter announcing her impending marriage, we see his demanding a re-shoot of the conclusion of Didi's movie despite the $50,000 price tag. After Kathleen's phone call and the second scene at the Malibu house with her, Stahr keeps an office full of people waiting as he writes draft after draft of a letter to her. And in marked contrast to his previously caring behavior, he is cold and ineffective at Didi's preview celebration, insisting on leaving early with Cecilia for the Malibu house, the site of his brief happiness. Finally, ecstatic over Kathleen's apparent agreement to go away with him for the weekend, he tells his secretary to cancel all of his appointments, including the one with Brimmer scheduled at Brady's home. At that very moment, he gets Kathleen's telegram; his smile at the cartoons he's been screening turns into a blank stare as he says, immobile, muttering, "Keep going." (263/127).

That final poleax is the blow that drives him to drink for the first time and to drunkenly attack Brimmer, who decks him, Brady again ominously watching through a window. Clearly caused by heartbreak, the scene provides Brady with enough to fire Stahr the next morning, the Board slavishly following New York's orders: "They've instructed me" Brady pontificates, "to tell you that they no longer hold you competent to negotiate with the writers. . . . They don't consider that trying to beat up the writer's representative is in the best interests of the company" (273/142). Though only as New York's puppet, Brady has won, and he's vengeful about it in a way he would never have dared before, advising Stahr that New York "said be sure to go see a doctor about your eye," blackened by Brimmer's punch.

Stahr has abandoned his balanced ability to cope with all comers, then, because he has lost Kathleen, but his professional fall carries with it a few positive implications for his potential personal growth. At first, Stahr has had no life beyond the movies, dwelling obsessively on his dead wife, whose picture is everywhere, over his shoulder at the office, in his bedroom, his study. Joss Marsh links that nostalgia to one of Fitzgerald's central problems, "modern man's removal from his direct experience into a half world of dangerous dreams," which can fracture relationships (102). But Stahr begins to struggle to learn to live in the present, outside the studio; after the first Malibu scene, we no longer hear much about Kathleen's resemblance to his dead wife. Stahr also makes an effort to get beyond his wish to dominate in his personal life as much as he does in his professional life, but that's finally ineffective because he cannot accept women as complex, independent equals. He wants them "perfect," like the screen's romantic icons. The film illustrates Victor Cahn's argument that in Pinter's version of competition between men and women, mystery about women troubles men "far more than it does his female characters" (7).

Monroe Stahr fails at love, loses his chance for two interrelated reasons. In the first place, his will, his courage to be, is not strong enough to force him into action when he is not assured of his own control; Kathleen's mystery, her secret life, perhaps her own ambivalence, places her beyond his limited experience and, like Prufrock, he simply can't risk, despite his desperate wish to do so. He cannot understand someone who is not of the film world, as he is, someone who wants a life different than his own, a "quiet life," as Kathleen reiterates. Secondly, Monroe Stahr is addicted to power, again because of his work; he attempts to dominate and control Kathleen at a number of points, sometimes successfully, but his final effort backfires, and he loses everything he cares about as direct result, personally and professionally. And then he dies.

There are three central scenes in this progression. After pejoratively establishing Stahr's initial fascination with Kathleen because of her resemblance to Minna Davis, the film shows her yielding to Stahr's very forceful pursuit after the Writer's Ball and agreeing to have lunch with him someplace where he is not known. Following a joyful idyll at a beach cafe, they end up at Stahr's unfinished house in Malibu, a typical Pinter image, going back that evening when Kathleen suggests a return, apparently overcome by passion. Millgate writes that the "most beautiful image of the book's sustained awareness of the ordinary queerness of experience is the scene of the consummation of Stahr's and Kathleen's love, which he finds a parallel for the opening image of the novel's earthquake sequence: everything in the novel "is afloat and moving, in an earnest and bumbling way that is at the same time a rapid drift toward the waste pipe. Nothing stands still and no one can afford to wait for things to be just right" (299).

In *The Last Tycoon*, too often at first Stahr typically waits; Kathleen acts. He does not try to approach Kathleen when she kicks off her shoes and lies on the grass; she's the one who kisses him first in the parking lot and suggests that they go back to the beach house. With delightfully romantic music in the background, we cut to the pair at night, Stahr bringing her a candle; back turned, she begins to take off her dress, covering herself with a blanket and coming toward him. He reaches behind him, weak-kneed, clutching a post. Dropping her dress, she embraces him, and then begins to undress him. They pull back and smile, the gentle music ends, we hear the surf, and cut to a shot of an electric heater; then we cut to their naked bodies, Stahr kneeling beside her head and kissing her. She looks up at him as he nestles a pillow under her head, and covers her with a blanket. By now, the moment is wondrous, natural, comfortable, full of hope for their future.

At this point, Kathleen wonders "when it's settled," adding that "there's a moment when you needn't, and then there's another moment when you know nothing in the world could keep it from happening" (241/85). That implies a good bit of very real experience, but it is also her credo, this yielding to powerful emotion, one which Stahr has not been able to live by. She goes on to say she knows why Stahr had liked her "at first," and asks about Minna Davis. He tells her that he doesn't remember "what we were like. She . . . became very professional. She was very successful. She answered all her fan letters. Everyone loved her. (Pause). I was closest to her when she was dying" (241-2/85). Stahr's lines suggest the kind of distance in his marriage which Pinter describes in those early notes. There's both an envy and a resentment in his description of Minna Davis' professional success. The lines about their closeness during her illness also suggest a recognition that she was actually someone different then, someone other than the professional persona she previously depended on.

As if in response to Stahr's admission, Kathleen gets up and playfully dons an apron, asking if the maid lives in or just comes for breakfast, adding that there would be lots of work to do looking after Mr. Stahr. At one level, this is a request for clarification, an opportunity for Stahr to respond, an offer to "live in" rather than being a passing fancy. But he cannot take advantage of the implied opportunity, instead questioning her about her plans for the future—"Are you going to stay in California?" The question is incongruous, jarring, a non-sequitur. And she does not reply. He pursues it: "What's the mystery?" and she refuses to tell him. Still, Monroe Stahr has made some progress. When Kathleen tells him he looks tired, he insists that he's not and "shows her" by beginning to make love to her again. Retrospectively, this scene is an emphatic contrast to his scene with Cecilia when she has offered herself to him in his office and he's told her that he's too tired to "undertake anything." And now, when Kathleen remarks that she looks like Minna Davis in her cheekbones, he says "No, it's here," as he begins to cover her body. The implied suggestion is that he is no longer so obsessed with the resemblance to Minna.

The next morning, though, he continues to pry into Kathleen's mystery, and she tells him the story of her marriage to a deposed king who had become a drunkard and tried to force her to sleep with his friends. She tells Stahr she should have left her king "long before." That deepens her mystery—why has she left him? when? what gave her the courage? is it true? But the scene concludes as he says "I don't want to lose you," and Kathleen replies, "I want a quiet life," certainly an implied rejection, now, of what he is (244/87). At the parking lot, their leave-taking is cold and anti-climactic until she suddenly goes to him, but Stahr cannot take advantage of this moment either, and their cars go off in separate directions, for the audience a gentle, sad foreshadowing.

When Stahr gets home, though, he's infatuated, ignoring those callers, taking a pill. When the Butler brings him the letter that Kathleen has claimed to have lost in the car, he doesn't read it at first, smelling its perfume as he puts it aside for a stack of scripts. The strange gesture emblematically suggests his cowardice, that his business life, steeped in illusion, carries elements with it of both obsession and escape from any full experience of reality. When he finally reads the letter, he starts up the stairs, switching off the lights himself, as we hear Kathleen, in voiceover, informing him that she is soon to be married and won't see him after today. She adds that she intends his interest to fade now, all at once. As the door of his bedroom shuts behind him, the emotional tone is bewilderingly sad.

But after we watch the screening of the rough cut of Didi's movie with its emphasis on choice and on a leave-taking that she does not really want, we see Stahr pick up the phone in his office to answer a call from Kathleen and cut to the Malibu house. Her call poses several interpretive possibilities. It may suggest that Kathleen's mood when she has composed the letter was much different than it was after their night of love at the beach, but it certainly emphasizes that she was lying when she said that she'd lost that letter in the car, that at least for the moment she chose to leave the letter with him despite that night at the beach. It also emphasizes that she cannot stick with the decision the letter communicates, that she must see him again, even though that means she will betray her fiancé, like Didi, a second time. That should set off bells of opportunity in Stahr's head.

But at the Malibu house in the late afternoon, Stahr just probes the mystery of the husband-to-be and then tries to dominate her. Kathleen replies to his questioning, haltingly, that the man is an American who took her away, presumably from her husband, and brought her here to live in his house. "He's an engineer," she adds. "He'll be back . . . next week." Indicated by Pinter's ellipsis, her brief pause both calls into question her truthfulness about that schedule and suggests its importance by centering our attention on it. When she adds that they are getting married, seemingly a redundancy, Stahr asks if she's in love with him. There is at least some courage there. And she replies: "Oh yes. It's all arranged. He saved my life. *Pause.* I just wanted to see you once more. *Pause.* It's all arranged" (256/112).

Pinter's dialogue here is typically subtle and evocative. Kathleen's repeated response to Stahr's question about love, "It's all arranged," coupled with "He saved my life," and her very pithy "Oh, yes," implies that she may not be in love with this man, that she is marrying him out of a sense of obligation. Retrospectively, Didi's returning to her husband because she "owes it to him" reinforces such a reading. Stahr's response, though, to this possibility is not to offer her his life, or to object to her going ahead with the plan. Instead, he attempts to control her, in marked contrast to that gentle lovemaking. He commands her to stop walking, to come back and to open her cape and to close her eyes. Though she hesitates at the cape command, she obeys. He traces first her face, then her throat, then her breasts, and finally her belly. As he does so, she opens her eyes, moves closer to him, and kisses him. He finally takes her in his arms. The scene clearly echoes that first shot of

Rodriguez embracing Didi after her call to her husband, when she has first asked him to leave and then asked him to stay. Stahr has taken advantage of the moment, here, but only in a limited, nearly hostile way. On one level, he means to underline their passion for each other as a reason for her not to marry; on another, though, he simply takes advantage of her own passionate nature, insistent on control, inarticulate about that *choice* offered him by her phone call and her ambivalence.

With the implication hanging in the air that they have made love once more, we cut to Stahr's car, driving rapidly along the road at night, clearly some hours after the scene at Malibu. Kathleen comments on how quickly night falls here, with no twilight, echoing *Godot* and emblematically labeling her own mood. Then, apparently a non-sequitur, she says "I suppose some parts of America are gentle" (257/113). The suggestion is that this experience, unlike the first, has not been. But Stahr simply replies, "Sure," and then changes the subject, asking if she's leaving California.

The line echoes both his earlier question to Kathleen and his repeated question to Cecilia about when she's going back to college, and similarly suggests his nervousness, his not knowing what to say, his ineptitude around "real" women. But Kathleen's response is "We might . . . I might . . . I don't know." The pauses and the progression again suggest that she may not be certain that she will marry at all, even now. In the film, at this point he suddenly stops the car. He says "Listen—" but doesn't complete the sentence. Kathleen says "What?" There's a pause, and Stahr says "Nothing." Kathleen turns to him, from across the seat. During a much longer pause, she looks at him as he stares straight ahead. And then he decorously drops her off a block from the engineer's house.

Kathleen's urging Stahr on, asking him what he means to say, subtly suggests that she would *like* him to say something. The novel's narrative is more specific: "They looked at each other and her eyes asked, "Shall I marry The American?" He did not answer" (114). Still, this Pinter scene, like the Fitzgerald, suggests the low point of Stahr's courage; in the face of any uncertainty, he is paralyzed, he cannot act. But the next day, as preface for the third central scene in this progression, we see him writing draft after draft on that blue stationery, ignoring all business in his mobbed office. His courage has returned to at least some degree. We never see the contents of that letter, but Stahr gets a call at his home in response. In a quiet voice, Kathleen tells him that she has gotten his letter. He says he must see her, asking her to come away for the weekend. She replies at first that "It's very difficult." Then she says she can't. At his repeated urging, she says "I'll tell you tomorrow." But he refuses to take that for an answer, commanding her again, "No. You must say yes now" (262/122). The camera cuts to Kathleen, in her kitchen nook, saying yes into a phone (262/123).

That phone in Kathleen's kitchen "catches" her in yet another lie, for she's told him at their leave-taking after the first Malibu scenes that she doesn't have one (244/89), perhaps to protect against the possibility of a call when her fiancé might be there. Stahr's behavior here echoes his attempts at domination during the second Malibu interlude, and he's ecstatic that it has apparently worked once more. We're not so convinced as he that his romantic script will evolve the way he's written it for himself, confident with little basis in reality. Her telegram about her marriage that next noon confirms our suspicions, but Kathleen's mystery remains intact, for perhaps, as in the novel, her fiancé simply comes home earlier than expected. On the other hand, she may have told a lie to be rid of Stahr, to pursue her obligation to the American, like Didi. Neither we nor Stahr will know, but the central implication remains the same—Stahr has lost his chance by not acting courageously when he had his opportunity, by "not saying" as Didi's song has it. This time the queer events that so often shape our reality have been profoundly negative.

The novel is much more specific about the implications of the slightly different scene it paints when Stahr asks her for that weekend: "It is your chance Stahr. Better take it now. This is your girl. She can save you, she can worry you back to life. She will take looking after and you will grow strong to do it. But take her now—tell her and take her away. Neither of you knows it, but far away over the night The American has changed his plans. . . . In the morning he will be here" (115).

The coda with Stahr's drunken and fruitless brawl with Brimmer follows rapidly, leading to his dismissal. We see Kathleen act out Stahr's second rendition of the tale of the mysterious girl with the purse, in the final moments burning Stahr's blue envelope instead of the gloves and embracing a man with light brown hair in a brown tweed jacket and brown shoes (158), decidedly not the elegant Stahr. Stahr stares into the camera and says, once more, "I don't want to lose you," and we see him walk into the darkness of that soundstage, a man at the end of a short life, bereft of all he has treasured.

The film version of Fitzgerald's unfinished novel appears fruitfully ambiguous in its conclusion on a number of levels, but the emotional mood of this ending, in general terms, is of tragic loss, both for the potential aesthetic promise of Hollywood and for the possibility of life-mending love that Stahr throws away through a want of courage. Less ambiguously, I'd suggest, Kazan and Pinter do provide an interpretive gloss by explicitly comparing Stahr to a very particular kind of Prufrock. At the second screening session, the one after Stahr has seen Kathleen on the head of the goddess, as he's seeking her phone number, the screen shows us a woman in high dudgeon asking a man in stentorian tones, "How dare you ask me that question." During the first Malibu sequence, Stahr places a pillow under Kathleen's head. She has previously remarked that the incomplete swimming pool at the Malibu house will require a "constant supply of nereids, to plunge and gambol" (238/79) as she ridicules Stahr about being here, alone with his movie projector. Through repetition and echo, Pinter calls our attention to the line three times.[11]

Briefly to refresh the reader's memory of Eliot, late in the poem his persona asks if it would have been "worth it, after all, / . . . among some talk of you and me, / . . . To have squeezed the universe into a ball / To roll it toward some overwhelming question, / . . . If one, settling a pillow by her head, / Should say: "That is not what I meant at all." Prufrock decides that no indeed, he does not have the courage to ask this lady with the pillow by her head that overwhelming question, and as a consequence he lingers in the chambers of the sea "By sea-girls wreathed with seaweed red and brown / Till human voices wake us, and we drown."

Like Prufrock, successful or no, Monroe Stahr has measured out a part of his life with coffee spoons, afraid of the mystery of women, of not knowing the answer to that question, afraid of intimacy and love beyond his romantic illusions. Those nereids will not sing for him, certainly, since he has been so afraid to dare that question. But even if we notice such a pattern of enriching allusion, or are convinced by my noticing it, *The Last Tycoon* is more complicated than most *carpe diem* poems, for it links the romanticism of an industry often reflective of our need to escape reality to the personal downfall of one of its titans. The industry that has absorbed Monroe Stahr's life finally destroys it.

In his recently published book, David Mamet writes: "Perhaps there was a Golden Age of Drama in the movies, perhaps not. And perhaps I delude myself to think that the business was once overseen by filmmakers rather than exploiters. The difference, to me, between those two categories is this: Each wants to make money, but the filmmaker intends to do so by making a film" (120–121). In *The Last Tycoon*, filmmakers Elia Kazan and Harold Pinter capture a wonderfully precise and evocative portrait of Hollywood during its time of crisis, at the beginning of the end of the Golden Age, by focusing narrowly, looking hard, at one of its most talented and creative captains and his personal strengths and weaknesses. It is both ironic and encouraging that in the difficult film climate of twenty years ago the two could make such a rich narrative film adaptation. They have managed to work honorably and well within those conditions that Stahr tells Boxley are always there in one way or another.

NOTES

1. I have used Edmund Wilson's 1941 edition of *The Last Tycoon* since that is clearly the version Harold Pinter worked from. I will mine Matthew J. Bruccoli's 1993 edition, *The Love of the Last Tycoon: A Western*, whenever appropriate.

2. See, for example, Crist, Kael and Farber.

3. Thanks to the wonderful staff in the Manuscript Room at the British Library and to the very helpful librarians at the American Film Institute. For a more complete analysis of the film materials in The Harold Pinter Archive at the British Library, please see the descriptive essay by Steven H. Gale and myself in *The Harold Pinter Review: Annual Essays 1995*. The Foundation at the University of Nevada, Las Vegas, provided funds for these research trips, for which I am very grateful.

4. Both Spiegel and Kazan later echo Pinter's ideas about not going beyond chapter 6. See Farber, 15, and Phillips 158–59. The Fitzgerald notes in the Wilson edition include plot lines expanding on the writer's union situation and detailing the increasingly melodramatic battle for control of the studio between Stahr and Pat Brady, a figure largely based on Louis B. Mayer. Both men take out murder contracts on the other; though Stahr decides on a transcontinental plane to abort his plan, ironically he dies when the plane crashes before he can cancel the hit. Though speculation, many critics agree with Ernest Hemingway in his letter to Maxwell Perkins: "Scott would never have finished it with that gigantic, preposterous outline" (Phillips 156).

5. See, for example, Repf.

6. Pagination throughout refers to Pinter's published script. The first numeral is the page number, the second Pinter's scene number. Where the dialogue in the film differs from the original, I will list only the scene number, quoting from my transcription.

7. Spiegel says that the inspiration for the guide sequence sprang from his taking Pinter on a Hollywood tour during a three-week visit. They met a guide with the studio for forty years, who told of Garbo often seeing him and complimenting him on his work, which made him cry (Alpert 11).

8. Boulting's casting and performance has evoked a good bit of negative criticism. Producer Spiegel says that Pinter's initial response to her tests was that he needed to find an actress, that Boulting couldn't get into repertory in London. Pleased with Boulting's work, in the interview Spiegel bets that Pinter is now eating his words (Alpert 14). In a 6 June 1996 letter to me, Pinter writes: "I thought the finished film did have a number of virtues but was destroyed at its very centre by the casting of the girl, who simply couldn't act."

9. In an unpublished 1984 interview, I asked Pinter about several such arresting images or scenes in his filmscripts, centering briefly on the one in *The Pumpkin Eater* where a mad Jamaican minister comes to Jo's distinctly upper class door. Pinter replied that our experience was indeed often that way, that "a mad Jamaican may appear at our door at any moment." That captures something of the same spirit of the "miracle of the queerness of experience" that Millgate finds in Fitzgerald, which I think runs throughout Pinter's canon.

10. "Eastwick" does not appear as a "named" character in the published script, surfacing in handwritten revisions in one of the two scripts at the American Film Institute.

11. None of these images occur in the novel. Stahr's action with the pillow appears in Pinter's published script as do the repeated references to the nereids. The screening clip with "How dare you ask me that question" does not appear in the published script nor in the scripts at the British Museum but is included in the handwritten revisions in the American Film Institute script.

WORKS CITED

Alpert, Hollis. *"The Last Tycoon." American Film.* March 1971, 8–14.

Cahn, Victor L. *Gender and Power in the Plays of Harold Pinter.* New York: St. Martins, 1993.

Ciment, Michael. "Visually Speaking: 'Reunion': Harold Pinter" (an interview). *Film Comment* 25 (1989), 20–22.

Crist, Judith. "Tycoon." *Saturday Review.* 11 Dec. 1976.

Esslin, Martin. *Pinter: The Playwright.* London: Methuen, 1984.

Farber, Stephen. "Hollywood Takes on 'The Last Tycoon.'" *New York Times.* 21 March 1976, 2:15.

Fitzgerald, F. Scott. *The Last Tycoon.* Ed. Edmund Wilson. New York: Charles Scribner, 1941.

The Love of the Last Tycoon: A Western. Ed. Matthew J. Bruccoli. New York: Cambridge, 1993.

Gale, Steven H., and Christopher C. Hudgins. "The Harold Pinter Archive in the British Library." *The Pinter Review: Annual Essays 1995.* Ed. Francis Gillen and Steven H. Gale. Tampa: Univ of Tampa, 1996.

Kael, Pauline. "Tycoon." *The New Yorker.* 29 Nov 1976.

Kazan, Elia. *The Last Tycoon.* Paramount. Screenplay, Harold Pinter. Sam Spiegel, Producer. Robert De Niro, Tony Curtis, Robert Mitchum, Jeanne Moreau, Jack Nicholson, Donald Pleasence, Ingrid Boulting.

Mamet, David. "The Screenplay." *Make Believe Town.* New York: Little, Brown, 1996, 117–125.

Marsh, Joss Lutz. "Fitzgerald, *Gatsby,* and *The Last Tycoon:* the 'American Dream' and the Hollywood Dream Factory—Part II." *Literature Film Quarterly* 20 (1992), 102–108.

Millgate, Michael. "Scott Fitzgerald as Social Novelist: Statement and Technique in *The Last Tycoon.*" *F. Scott Fitzgerald: Critical Assessments, Vol. III.* Ed. Henry Claridge. Near Robertsbridge, East Sussex: Helm, 1991. 283–9.

Noss, John B. *Man's Religions.* New York: Macmillan, 1967.

Phillips, Gene D., S.J. *Fiction, Film and F. Scott Fitzgerald.* Chicago: Loyola, 1986.

Pinter, Harold. *The Last Tycoon.* Typescript. The Mayer Collection. The American Film Institute.

———. *"The Last Tycoon."* The Pinter Archive at the British Library. Typescripts, correspondence, notes. Boxes 30–32.

———. *The Last Tycoon. The French Lieutenant's Woman and Other Screen Plays.* London: Faber, 1982. 191–277.

———. Letter to the author. 6 June 1996.

———. *Lolita.* An unpublished screenplay. Author's collection.

Repf, Joanna E. *"The Last Tycoon* or 'A Nickel for the Movies.'" *Literature/Film Quarterly* 16 (1988), 78–81.

Silver, Charles, and Mary Corliss. "Hollywood Underwater: Elia Kazan on *The Last Tycoon.*" *Film Comment.* Jan-Feb. 1977, 40–46.

Hollywood as Text in the Plays of Christopher Hampton, with Reference to David Rabe and Others

Kimball King

The title of Englishman Christopher Hampton's, *Tales from Hollywood* (1982) is derived from the German writer, Odon von Horvath's, *Tales from the Vienna Woods* (which Hampton had translated in 1970) and that of the Andrew Lloyd Webber-Christopher Hampton stage musical collaboration *Sunset Boulevard* is adapted from Billy Wilder's 1950 film of the same name. However, neither work is a conventional allusion to what preceded it. In both cases the recent Hampton plays are woven out of literary and filmic lore, a composite of images, stories and cultural myths which constitute "Hollywood" in the public imagination. That Hollywood is an American, or more accurately an international "dream factory" town, which alternately mixes the promise of quick wealth, gratification of the senses and escape from the mundane with ruthless savaging of individuals, moral decadence and cheap glamour. The social structure is a pyramid whose highly visible and publicized top layers are supported by masses of disappointed, embittered and equally corrupted slave laborers. One particular scene in the staged *Sunset Boulevard* is a technical tour de force in that Norma Desmond's vast high-ceilinged mansion literally rests on top of the meager apartment of underling New Year's Eve revelers. The pyramid of Hollywood success is blatantly illustrated and an imposing staircase in Norma's mansion stretches further upward toward the star's lofty bedroom suite.

Yet a powerful misogyny infiltrates "Hollywood" plays. In David Mamet's *Speed-the-Plow*, two Hollywood "idea men" (a misnomer if there ever was one) place bets on the potential seduction of their secretary, whom they callously discard at the play's conclusion. In Arthur Kopit's *Road to Nirvana*, the female protagonist, who as the actress Nirvana is both "nervy" and vulnerable as a "raw nerve," is a ruthless satire of a sexy but talentless Madonna, all packaging and "no goods." And finally in David Rabe's *Hurlyburly* we listen in horror to the tale of a bored, violent lover who impatiently shoves his mistress of the moment out of a moving automobile.

So, too, in Hampton's plays, the female characters, while marginally more sympathetic and considerably more complex are easily destroyed by pressures of the industry. In *Tales from Hollywood*, Nelly Mann, Heinrich's wife and sister-in-law to the better known novelist, Thomas Mann, is alcoholic, erratic and professionally unsuccessful. Her eventual suicide is recorded as a great relief to her socially ambitious in-laws, forever anxious about her being a potential embarrassment to them. The second wife of the man known primarily in America for writing *The Blue Angel* ("My entire American reputation," he quips in the Hampton play, "stands on the legs of Marlene Dietrich") has himself been drawn to a woman primarily distinguished for her destructive capabilities.

In *Sunset Boulevard*, Norma Desmond becomes a rich, famous, silent screen star but ends as a reclusive has-been for more than half of her life, following the advent of the "talkies." The elaborate theater program of the London and Broadway productions suggests that biographically Norma is a composite of Gloria Swanson, who played Norma in the 1950 Wilder film, Mary Pickford, once "America's Sweetheart" but later forgotten, and the lovely but narcissistic Greta Garbo. Norma's self-delusions and monstrous selfishness suggest that the power of Hollywood to transform individuals into icons can also turn an unspoiled seventeen-year-old girl into a damaging as well as a damaged fifty-year-old predator. The Norma Desmond saga is particularly intriguing. Gloria Swanson was still chic and beautiful at 50 when director Wilder reintroduced her to a new generation of moviegoers. She and audiences took her own perpetual glamour and mysterious ways seriously. By the 1970s when Hampton was a student at Oxford, albeit already a published and performed playwright, the movie *Sunset Boulevard* had become a great "camp" classic and Swanson was regarded as a now over-the-top, would-be movie queen. Female impersonators selected passages of dialogue from the film with which to regale night-club audiences. In particular, "I am big; it's the pictures that got small"; "We didn't need dialogue; in those days we had faces"; "A Great Star has great pride"; and finally and especially, "I'm ready for my close-up, Mr. DeMille," all became famous preludes to appreciative laughter like Bette Davis's "Fasten your seat belts, it's going to be a bumpy evening" or "What a dump!" This camp legacy of the movie *Sunset Boulevard* has been incorporated into the latest musical production along with an implicit satire of the silent film genre. During the early years of commercial film the stars were dressed lavishly for every appearance. In 1919 a Paris couturier created a dress for Swanson entirely of pearls and egret feathers. However, Wilder selected chic black clothing for his star who wore a possibly excessive number of diamond bracelets primarily to conceal the scars on her frequently slashed wrists. The musical version, however, perpetuates the camp legacy of ostentation. Norma, dressed like a drag queen in feathered hats, gold lamé and numerous furs, including a whole leopardskin outfit, looks far more ludicrous than chic.

Mindlessness, solipsism, greed and posturing are leitmotifs of the Hollywood saga. We are not surprised in *Tales from Hollywood* when Horvath upon his arrival in America meets a studio executive named "Mr. Money," when the trade newspaper *Variety* worries about the rise of Nazism ("Hitler's reshuffling of Central Europe represents a loss of $2^1/2$ to 3 percent of total foreign film income") and when the wealthier denizens of Los Angeles demonstrate their "patriotism" by firing their Japanese gardeners. Not only playwrights but novelists harbored similarly negative assessments of Hollywood. Henry Miller, writing in the *Air-Conditioned Nightmare* in the 1930s, records the philistinism of movie moguls—most of them proving their philistinism by never having heard of him. Walker Percy, fifty years later, refers generally to "the Los Angelization of America" as a continual "dumbing down" of natural IQ combined with a terrifying homogeneity that makes every American town resemble every other.

The issue has always been whether Hollywood has captured the American ethos and viewers are horrified by its enlargement on the screen or whether the filmmaker's failure of moral imagination—since technically they have continued to grow in many ways—has shaped our own and perhaps universal expectations of life. The question is similar to the issue of language preceding thought. Playwrights in the 1980s and 1990s appear to be deconstructing the Hollywood Dream Machine, but they have, at the same time, tacitly permitted individuals to escape ethical responsibility by pleading "innocent by virtue of having been brain-washed."

In England the division of stage and film is much less decisive than in the United States. The distance from London to Pine Wood Studios, say, is such that actors can appear simultaneously in a stage play, television film or cinematic production—as Jeremy Irons did, for example, when he starred in the movie version of *French Lieutenant's Woman* at the same time that he completed a role in television's *Brideshead Revisited*. While *Tales from Hollywood* was commissioned for the Mark Taper Forum in Los Angeles, Hampton's reputation in the theater depends upon successful productions of his works in London and New York. There is an element of East Coast disapproval or snobbery concerning the West Coast in most stage plays with Hollywood settings. (Such artists owe their reputation and hence their loyalty to some other geographical space than LA). If one believes the movement of American culture and commerce has had a westward thrust, one might expect the evasive American dream to reach fruition in Hollywood. But frustrated Californians—and one thinks of Steinbeck's old men, sitting on California beaches desperately scanning empty Pacific horizons—transferred their fantasies to the movies instead of improving their actual surroundings. Movies provided Americans, as Norma and Max are fond of repeating in *Sunset Boulevard*, "with new ways to dream."

One cliché concerning Hollywood is the dearth of serious artists who are committed to raising the consciousness and cultural sophistication of the masses. *Tales from Hollywood* shows that even the most high-minded artists like Brecht, and to some extent Heinrich Mann (Thomas is consistently depicted as a supercilious and pedantic opportunist in the play) are unable to make an impact on the film industry and by implication on the moviegoing public. Hampton acknowledges the economic realities of a medium which derives its profits from conferring pleasure upon ticket-purchasers, but he also suggests that the support the masses required for cinematic success, in contrast to the more highly evolved demands of a relatively privileged, better educated, legitimate theater audience necessitates compromises and perhaps even contamination by yielding to popular tastes.

Yet instead of being repulsed by a largely uneducated, thrill-seeking audience, Hampton's "fictitious" Horvath finds movie audiences and individual attitudes oddly appealing as he indicates when he describes his reactions to Hollywood: "I had always loved what was strange and half-finished. I love gullibility, cheap religious mementos, plastic, superstitions, pornography without spelling mistakes, girls dressed as mermaids, streets without end, the ethics of the fairground, the bright smiles of the no-hopers, motiveless friendliness, the pleasure of nomad's land. In short, after two years in Los Angeles, I knew I was home." Earlier in the play he had described his philosophy of writing to another émigré: "I just write about ordinary people, how bizarre they are. I write about life, as regrettable as it is. I write about the poor, the ignorant, about victims of society, women especially. The Left attack always: they say 'easy pessimism'. But they love the people without knowing any people. I know the people, how terrible they are, and still I like them."

In a 1991 interview with John Lahr, Hampton echoes Horvath's philosophy of writing: "Rather than exalt the people and say how wonderful they are, it's perhaps better to say that some people are terrible and I understand that and I like them anyway." Therefore the playwright has chosen Horvath to be his spokesperson, positing an alternative to Bertolt Brecht's approach to theater; but ironically undercutting this bond with his protagonist. Hampton makes Horvath a Brechtian-style narrator who conveys the author's intentions to the audience.

There is actually an "overabundance of sources" on the exiled German writers who came to Hollywood at the end of the 1930s as Siegfried Mewes points out. Hampton clearly could not include the experiences of them all in his play. His principal characters, therefore, become the Mann brothers and Brecht. Most of the situations in the plays actually occurred although not necessarily in the order in which Hampton arranges them. Hampton's most significant departure from history was his decision to make Odon Von Horvath the narrator and central protagonist of his drama. Horvath, in fact, was struck dead by lightning in 1938 and was one of the few major German writers never to come to Hollywood. He was also the only character in the play to have had former links to the Nazi Party, an allegiance which he later finds more embarrassing than deplorable and which sets him further apart from artists who came to America primarily to escape Hitler. Having translated Horvath's *Tales from the Vienna Woods* in 1977, however, Hampton considered the real Horvath to be greatly talented and believed the anachronism of placing him as an interpreter of events in a play would cast a potentially tragic story of misunderstood artists in an ironic and occasionally comic perspective.

In particular, Horvath becomes a foil to Bertolt Brecht, the only giant among the playwrights to be evaluated in this theater piece. Hampton personally has expressed skepticism about didactic theater and especially about Marxian political theater. Curiously, however, he casts his own play in a post-Brechtian mode. The narrator Horvath not only explains the action of the other characters who were real people and unlike himself present in the Hollywood scene, but he also carries on a dialogue at times with the play's audience. Projections of famous

California landmarks, including the Warner Brothers logo, combine with musical selections from Looney Tunes in a drama whose short scenes of Hollywood life are designed to provoke an instant critique of political and social forces, all tending to create an *alienation-effect*. Hampton, himself, skeptical about the power and even the appropriateness of Brecht's political theater, appears to pay homage to the man whose methods he questions.

Although Hampton is an English playwright, all writers whose original reputations have been built upon stage productions are "foreigners" to Hollywood. The American, David Rabe, wrote a series of plays decrying American's involvement in Vietnam prior to his coming to Hollywood with *Streamers*, his adaptation of Broadway materials for a Robert Altman film. Hollywood has typically ignored thorny issues—such as Communism and Nazism in the 30s and Vietnam in the 60s—and has waited until such topics could be dealt with retrospectively and were therefore bankable and only controversial in an academic sense. Interestingly, *Hurlyburly*, which in 1984 was based on Rabe's personal experiences in Los Angeles over the preceding decade was cast with big well-known movie stars in its successful Broadway production. Sigourney Weaver, Bill Hurt, Harvey Keitel and Christopher Walken brought an aura of Hollywood-style celebrity to the Eastern theater establishment's Ethel Barrymore Theater in New York.

Rabe has pointedly declared that *Hurlyburly* is less about Hollywood than gender identity problems in a capitalistic culture, but Robert Scanlon is doubtless correct when he underscores the importance of the movie industry setting, noting that "Hollywood isn't just a place on the map. It is a place and an idea deliberately created in the same way that cocaine is made (Scanlon, "Fighting Saints" 209). While *Hurlyburly*'s characters are Hollywood "insiders," as it were, they pathetically cling to media-generated images of masculinity and success. They earn their living by perpetuating stereotypes on the big screen, but they are also victims of that stereotyping, shaping the common value system of the "outsiders" as well. Toby Zinman, drawing an analogy between Rabe's protagonists and the two dimensional characters of comic strips, points to the failure of the principal character, Eddie's, attempt in *Hurlyburly* to find a solution to his (and by extension society's) communication breakdown because his self-conscious role-playing omits any expression of genuine emotion.

Possibly Sam Shepard more than any other playwright has suggested (in *Angel City*, in particular, and to a lesser extent in *True West*) that while Hollywood provides the myths we think we need, these myths are always artifice, never a mirror of what is taking place or what has ever taken place. Most plays about Hollywood yearn nostalgically for a hero with a moral core. Traditionally, playwrights and actors have attempted to create real people on the stage and subjects centered in a world that makes sense. After the transformations of the theater that took place in the 1950s with Absurdism, earlier notions of dramatic character have been altered. Yet many dramatists still create characters who espouse a system they themselves would encourage. Hampton may well be one of these, having a command of language and ideas shaped by his extensive reading of canonical western writers, especially the German and French masters. It is unlikely that he would write a stage direction similar to Shepard's in *Angel City*: "The term character would be thought of in a different way in this play. Instead of the idea of a "whole character" with logical motives behind his behavior which the actor submerges himself into, he should consider instead a fractured whole with bits and pieces flying off the central theme. In other words, more in terms of collage construction, of jazz improvisation."

Lacking a vocabulary to define their predicaments, Shepard's characters, like Rabe's, often select clichés from popular culture, which both influence and are influenced by movies and other media. There is something wonderfully subversive about the genre of the Hollywood stage play because it uses the phenomenon of a serious and respectable media event for the purpose of undermining a popular but intellectually suspect form of entertainment. The "players" in Angel City cherish the dreams and desires that have been created by the dream-factory in which they are laborers. Lanx hopes to become a successful prize fighter who then sells his "bio" to movies; Tympani fantasizes the set of a diner which has entered his imagination from watching old movies. Finally, Wheeler dreams of a cataclysmic event which appears to emerge from his subconscious, until we realize that his subconscious has been structured by the films he has seen. This imagined event which he says will result in "mass hypnosis. Suicide. Autodestruction. Something which will open entirely new fads in sado-masochism." But moviegoers have already been hypnotized. That is Hollywood's contribution.

WORKS CITED

Hampton, Christopher. *Tales from Hollywood*. London: Faber and Faber, 1983: 28–29.

Lahr, John "Interview with Christopher Hampton." *Light Fantastic: Adventures in Theatre*. New York: Dial Press, 1996: 37.

Mewes, Siegfried "The Exiles on Stage: Christopher Hampton's *Tales from Hollywood.*" Ed. Robert Gross. *Christopher Hampton: A Casebook.* New York: Garland Publishing, Inc, 1990: 96.

Scanlon, Robert. "Fighting Saints: The Idea of Hurlyburly" in *David Rabe: A Casebook.* Ed. Toby S. Zinman. New York: Garland Publishing Inc., 1991: 209.

Shepard, Sam . *Angel City, Curse of the Starving Class and Other Plays.* New York: Urizen Books, 1981: 6.

Webber, Andrew Lloyd, and Christopher Hampton. *Sunset Boulevard.* London: Faber and Faber, 1993: 11.

Zinman, Toby S. "David Rabe's Comic Book Characters." *David Rabe: A Casebook.* Ed. by Toby S. Zinman. New York: Garland Publishing Inc., 1991): 3–17.

The Clash of Verbal and Visual (Con)Texts: Adrienne Kennedy's (Re)Construction of Racial Polarities in *An Evening with Dead Essex* and *A Movie Star Has to Star in Black and White*

E. Barnsley Brown

Since her playwriting career began under the tutelage of Edward Albee in the early sixties, Adrienne Kennedy has opened up a dialogue in her plays between visual and verbal representational systems and the ideologies from which they originate. This dialogue simultaneously embodies and renounces the history of racial oppression in the United States and is most pronounced in her multimedia examination of the documentary genre, *An Evening with Dead Essex* (1973), as well as her metadrama about filmic fact and fiction, *A Movie Star Has to Star in Black and White* (1976).[1] While Kennedy ascribes her limited critical success to the fact that her plays are "abstract poems" (Diamond "Interview") and thus do not easily fit into an American theater tradition dominated by realism, her lack of widespread popularity can be attributed to her uncanny ability to make her audiences feel ill at ease, both through the form and content of her plays. She avows in a recent interview, "My plays made people uncomfortable so I've never had a play done in [my hometown of] Cleveland, never" (Diamond "Interview" 157). The volatile content of Kennedy's plays—her (not so) standard theme of a history of racial and sexual abuse leading to fragmentation and even death—does not make her plays either light viewing or reading. In effect, it is Kennedy's ability to shock and shake her audience that constitutes her riveting power as a writer as well as the grounds upon which her work is sometimes dismissed.[2]

Quite obviously, Kennedy does not fit easily into any established categories. She writes against the realistic tide that has dominated both

American and African American drama. And while her work has been described alternately as avant-garde, expressionistic, surrealistic, absurdist, symbolist, as well as evocative of Artaud's theatre of cruelty, these labels do little to encompass the startling originality of her plays.[3] As Robert L. Tener concludes in "Theatre of Identity: Adrienne Kennedy's Portrait of the Black Woman," "Set in the surrealistic theatre of the mind, her dramas are rich collages of ambiguities, metaphors, poetic insights, literary references, and mythic associations, all of which provide a dramatic form unique to Miss Kennedy" (1). Yet this "surrealistic theatre of the mind" operates not as a "rich collage," as Tener suggests, each element harmonizing with the others to create a synergistic effect, but rather as a (con)textual war zone in which verbal and visual representational systems clash through ironic juxtaposition and incongruity, with fragmentation serving as the governing aesthetic.

Indeed, Kennedy's plays are psychic landscapes, embodying in both content and form the fragmented consciousness that results from living as a "minority" in a white-dominated society. Kennedy has even referred to her plays as "states of mind" (quoted in Cohn, *New American,* 1st. ed. 108), a statement that might be revised to specify "states of *her* mind" since she contends, "Autobiographical work is the only thing that interests me, apparently because that is what I do best. . . . I see my writing as being an outlet for inner, psychological confusion and questions stemming from childhood" ("Growth" 42).[4] Yet, in spite of this autobiographical base, it is very clear that Kennedy's plays articulate a larger history, a history of race and racial polarity, and in particular, of miscegenation.[5]

Kennedy realized early on that representations of race should focus on whiteness as well as blackness, and writes of the intuitive sense of a divided heritage that finally found expression in *Funnyhouse of a Negro* (1964)[6] and her other plays. She recalls,

> I'd often stare at the statue of Beethoven I kept on the left-hand side of my desk. I felt it contained a "secret." I'd do the same with the photograph of Queen Hatshepsut that was on the wall. I did *not* then understand that I felt torn between these forces of my ancestry. . . European and African. . . a fact that would one day explode in my work. (*People Who Led* 96)

In *Funnyhouse of a Negro,* Kennedy thus presents her protagonist as a product of miscegenation, of the presumed rape of her white mother by her black father. In the play, the protagonist, Sarah, attempts to pass for white, to claim that half of her heritage while rejecting the black side of her heritage. Sarah, like Clara in *The Owl Answers* (1963), occupies a liminal space between blackness and whiteness, and hence can find neither a place to belong in either race nor a unified conception of self. Kennedy thus uses her mulatta protagonists to represent the fragmented psyche/self (de)constructed by racial polarities.

As such, Kennedy's writing reconstructs the usually ignored (and taboo) history of racial mixing that has characterized North American society, but is rarely represented in canonical literature. She writes of her childhood in her postmodern autobiography, *People Who Led to My Plays* (1987), "'My mother often said that most of the white people of Montezuma's families came from England. I realized dimly that this meant some of our ancestors too had come from England, since, like most 'Negro' families in the town, we had white relations as well as 'Negro.' I became very interested in "England" (22). To the young Adrienne, England represented neither a colonial force nor the specter of white oppression of blacks, but rather a legitimate part of her heritage about which she was curious.

Only later while at Ohio State did Kennedy experience intense racial oppression from peers, teachers, and even the administration with its expected majors for black students.[7] In particular, Kennedy reports that the overt racial hatred of her dorm mates proved paradoxically to be a source of inspiration: "This dark reality was later to give great impetus and energy to my dreams" (*People* 69). She returns to this theme in her introduction to her radio play, "The Dramatic Circle": "There's no doubt that I see life as tragic. . . . I do feel oppressed by white American society. . . . A lot of my energy comes out of that feeling of oppression, and from trying to break through being overdefined by another group of people" (190). Eschewing the realistic dramatic structure in favor of "a kaleidoscope of imaged scenes" (Benston "*Cities*" 237) thus became Kennedy's method of rejecting and subverting a stilted dramatic tradition whose underpinnings lie in the dominant Eurocentric ideology.[8]

While Kennedy formally rejects a realistic form in favor of the Nommo or poetic/prophetic/psychic force of language in some of her shorter plays—*A Lesson in a Dead Language* (1970), *A Rat's Mass* (1966), *Sun* (1968) and *The Beast Story* (1965)[9]—in *An Evening with Dead Essex* (1973), she turns to the metadrama to formally suggest the (de)construction of selfhood within a racially polarized arena.[10] Here, the director and cast of the play within the play are faced with constructing a documentary performance piece about Mark Essex, the young black Vietnam veteran who in 1972 shot and killed six people and wounded twelve others from a Howard Johnson's roof before being shot by the police. Kennedy suggests the impossibility of the cast and crew's task by the fact that the very subject they are trying to construct is absent. Hence, the title of the play holds a double irony; Essex is, in fact, "dead," but what about his representation in the performance piece itself? This narrative of Essex, this "evening" the cast and crew are assembling, is also dead since it can never capture the essence of the subject-in-process, in this case, Essex. [11]

The problem of representing Essex accurately is further complicated by the fact that all the cast and crew have to work with are newspaper clippings, photographs, and slides, out of which they literally have to piece together a narrative of Essex's life and death. [12] When asked how she came up with this multimedia dramatic form, Kennedy replied, "I was trying to capture how you feel when you hear all that on television" (Betsko and Koenig 256). The audience, like the cast and crew of the play within the play, must sift through the many images, the many versions, of Essex to attempt to penetrate the truth of his existence and identity.

Indeed, Kennedy's use of media representations of Essex calls into question their veracity, a theme also suggested by her emphasis on the projectionist's race: "All [the characters] are black *except* the projectionist who is white" (66). She underscores this again while setting the scene: "To the rear with his back to the audience is the Projectionist (the only white character) at the projector" (66). While the projectionist follows the orders of the director of the play within the play, it is clear that "He is the one who flashes the pictures on the screen" (66). In other words, he has control over the assembling of the documentary and is thus an embodiment of the media's power over the mechanisms of representation.

Indeed, although Kennedy reports that throughout, the projectionist experiments with photos but always returns to what the director wants (69), it becomes clear that at key points, the projectionist undermines the acting and direction with his pictures on a screen which is "slightly bigger than everything else" (66). The very size of the screen itself attests to the power of the media and its claim of "documenting" Essex's life. In effect, when the projectionist "flashes slain Essex [as if by mistake]" while the cast is singing an idealistic version of "My Country Tis of Thee" (69), Kennedy suggests through ironic juxtaposition that the text the projectionist is constructing (i.e. Essex as crazed sniper)is quite different from the text the cast and director are constructing (i.e. Essex as victim who is driven to victimize by racism).[13]

Kennedy shows these disparate texts clashing again near the end of the play when a struggle for control over the visual narrative of Essex's life ensues. At this point, the projectionist once again flashes the body of slain Essex and moves to a close-up of Essex's face. After a pregnant silence, the director "very quietly" insists, "Show him as a boy again" (76). While the projectionist wishes to focus on Essex's death, particularly his body riddled with bullets after being shot over and over by the police, the director and cast are more concerned with representing Essex's life, with revealing the subtle racism and overt hatred that brought him to the breaking point in which he crossed from sanity to insanity.

Thus in the play, the cast tries to recreate Essex's life, particularly his experience in Vietnam, to reach some understanding of his final violent act. The director encourages his cast, "O.K this is it. We're there now. We're with him" (76). Yet the impossibility of truly being with Essex is emphasized by the empty screen, an inscription of Essex's absence, that fills the stage. Indeed, although the cast reads from clippings that recount the news "story," Kennedy suggests that Essex is no more present in these clippings than in the play's final image of him as an "American sailor" (78). As the verbal text ends with a reading from the Bible, thus inscribing the institution of religion and its discourses, so Essex's body is institutionalized as he is dressed in the generic Navy uniform. Kennedy suggests that although the verbal and the visual text vie for control over the narrative in *An Evening with Dead Essex,* neither can successfully document the truth(s) of his life and/or death. He remains a cipher that can only be "read" in the silences that Kennedy uses to punctuate the piece.

Toby Silverman Zinman thus concludes that in Kennedy's metadrama, the author inscribes the impossibility of evoking Essex:

> Having partially freed herself from the chains of theatrical "exactitude" (i.e. conventional realism, i.e., a play about Mark Essex in New Orleans, with predictable expository passages about his childhood, tour of duty in Vietnam, etc.), *Dead Essex* shows us that Essex cannot be evoked from photographs any more than Essex can be evoked from the newspaper accounts, or from the theatre company's homage. (11–12)

Zinman contends that, "The play seems empty not because of Essex's absence but because Kennedy has not found a satisfying way to present absence on stage" (12). However, Kennedy has in fact inscribed absence successfully, so successfully that the audience is left both literally and figuratively in darkness concerning "Dead Essex."

In effect, the audience is forced to search for Essex in the excruciating silences Kennedy scripts into the play as well as the play's more covert subtexts, only to find that the documentary genre cannot, in fact, document: "Just as people in Essex's life and death may have attached meaning to his existence (martyr? psychopath? revolutionary? racist? etc.?), so the theatre group in creating their documentary tribute tries to interpret a life and necessarily fails, just as the audience/readers try to interpret their interpretations and necessarily fail" (Zinman 8). Kennedy's (de)construction of Essex's selfhood is achieved as she involves the audience in untangling an elusive web of visual and verbal imagery in which Essex can be glimpsed but never caught and fact and fiction are indistinguishable.

The dialogue between visual and verbal representations that Kennedy undertakes in *An Evening with Dead Essex* becomes even more apparent in *A Movie Star Has to Star in Black and White* (1976) as Kennedy jarringly reveals incongruities in verbal versus visual texts.[14] Here by juxtaposing clips from classic American movies such as *Viva Zapata!* (1952), *Now, Voyager* (1942), and *A Place in the Sun* (1951) with scenes in the life of her protagonist, Kennedy rewrites the family drama to create an uncomfortable disparity between the public, white-dominated sphere of movies and the private domestic sphere of an ordinary black family.

Invoking the iconic status of the Columbia Pictures Lady as well as actors and actresses such as Bette Davis, Montgomery Clift, Elizabeth Taylor, and Marlon Brando, Kennedy juxtaposes these cultural icons with Clara and her family so that they are in dialogue with each other, commenting upon one another. In the first scene, for example, Kennedy juxtaposes a long dialogue by Bette Davis on the set of *Now, Voyager* with monologues by Clara's mother and father. Yet as Bette Davis begins to speak, it becomes evident that her stream of consciousness actually consists of Clara's own troubled ruminations:

> I've always felt sad that I couldn't have been an angel of mercy to my
> father and mother and saved them from their torment. . . .
>   The one reality I wanted never came true. . . to be their angel of
> mercy to unite them. I keep remembering the time my mother

> threatened to kill my father with the shot gun. I keep remembering
> my father's going away to marry a girl who talked to willow trees.
> (83)

The regretful tone of this confessional monologue is contrasted with the
stark reality of the mother's history, a history of racial oppression that
is at once private as well as public:

> In our Georgia town the white people lived on one side. It had
> pavement on the streets and sidewalks and mail was delivered. The
> Negroes lived on the other side and the roads were dirt and had no
> sidewalk and you had to go to the post office to pick up your mail . . .
> In the center of Main Street was a fountain and white people drank on
> one side and Negroes drank on the other.
>   When a Negro bought something in a store he couldn't try it on.
> A Negro couldn't sit down at the soda fountain in the drug store but
> had to take his drink out. In the movies at Montefore you had to go in
> the side and up the stairs and sit in the last four rows.
>   When you arrived on the train from Cincinnati the first thing you
> saw was the WHITE AND COLORED signs at the depot. White
> peple had one waiting room and we Negroes had another. We sat in
> only two cars and white people had the rest of the train. (84)

In this world, racial polarity is the means of social organization and
blacks and whites have separate but not equal resources and facilities.
   As Clara's mother continues to detail the historical realities of life
in the Jim Crow South, it becomes clear that this is no romanticized
version of history. Just as an incongruity exists between the glamorous
white actress, Bette Davis, speaking lines about Clara's mother
threatening to kill her father with a shotgun, Clara's mother is out of
place on the luxurious ocean liner set of *Now, Voyager.*[15] With the
clashing of verbal and visual (con)texts, Kennedy draws attention to the
representation of race, a construction which is contingent upon the
construction of difference.
   At one level, Kennedy's project in *A Movie Star Has to Star in
Black and White* has an undeniably revolutionary agenda; it inscribes a
black family within the most public of spheres, that of film.[16] Yet
simultaneously, the effect of this inscription is to draw attention to its
implausibility. Kennedy demonstrates that, in reality, as the title of the
play suggests, a movie star *has* to star in black and white; just as the
stage directions in the play designate that "all the colors are shades of

black and white" (80), one can never escape racial polarities in a culture
whose very laws and socio-cultural organization are built upon them.

The trope of "black and white" in the title itself conflates the
different texts present in the play: the cinematic text of classic black
and white movies, the written text inscribed in black on the white page,
and the dynamic of racial segregation that informs the play. Hence, in
the vortices where these texts intersect and collide, we find the play's
dramatic tension. Linda Kintz suggests that the characters of *A Movie
Star* themselves function as such vortices in her excellent study, *The
Subject's Tragedy: Political Poetics, Feminist Theory, and Drama:*

> The characters are very specifically represented as mixtures, or,
> rather, sites that constantly and relentlessly metamorphose to bring
> together technologically available images and presentational bodies,
> as the presentational bodies of actors are brought into relationship
> with characters whose figurations layer several other kinds of cultural
> reproduction. (182)

Kennedy, in effect, creates a veritable *body* politic as she interrupts the
(white) social order represented in classic Hollywood films to inscribe
another social order in which the trials of a black family are
(re)presented through the lens of American film.

The white social order in these classic films is in fact what Linda
Kintz calls the "sanitized spectacle,"[17] a romanticized world in which
decorum reigns, women are pure and ladylike, and men are brave and
chivalrous. Thus Kennedy revises the pristine wedding night scene in
Viva Zapata! in which Josefa (played by Jean Peters) teaches her new
husband, General Zapata (played by Marlon Brando), to read. While in
the film, Josefa, appropriately clad in pure white, and Zapata share a
few innocent (and brief) kisses and generic appellations such as
"darling," they share little else in the marriage bed—certainly not the
torrid sexuality one has come to expect of today's Hollywood features.
Yet, in Kennedy's version, the bedsheets are black rather than white,
and Jean Peters is bleeding profusely when she stands up before falling
back onto the bed. It is interesting here that Kennedy refers to Peters by
her actual name in the script rather than the character she ostensibly is
playing. In this way, Kennedy invokes Peters's iconical stature and
idealized beauty only to deflate them; Peters is, after all, an ordinary
woman who bleeds, whose body sullies the dark sheets so that, "From
now until the end MARLON BRANDO continuously helps JEAN PETERS
change sheets" (*Movie Star* 92). Kennedy thus debunks the

romanticized versions of a white(ned) world and its Eurocentric ideals of beauty as represented in classic Hollywood films.

Not only does Kennedy signify on classic films, but the intertextuality of *A Movie Star* also results from her references back to her earlier play, *The Owl Answers*. In effect, Clara in *A Movie Star* is writing a play during the play, and this turns out to be *The Owl Answers*, as evident in the following speech transcribed exactly as on page 43 of that earlier work:

> They are dragging his body across the green his white hair hanging down. They are taking off his shoes and he is stiff. I must get into the chapel to see him. I must. He is my blood father. God, let me in to his burial. I call God and the Owl answers. It haunts my Tower calling, its feathers are blowing against the cell wall, speckled in the garden on the fig tree, it comes, feathered, great holloweyed with yellow skin and yellow eyes, the flying bastard. From my Tower I keep calling and the only answer is the Owl, God. I am only yearning for our kingdom, God. (*Movie Star* 89)

With this innovative twist on the metadrama—namely, a dramatic protagonist who is writing a play—Kennedy emphasizes the construction of subjectivity. In effect, Clara strives to write/right the script of her life in *A Movie Star Has to Star in Black and White*. In a very real sense, the script is indistinguishable from her life, as Kennedy has Clara express:

> Eddie [Clara's husband] says I've become shy and secretive and I can't accept the passage of time, and that my diaries consume me and that my diaries make me a spectator watching my life like watching a black and white movie.
>
> He thinks sometimes. . . to me my life is one of my black and white movies that I love so. . . with me playing a bit part. (99)

Yet Clara neither watches her life as a spectator nor plays a bit part in it; rather, Kennedy shows that she scripts cultural icons into her own family drama and thus creates a narrative in which she is simultaneously both present and absent, both represented and (re)presented.

Indeed, Kennedy has Clara re-present her story by inhabiting the bodies of white actors and actresses, scripting them to speak *her* lines in a bold gesture of reverse colonization. While the bodies of African

American women have been colonized since slavery, here Kennedy has her protagonist colonize white bodies for her own purposes.[18] This tactic creates a kind of schizophrenia in the viewing audience, and Kennedy uses it to both draw attention to as well as to deconstuct constructions of race. Elin Diamond explains,

> The white spectator might expect the ironic disjunction between movie image and theatrical performance, but the whiteness of the performers enters into consciousness when, and only when, they speak the life of the *visible* black woman. Colonized by these glamorous images, Clara/Kennedy in turn remakes and re-presents them in a context that bears the materiality of her consciousness, if not her color—which is precisely the point. ("Rethinking" 95)

Contrasting the visual text of the body with the verbal text, the narrative of Clara's family's life, Kennedy challenges a social system based on the racial marker of color, and creates a script that hovers between black *and* white—another implication of the wording of the title of the play—to encompass that liminal space, (inter)textually.

Alisa Solomon believes that Kennedy's earlier plays are therefore dialogistic at root since in them, "Dialogue takes place not through the conversational exchange of characters addressing each other, but through the fluid interplay of visual and verbal imagery" (Solomon xiv). Thus, though rarely performed, they become much more readable in performance, as Jeanie Forte speculates: "Reception of the performance text thus might outstrip the political impact of the dramatic text, allowing for a higher degree of visual readability" (Forte 125). As opposed to Kennedy's more recent works—*The Alexander Plays* (1992) and a dramatic adaptation of *People Who Led to My Plays* (1992)—which allow the verbal text to preside as characters recount and remember violence that is not presented in images on stage, Kennedy's earlier works prompt a consideration of selfhood as necessarily fragmented, a point that is both visually and verbally underscored.[19] Furthermore, her focus on the body as an integral element in a play's visual text has opened up new ground for the work of playwrights such as Ntozake Shange whose work derives from an aesthetic born in the black female body, as it is re-membered. Kennedy's vision, although decidedly less optimistic than Shange's, both deconstructs and reconstructs racial polarities, visually and verbally (con)textualizing the history of race, a history riddled with (t)races of subjectivity.

NOTES

1. For an interesting account of Kennedy's first experience with playwriting in Albee's workshop in which she was the only black woman as well as a vivid account of her career-changing interaction with Albee, see her article, "Becoming a Playwright," *American Theatre* 4.11(1988): 26–7.

2. It should be noted, however, that interest in Kennedy's work is now growing as evidenced by the recent Adrienne Kennedy festival. See Philip Kolin, "The Adrienne Kennedy Festival at the Great Lakes Theater Festival: A Photo Essay." *Studies in American Drama. 1945-Present* 8.1 (1993): 85–94. Indeed, out of the four major 20th-century black American women dramatists generally recognized by the theater establishment—Alice Childress, Lorraine Hansberry, Ntozake Shange, and Kennedy—Kennedy is now receiving the most attention, followed by Shange. Still, plays by Kennedy rarely show up on university syllabi, even if they are now being produced more often.

3. See the following: Lorraine A. Brown, "'For the Characters Are Myself': Adrienne Kennedy's *Funnyhouse of a Negro*," *Negro American Literature Forum* 9.3(1975): 86; Kimberly W. Benston, "*Cities in Bezique:* Adrienne Kennedy's Expressionistic Vision," *CLA Journal* 20.2(1976): 237; Ruby Cohn, "Black on Black: Childress, Baraka, Bullins, Kennedy" in *New American Dramatists. 1960–1990,* 2nd ed. (New York: St. Martin's P, 1991), 117; William R. Elwood, "*Mankind* and *S u n:* German-American Expressionism," *Text and Presentation: The Journal of the Comparative Drama Conference* 11(1991): 9–12 as well as his "Adrienne Kennedy through the Lens of German Expressionism" in *Intersecting Boundaries: The Theatre of Adrienne Kennedy,* eds. Paul K. Bryant-Jackson and Lois More Overbeck (Minneapolis and London: U of Minnesota P, 1992), 85–92; Elinor Fuchs, "Adrienne Kennedy and the First Avant-Garde" also in *Intersecting Boundaries: The Theatre of Adrienne Kennedy,* 76–84.

4. In the introduction to her radio play, "The Dramatic Circle," Kennedy even traces the inspiration for her characters to four members of her immediate family: "I've learned over the years that there are four women who fascinated me . . . my mother, my aunt, my grandmother and my great-aunt. I was always studying them, how they spoke. I think, in many ways, I'm always trying to recreate those women as a part of my main characters. I'm always trying to recreate a synthesis of those women to make a statement, and of course to add myself" (191). See Kennedy's introduction "The Dramatic Circle," *Moon Marked and Touched by Sun: Plays by African-American Women,* ed. Sydne Mahone (New York: Theatre Communications Group, 1994), 189–191.

5. Kennedy has in fact identified the history of race as "the predominant question" of her existence. Refer to page 189 of her introduction to "The Dramatic Circle," *Moon Marked and Touched by Sun: Plays by African-*

American Women, ed. Sydne Mahone (New York: Theatre Communications Group, l994).

6. All dates given in parentheses throughout the article are dates of first production unless otherwise indicated. In this case, although *Funnyhouse* was written and produced in the workshop Kennedy took with Albee in 1962, its first major production was at the Actor's Studio in 1964.

7. Kennedy offers a fictionalized version of this oppression in a recent play, *The Ohio State Murders* published in *The Alexander Plays* (Minneapolis: University of Minnesota Press, 1992), 25–63.

8. For excellent discussions of the ideological bases of realism, refer to Elin Diamond, "Mimesis, Mimicry, and the 'True Real," "*Modern Drama* 32.1(1989): 60–61 as well as Jeanie Forte, "Realism, Narrative, and the Feminist Playwright—A Problem of Reception," *Modern Drama* 32.1(1989): 116–17.

9. See Paul Carter Harrison, *The Drama of Nommo* (New York: Grove P, 1972), in particular, his discussion of Kennedy's work on pages 216–20. Although Harrison touts Kennedy as "one of the most inventive black dramatists on the Babylonian scene" and asserts that her plays demonstrate Nommo force (216), his discussion is problematic in that he contends that Kennedy's works "unconsciously" manifest "the sensibility of the African continuum" (216). His critique thus exemplifies the traditional critical tendency to consider the work of women writers as unconscious and to ignore the formal crafting of their work.

10. All of these shorter plays except *A Beast Story* are included in *Adrienne Kennedy in One Act* (Minneapolis: U of Minnesota P, 1988). *A Beast Story* is anthologized in *Kuntu Drama: Plays of the African Continuum,* ed. Paul Carter Harrison (New York: Grove P, 1974), 191–202. For interesting critical discussions of these plays, see *Intersecting Boundaries: The Theatre of Adrienne Kennedy,* eds. Paul K. Bryant-Jackson and Lois More Overbeck (Minneapolis and London: U of Minnesota P, 1992). Other useful essays include the following: Rosemary K. Curb, "'Lesson I Bleed': Adrienne Kennedy's Blood Rites" in *Women in American Theatre,* rev. ed., eds. Helen Krich Chinoy and Linda Walsh Jenkins (New York: Theatre Communications Group, 1987), 50–56; William R. Elwood, "*Mankind* and *Sun:* German-American Expressionism," *Text and Presentation: The Journal of the Comparative Drama Conference* 11(1991): 1–5; Kimberly W. Benston, "*Cities in Bezique:* Adrienne Kennedy's Expressionistic Vision." *CLA Journal* 20.2(1976): 235–44.

11. This interpretation is supported by the director's line in the play, "Think we'll finally call it an evening. . . With Dead Essex or a documentary of

Mark Essex—dead" (68). The syntax here implies that the documentary is, in some sense, dead like Essex, for it cannot give presence to his absence.

12. Interestingly, their attempt to construct a piece on Essex using photographs, newspaper clippings, and slides mirrors Kennedy's own creative process in which she attempts to make associations between images in her mind. For example, *Funnyhouse of a Negro* was inspired by Kennedy's visit to a Coney Island funnyhouse, particularly by the figures of the funnyhouse figures outside. Thus, when Michael Kahn was to direct *Funnyhouse* in 1964, Kennedy tried to give him a sense of the images that had inspired the play. See Howard Stein, "An Interview with Michael Kahn" in *Intersecting Boundaries: The Theatre of Adrienne Kennedy* (Minneapolis and London: U of Minnesota P, 1992): "I think it was clear that the image of the play was that it was taking place in a kind of Coney Island Chamber of Horrors and the Funnyhouse Man. . . or the Funnyhouse Woman. . . were really played like those figures that laugh in booths. . . . When I first met Adrienne, instead of explaining the play to me, she brought me loads and loads of photographs and reproductions of paintings. From that I really understood what the power of the images were for her" (191). Kennedy's plays thus bring together images in dialogue and even direct confrontation with each other and with the audience itself.

13. Here it is important to note Kennedy's wording in her stage directions. By emphasizing "as if by mistake, in square brackets, she suggests that indeed the projectionist is flashing the slide of slain Essex on purpose. This reading is supported by a later point in the play discussed above in which the projectionist again returns to this slide.

14. Kennedy does, to some extent, undertake this dialogue between verbal and visual texts in all of her plays, often using one to emphasize or undercut the other; however, in *An Evening with Dead Essex,* her multimedia approach formally suggests the interplay between visual and verbal, an interplay that she reveals more directly in *A Movie Star Has to Star in Black and White* by juxtaposing scenes from classic movies with her protagonist's life experiences.

15. Elin Diamond points out this incongruity using a personal anecdote in "Rethinking Identification: Kennedy, Freud, Brecht," *The Kenyon Review* 15.2(1993). Evidently, Kennedy delivered a speech to a university audience in which she asserted, "As long as I can remember I've wanted to be Bette Davis," a comment that made the audience laugh since, "The subject of the enunciation not only did not resemble her model, but it was also unacceptable in the cultural discourses through which we think, speak and most of all see, that she could represent her" (90). Diamond thus concludes that Kennedy is suggesting "the radical power of identification to override the constraints of identity" (90), a point confirmed by Kennedy's autobiography in which she draws inspiration

from various cultures, cultural icons, and texts. Kennedy is challenging us to see beyond socio-cultural constraints to claim a truly multicultural heritage.

16. To present a black family as an appropriate subject for a family drama, to place them center stage, was itself a radical act as suggested in Kennedy's autobiography, *People Who Led to My Plays* (New York: Theatre Communications Group, 1987). Kennedy ruminates after seeing Wilder's *Our Town*, "Was what our family did important enough to write about? To read about?" (60) and then answers her own question on the next page: "After we saw *The Glass Menagerie*. . . I didn't understand for a long time that it was that summer evening when the idea of being a writer and seeing my own family onstage caught fire in my mind. But I wrote no play for years" (61). When Lorraine Hansberry had success on Broadway with *A Raisin in the Sun*, Kennedy was given renewed hope that indeed her subject matter was appropriate and significant.

17. See Kintz, "The Sanitized Spectacle: What's Birth Got to Do with It? Adrienne Kennedy's *A Movie Star Has to Star in Black and White*," *Theatre Journal* 44.1(1992): 67–86. More analysis along these lines can also be found in Kintz's chapter on Kennedy in *The Subject's Tragedy: Political Poetics. Feminist Theory, and Drama* (Ann Arbor: U of Michigan P, 1992), 141–94.

18. For an excellent discussion of the historical colonization of the black female body, see Hazel V. Carby, "'On the Threshold of Woman's Era': Lynching, Empire, and Sexuality in Black Feminist Theory," *Critical Inquiry* 12.1(1985): 262–77.

19. See *The Alexander Plays* (Minneapolis: U of Minnesota P, 1992) as well as Philip Kolin's description of Kennedy's adaptation of her autobiography in "The Adrienne Kennedy Festival at the Great Lakes Theater Festival: A Photo Essay," *Studies in American Drama. 1945-Present* 8.1(1993): 85–94. For helpful discussions of *The Alexander Plays*, see Alisa Solomon's foreword to them as well as Lois More Overbeck, "The Life of the Work: A Preliminary Sketch" in *Intersecting Boundaries: The Theatre of Adrienne Kennedy*, eds. Paul K. Bryant-Jackson and Lois More Overbeck (Minneapolis and London: U of Minnesota P, 1992), 36–7.

WORKS CITED

A Place in the Sun. Dir. and prod. George Stevens. Perf. Montgomery Clift, Elizabeth Taylor, Shelley Winters, Anne Revere, Keefe Braselle. Paramount Pictures, 1951.

Benston, Kimberly W. "*Cities in Bezique:* Adrienne Kennedy's Expressionistic Vision." *CLA Journal* 20.2(1976): 235–44.

Betsko, Kathleen, and Rachel Koenig, eds. Interview with Adrienne Kennedy. *Interviews with Contemporary Women Playwrights.* New York: Beech Tree Books, 1987. 246–58.

Bryant-Jackson, Paul. K., and Lois More Overbeck, eds. *Intersecting Boundaries: The Theatre of Adrienne Kennedy.* Minneapolis and London: U of Minnesota P, 1992.

Carby, Hazel V. "'On the Threshold of Woman's Era': Lynching, Empire, and Sexuality in Black Feminist Theory." *Critical Inquiry* 12.1 (1985): 262–77.

Cohn, Ruby. "Black on Black, Baraka, Bullins, Kennedy." *New American Dramatists. 1960–1980.* New York: Grove P, 1982. 94.116.

———. "Black on Black: Childress, Baraka, Bullins, Kennedy." *New American Dramatists. 1960–1990.* 2nd ed. New York: St. Martin's P, 1991. 103–23.

Curb, Rosemary K. "'Lesson I Bleed': Adrienne Kennedy's Blood Rites." *Women in American Theatre.* Rev. ed. Eds. Helen Krich Chinoy and Linda Walsh Jenkins. New York: Theatre Communications Group, 1987. 50–56.

Diamond, Elin. "An Interview with Adrienne Kennedy." *Studies in American Drama. 1945-Present* 4(1989): 143–57.

———. "Mimesis, Mimicry, and the 'True Real'." *Modern Drama* 32.1(1989): 58–72.

———. "Rethinking Identification: Kennedy, Freud, Brecht." *The Kenyon Review* 15.2(1993): 86–99.

Elwood, William R. "Adrienne Kennedy through the Lens of German Expressionism." *Intersecting Boundaries: The Theatre of Adrienne Kennedy.* Eds. Paul K. Bryant-Jackson and Lois More Overbeck. Minneapolis and London: U of Minnesota P, 1992. 85–92.

——— "*Mankind* and *Sun:* German-American Expressionism." *Text and Presentation: The Journal of the Comparative Drama Conference* 11(1991): 9–12.

Forte, Jeanie. "Realism, Narrative, and the Feminist Playwright—A Problem of Reception." *Modern Drama* 32.1(1989): 115–27.

Fuchs, Elinor. "Adrienne Kennedy and the First Avant-Garde." *Intersecting Boundaries: The Theatre of Adrienne Kennedy.* Eds. Paul K. Bryant-Jackson and Lois More Overbeck. Minneapolis and London: U of Minnesota P, 1992. 76–84.

Harrison, Paul Carter, ed. *Kuntu Drama: Plays of the African Continuum.* New York: Grove P, 1974.

———. *The Drama of Nommo.* New York: Grove P, 1972.

Kennedy, Adrienne. *Adrienne Kennedy in One Act.* Minneapolis: U of Minnesota P, 1988.

————. "A Growth of Images." *The Drama Review* 21.4(1977): 41–8.

————. *A Movie Star Has to Star in Black and White. Adrienne Kennedy in One Act.* Minneapolis: U of Minnesota P, 1988. 79–103.

————. *An Evening with Dead Essex. Theater* 9.2(1978): 66–78.

————. "Becoming a Playwright." *American Theatre* 4.11(1988): 26–7.

————. *Funnyhouse of a Negro. Adrienne Kennedy in One Act.* Minneapolis: U of Minnesota P, 1988. 1–23.

————. *People Who Led to My Plays.* New York: Theatre Communications Group, 1987.

————. *The Alexander Plays.* Minneapolis: U of Minnesota P, 1992.

————. "The Dramatic Circle." *Moon Marked and Touched by Sun. Plays by African-American Women.* Ed. Sydne Mahone. New York: Theatre Communications Group, 1994. 189–210.

————. *The Owl Answers. Adrienne Kennedy in One Act.* Minneapolis: U of Minnesota P, 1988. 25–45.

Kintz, Linda. "The Sanitized Spectacle; What's Birth Got to Do with It? Adrienne Kennedy's *A Movie Star Has to Star in Black and White.*" *Theatre Journal* 44.1(1992): 67–86.

————. *The Subject's Tragedy: Political Poetics, Feminist Theory, and Drama.* Ann Arbor: U of Michigan P, 1992.

Kolin, Philip. "The Adrienne Kennedy Festival at the Great Lakes Theater Festival: A Photo Essay." *Studies in American Drama. 1945-Present* 8.1(1993): 85–94.

Now, Voyager. Dir. Irving Rapper. Prod. Hal B. Wallis. Perf. Bette Davis, Paul Henreid, Claude Rains, Gladys Cooper, Bonita Granville, Ilka Chase. Warner Bros., 1942.

Overbeck, Lois More. "The Life of the Work: A Preliminary Sketch." *Intersecting Boundaries: The Theatre of Adrienne Kennedy.* Eds. Paul K. Bryant-Jackson and Lois More Overbeck. Minneapolis and London: U of Minnesota P, 1992. 36–7.

Solomon. Alisa. Foreword. *The Alexander Plays.* By Adrienne Kennedy. Minneapolis: U of Minnesota P, 1992. ix–xvii.

Stein, Howard. "An Interview with Michael Kahn." *Intersecting Boundaries: The Theatre of Adrienne Kennedy.* Eds. Paul K. Bryant-Jackson and Lois More Overbeck. Minneapolis and London: U of Minnesota P, 1992. 189–98.

Tener, Robert L. "Theatre of Identity: Adrienne Kennedy's Portrait of the Black Woman." *Studies in Black Literature* 6.2(1975): 1–5.

Viva Zapata! Dir. Elia Kazan. Prod. Darryl F. Zanuck. Perf. Marlon Brando, Jean Peters, Anthony Quinn. Twentieth Century Fox, 1 952.

Zinman, Toby Silverman. "'in the presence of mine enemies': Adrienne Kennedy's *An Evening with Dead Essex." Studies in American Drama 1945-Present* 6.1 (1991): 3–13.

Hollywood as Inspiration for the Stage: The Gay Playwrights' Perspective

Robert Gross and Kimball King

While the theatre's view of Hollywood has largely been negative, ranging from comic condescension to moral indignation, it is important to note that this view has largely been fashioned by heterosexual males. Hollywood, however, has played a very different role in gay theatre. Drawing on a tradition of female impersonation and camp, gay playwrights are less inclined to explore the seamy side of Hollywood production, than to appropriate the plots, stars, and stylistic excesses of Hollywood movies for their own purposes. Rather than perpetuating the myth of the Noble Stage vs. Venal Movies, both Broadway and Hollywood are merged into a larger world of Glamorous Performance.

Playwright, actor and director Charles Ludlam, founder of the Theatre of the Ridiculous Theatrical Company, was a movie enthusiast who saw no tension between the productions of Hollywood and Broadway. In fact, he quite rightly saw early movies as important documents of stage acting style: "You see in early films what stage acting was. You see how fantastic it was, its expressive possibilities and the prowess of those actors. It's just extraordinary" (Ludlam, *Ridiculous*, 209).

Ludlam's first produced play, *Big Hotel* (1966), not only takes its premise from Vicki Baum's *Grand Hotel*, a Hollywood film with Broadway roots, but also adds a collage of other cultural figures— Bartok's Miraculous Mandarin, Du Maurier's Trilby and Svengali, history (and Hollywood's) Mata Hari, Broadway (and Hollywood's) Lupe Velez, and, in homage to Greta Garbo's tragic ballerina in the film of *Grand Hotel*—Mme. Birdshitskaya, Ludlam appeared in one of his favorite roles, "the madly chic Norma Desmond" of *Sunset Boulevard* (Ludlam, *Plays*, 11). With a rich amalgam of archetypal figures performing in a variety of performance styles—theatre, vaudeville, film and drag show—*Big Hotel* is a fascinating pastiche of what Ludlam called "ecological theatre": "we take the abandoned refuse, the used images, the shoes from abandoned shoe factories, the clichés, and search for their true meaning. We are recycling culture. If you learn to use the waste of society you cannot make yourself very prosperous but bring an era of prosperity for everyone" (Ludlam, *Ridiculous*, 32). Breaking from the dominant stage exploration of Hollywood through realistic conventions (Odets, Behrman, Mamet, Hampton), Ludlam boldly collages images and styles from Hollywood films, putting him in a post-modernist tradition that includes Marcel Duchamp, Hannah Höch, Robert Rauschenberg, and Jess Collins.

All of Ludlam's plays grow from a rich humus of performance history, but some are particularly indebted to Hollywood. *Bluebeard* (1970) echoes Marlowe's *Doctor Faustus*, but draws primarily on the conventions of horror films, especially, *The Island of Doctor Moreau*. *Hot Ice* (1974) reworks characters and situations from Raoul Walsh's gangster classic *White Heat. Exquisite Torture; A Romantic Ecstasy* (1982) takes its inspiration from Pirandello's *As You Desire Me* and the Hollywood adaptation with Greta Garbo. *The Artificial Jungle* (1986) harks back to such film noir classics as *Double Indemnity* and *The Postman Always Rings Twice*, as well as to their literary prototype, Emile Zola's *Thérèse Raquin*. In these plays, Hollywood's stage-indebted material is returned to its theatrical origins.

The gender anxieties that suffuse *The Big Knife* and *Speed-the-Plow* are absent from Ludlam's theatre. In his frequent use of cross-gender casting, masculinity and femininity become roles, rather than immutable realities. Ludlam noted that his portrayal of the macho police officer Buck Armstrong in *Hot Ice* is as much a drag role for him as playing a woman (Ludlam, *Ridiculous*, 49). In the Ridiculous Theatre, one is encouraged to indulge as many different imaginary identifications as possible.

To understand gay theatre's appropriation of Hollywood materials, one need only to look at Ludlam's *Camille: A Travesty on La Dame aux Camélias* by Alexandre Dumas, Fils which he produced in 1973 at the age of thirty. Dumas's original stage play, written in 1855, was "discovered" by Hollywood producers and transformed several times into movies. The first film starred Alla Nazimova and Rudolph Valentino, the next featured Norma Talmadge and Gilbert Roland and the most famous version became a vehicle for the talents of Greta Garbo and Robert Taylor. Both the silent films and the Garbo-Taylor "talkie" describe the same tragic love affair of a beautiful but tubercular Parisian courtesan and her young, aristocratic lover whom she forsakes at his father's request, only to be reunited with him on her deathbed. The melodrama, with its star-crossed lovers and inevitable tragic ending, inspired not only Verdi's opera, *La Traviata*, but also became a romantic archetype of self-sacrificing love and unwavering devotion.

The cinema's mass-marketing has introduced more audiences to Camille's romantic ingredients than any stage or operatic version of the story. Theatre-goers who saw one of the five hundred performances of Ludlam's *Camille* were most probably prepared by their familiarity with the famous Garbo film. Doubtless, this contributed to the drollery of the event, because the playwright himself impersonated the ill-fated Marguerite Gautier in drag. A bald, hirsute man with a large nose, Ludlam was in appearance a ludicrous contrast to the incomparably beautiful Greta Garbo. Yet the audience which initially laughed at his infamous female impersonation was ultimately moved to tears when his character died in the arms of the wronged but ever-faithful Armand. Ludlam went so far as to suggest that the gender of the actor or actress personifying Camille is irrelevant: "the most profound theme of the theatre is role-play but roles are interchangeable, that personality is an artifice in life and that it can be changed or interchanged. I believe that is the message of the theatre." (Ludlam, 45) Thus Ludlam led his audience from comedy to believable melodrama by exploiting an enduring theatre and film legend.

Hollywood had attempted, with considerable success, to take the original play of Dumas and transform it into three separate movies, which would come to epitomize in the public imagination the highly romanticized suffering of thwarted lovers. Rather than see Hollywood overshadow or even eradicate Dumas' original contribution, Ludlam attempted to reclaim for the stage the heartbreaking drama which had been created for it. Rising to the challenge of Hollywood's "misappropriation," Ludlam was inspired to question the nature of relationships that endure or fail and the standards of society that clash with an individual's quest for fulfillment. The visual joys of the cinematic medium had provided his primary creative stimulus.

Ludlam's imaginative use of the Hollywood mystique for a queer theatre that is characterized by bold theatricality, cross-gender casting and camp strategies has continued to have an impact after his death. The Ridiculous Theatre Company continues its work under Everett Quinton.

Following Ludlam, female impersonator and playwright Charles Busch has re-appropriated plots and characters from the movies in such comic vehicles as *The Lady in Question* and *Red Scare on Sunset*. In

Red Scare on Sunset, Busch satirizes the era of Hollywood blacklisting. The political climate which marginalized left-leaning celebrities in the 1950's is regarded by even important observers today as a shameful episode in Hollywood's history. During blacklisting, hysteria and paranoia over the growing power of Communism in American life in the early days of the Cold War wrecked the careers of many actors, directors and other movieland professionals. Beginning with its first scene in the beach house of movie stars Mary Dale and Frank Taggart, *Red Scare* uncovers a communist conspiracy to take Hollywood completely in its thrall. Encouraged by a red-baiting journalist, Pat Pilson, Mary Dale begins to suspect everyone in Hollywood of Marxist tendencies, including her own husband. Not content with stirring up Mary's anti-Communist fervor, her friend Pat is a committed homophobe as well, referring to Mary's butler as a "pansy" and implying that her husband, Frank, may be bisexual. The playwright sees parallels in red-baiting and gay-bashing; both actions derive from the self-righteousness of fascistic "right-wingers."

In fact, there are homoerotic undertones in the butler's relationship with Frank, whom Mary explains, "many nights . . . (has) had to strip Frank naked and hold him under a shower" (*Red Scare*, 23). Furthermore, Frank, who changed his name to conceal Russian parentage and who accidentally killed a friend in childhood, embarks on an affair with the mysterious Marta Towers, later revealed to be a black-mailing communist recruiter. Ultimately, Pat Pilson herself becomes a victim of the conspiracy when an ex-lover forces her to join with the communists or else face exposure as a willing participant in pornographic movies. Both Taggart and Pilson are saved from blackmail and corruption when Mary Dale emerges heroically to give the names of those "we know to be disloyal." (*Red Scare*, 95) In her final speech, Mary Dale stands at a podium before U.S. senators and submits for blacklisting the names of her husband and closest friends. Busch's stage directions specify that "patriotic music swells and eventually drowns out her speech" (*Red Scare*, 97). It is unique to have a play, even such a broad satire, that demonizes Hollywood liberals and exalts conservative bigots. As Busch has noted, most of the red-baiting movies of late Forties and Fifties were right-wing propaganda: *Red Menace*, *I Married a Communist*, and *My Son John*. He adds "I thought it would be mad fun to dramatize it (this play) from the point of view of the hysterical right" (*Red Scare*, author's note). He was surprised when some members of his audiences "took the play at face value and assumed, because I was playing the role of Mary Dale, that I shared her beliefs and was advocating blacklisting. Here I was performing in drag. How could I be championing the suppression of creative freedom?" (*Red Scare*, author's note). In the case of *Red Scare on Sunset*, Busch uses the Hollywood milieu as a situational resource, but the true object of his satire is the widespread complacency and hypocrisy of seemingly patriotic Americans in the days following World War II.

Still later, in Toronto, playwright, actor and director Sky Gilbert would also begin to work in this tradition, most famously in his 1988 *Lola Starr Builds Her Dreamhouse*, in which "film legend" Lola Starr (originally played by Gilbert himself) triumphs over adversity to create a decidedly non-traditional family in her new home—a renovated vaudeville theatre. Here the model seems to be the domestic melodramas of the 1940s and 50s—Lana Turner"*See*" in *Imitation of Life* comes to mind more than once. And one must not forget Manuel Puig, whose *Kiss of the Spiderwoman* is set in a South American prison and not in Hollywood. However, the homosexual protagonist maintains his own sanity and makes life bearable for his revolutionary cellmate, by describing the plots of old Hollywood films. Of course, his reaction to female movie stars is ambivalent; for while he derives strength from their glamour he also fears their inherent "deadliness." Thus, for gay playwrights, the attention-grabbing spectacle of Hollywood lore and the rich iconography of its visually and emotionally compelling landscape often provides a framework of allusions to a popular culture which stimulates rather than diminishes creativity on the legitimate stage.

WORKS CITED

Busch, Charles. *Red Scare on Sunset.* New York: Samuel French, 1991.

Ludlam, Charles. *The Complete Plays of Charles Ludlam.* New York: Harper and Row, 1989.

Ludlam, Charles. *Ridiculous Theatre: Scourge of Human Folly: The Essays and Opinions of Charles Ludlam.* Ed. Steven Samuels, New York: Theatre Communications Group, 1992.

The Matter of Bodies:
Women, Pornography, and Hollywood in Marlane Meyer's *Etta Jenks*

Leslie Frost

In "Pornography: On Morality and Politics," the anti-pornography feminist Catharine MacKinnon writes that obscenity laws rest on a conception of pornography that is "not about women at all, but about sex, hence about morality" (196). MacKinnon differentiates between a feminist concern with power and powerlessness, and a legal concern with virtue and vice. While she represents a polarized, anti-pornography view, MacKinnon articulates a more general concern in her clear separation between the legal, and public, discourse of morality and the feminist focus on power relations and the political. Like Andrea Dworkin, MacKinnon insists that gender inequality is a "sexual reality" of which pornography "is a core constitutive practice" that forces sex on women for profit (198). This construction of power relations within patriarchy rests on clear gender dynamics of power vs. powerlessness and a female sexual identity that is male constructed and controlled. But such clear gender dynamics require a compliant and victimized female body on which to operate, and it is precisely upon this body that feminist arguments find themselves situated.[1] This essay will explore Marlane Meyer's 1986 play *Etta Jenks* as it articulates the relationships between womens' bodies, power dynamics, and morality in the pornographic film industry and Hollywood. The play offers a critique of pornography's sexual politics and, by implication, a critique of the Hollywood of which pornography is the shadow. Exploring similar issues to those which have formed the theoretical framework of the feminist pornography debate, *Etta Jenks* takes a firmly anti-pornography stance.

If public discourse on obscenity is a morality tale and the pornographic film industry plays the Cain shadowing Hollywood's starring Abel, then *Etta Jenks* wraps that relationship around a narrative that focuses on feminist issues of gender and the political. In the play, glamour girls not good enough for the sun-kissed God-loved boy but dazed by the promise of his smile hurl themselves into his brother's clutches, and stay there (slowly sliding to the realization that in the dark both brothers look the same anyway). The treatment the women receive, as well as the choices they make, is always posed against a backdrop on which the relationships between pornography and women and Hollywood and women are played out. So while the narrative foregrounds gender and power within the pornographic film industry, *Etta Jenks* also concerns itself with the complex relationship between body, identity, desire, and Hollywood. The promise of a Hollywood never even glimpsed within the play illuminates the decisions made by the women characters; the image of women Hollywood promotes, the dream of becoming an icon of womanhood, creates an Etta Jenks. Protagonist Etta makes it in pornographic movies because she can't make it in Tinseltown—and she can't imagine herself as anything other than a movie star. "Maybe you shouldn't be in the movies," says her friend Sheri. "It's my only dream, Sheri," Etta replies (12).

Staged between the whistle of an arriving train and the whistle of a train departing, the one-act play has 19 scenes, a staccato beat of change as antithetical to the journey motif suggested by the opening whistle as is the anapestic midwestern thud of Etta Jenks' name. Etta, who is not sure what city she's in when she steps off the train, is still on the platform when a sleazeball named Clyde oozes up to her promising good times and money if she'll just follow him. Etta shakes him off by offering her trust instead to the baggage handler, who promises her a room with his brother. But if her actions in the first scene raise assumptions of Etta's naivete and "virtue," the assumptions are quickly unsettled. Living with the baggage handler's blind brother, and sleeping with the deaf baggage handler, she quickly discovers how difficult it is to break into the movies (and to get paid in theater) and breezily arranges to test for a pornographic movie to raise money. Just before she goes to meet its producer, Etta talks about the decision with blind Sherman and Sheri:

> ETTA: I could use a hundred dollars a day.
> SHERMAN: Pornography in its focus on the genital experience creates an ultimately carnal mind that is necessarily death oriented since the body is always in a progressive state of decay. The earth begins to crawl up inside you . . .

SHERI: Ugh.
ETTA: We're dying anyway, who cares? (13)

As the lines suggest, this scene establishes that Etta isn't some 19th-century sentimental heroine whose fall from virtue leads to ruin and death, but a protagonist of Sister Carrie-like adaptability and toughness. This characteristic is emphasized later in the same scene when Sherman defines the films made by the producer Etta will approach:

SHERMAN: The difference between erotic art and Ben's business is
the difference between gourmet dining and eating fifty pounds
of raw sewage in one sitting.
ETTA (Sneaking a cigarette): What do you think of the name Lana,
Sherman? (14)

As Lana, Etta not only makes pornographic movies, she briefly becomes the mistress of their producer. After he flees to Mexico to avoid paying his debts, and abandons Etta there, she works as a hooker. When she enters Scene 11 with her arm in a sling and with blackened eyes, again the play sets up the audience to expect her downfall. Instead, Etta is offered work as a "talent coordinator" bringing girls into the studio, and when the financial rewards of the job reach the right level, she accepts. Her friend Sheri, in a scene from which Etta is absent, is offered a job in Mexico. Sheri is never seen again, and Etta presumes that she is killed in a snuff film made by the same producer for whom Etta worked. Outraged, she travels to Mexico to make sure the producer really made the movie. He admits to filming Sheri, saying "We were making a movie. What is visible becomes invisible. Her hair, skin, her eyes go transparent and she vanishes" (51). Thinking the producer is constructing a gruesomely elaborate poetic metaphor for Sheri's death, Etta revenges her friend's death by having him killed.

After the producer's murder, Etta decides to leave the business, but while she is packing up, a young woman, Shelly, arrives to ask for help getting into pornographic films. When Etta tells Shelly she won't help her, the young woman tries to change her mind by explaining that she'd been sent by someone who claimed good friendship with Etta:

SHELLY: She does these seminars down in Mexico on out-of-the-
body experience. I saw her do it in front of a bunch of people,
she got real light, like you could see through her and then . . .
poof. it teaches you how meaningless the body is and how it's

never the thing you remember about people? (Beat) Their
bodies? Hello? Hey (58).

As the series of questions suggests, Etta is no longer listening. She is
remembering:

> ETTA: You know, I took this test when I was a kid ... It was a
> perception test. 'Cause I was quiet my teacher thought there was
> something wrong with me. They show you a bunch of pictures,
> scenes of daily life, and they ask you what's happening to see if
> you know. And I can remember this one picture, of a woman,
> floating in the air, and this magician was pointing at her with his
> wand. And they asked me what was happening. And I said the
> woman is dead, she's floating to heaven, but my teacher shook
> her head and said, no Etta, this is magic, this is a trick. But what
> if we were both wrong?

Her metaphysical speculations are quickly subsumed by the business at
hand: Shelly undresses for Etta; Etta tells her she could quickly make a
fortune and retire, to drift, but warns her that the business, "it's not for
everybody" (60). After sending Shelly away, Etta stands alone on the
stage. Through the sound of an approaching train, she says: "You have
to like to travel. That's the trick to drifting. People you call friends
become strangers, one day familiar the next day better forgotten. You
can't want anything, you can't keep anything, because everything ...
disappears" (60). And with those words, Etta vanishes as the light goes
black and the sound of a train roars by.

    As the synopsis suggests, *Etta Jenks* explores a relationship
between an existentialist conception of individual freedom and women
trapped in, to evoke Judith Butler's phrase, bodies that do not matter.[2] It
shows not women victimized by pornography, or subjugated by men,
but women trapped within bodies that evoke an enforcing gaze which is
interiorized by the women characters. Sheri longs to escape her body
and Etta, initially, to enshrine hers; both desires take them to Los
Angeles and the world of images and fantasy. Hollywood sells the
fantasy of womanhood, a fantasy based on the spectacle of the female
body as the object of male desire. This fantasy seduces Etta; *Etta Jenks*
never declares why movie stardom is her goal, it merely draws the lines
between the women's fantasies of film success and their identity as
desirable bodies. Thus, while Etta never becomes a movie star, and the
machinations of Hollywood play no part in the play, the film industry

legitimizes a conceptualization of female subjectivity that creates a space for pornography's use of their bodies.

References to iconographic movie legend Grace Kelly emphasize the presence of Hollywood. For example, after watching a pornographic film involving children and dogs, one of the men says, "Remember dècolletage, Benjamin? . . . A flash of thigh, a bare shoulder. Evening gowns, Grace Kelly, a single strand of pearls?" The mention of Grace Kelly, the screen ice queen whose elegant beauty has epitomized the glamour of women in film strikes a discordant note into an already jarring scene. But while the question seems to oppose what Grace Kelly represents to the sex between children and dogs, it in fact places her on a continuum with them. Both represent female sexuality as a perpetually available enticement to men. Etta wants to be Grace Kelly; she becomes the flash of thigh, the bare shoulder, the spread legs and nude form; recognizing that both Hollywood and the pornography industry sell women's bodies, she sets her sights low on the continuum as if it were a ladder she could climb.

Decisions Etta makes drive the narrative of the play, but consistently undermining Etta's agency are the reminders of bodily practices that constrict those choices. She chooses to make a pornographic film, to become the mistress of the producer, to work as a "talent coordinator" and to leave the pornography film business at the end of the play. Posed against this freedom to act are the actions done to her body. If Etta does breezily decide to make a pornographic movie, a young woman convinced of her bright future, a young woman who likes sex, she is changed from that experience. She gets a disease that makes her body painful to her. She begins to hate men, and to deny her own sexuality. During a long conversation between Sheri and Kitty about dematerializing, they sponge down Etta's body between filming takes.

> SHERI: I was just telling Kitty about disappearing the body.
> ETTA: My hands smell like feet.
> SHERI: I read about this yogi in India.
> ETTA (SHE starts to sit down, grimaces): God, does anyone else have
>   this infection . . . ?
> KITTY: It's a fungus, everybody has it (18).

When Etta enters Scene 11, she has a black eye and a broken arm. Although decisions Etta makes drive the narrative of the play, her body is constantly presented as diseased and broken; like the flash of tit revealed when the women remove their shirts for inspection that signals the body as exchange object, her broken arm serves as synecdoche for the violence that is possible to women's bodies.

Her diseased body is imaged when the second producer, Spencer, tries to convince her to become a procurer and forces Etta, already a widely known porn star, to think about herself in terms of her Hollywood dream.

> SPENCER: When you imagine yourself up there on the wide screen, with the big stars, what do you see? . . . In you head, in your heart, in your imagination, think. People are sitting there in the dark, eating popcorn, what do they see?
>
> ETTA takes a long beat to see what SHE actually thinks.
>
> ETTA : Lana. They see Lana. Her body makeup is streaked with sweat 'cause she's running a temperature from an infection she can't seem to get rid of. She's smiling at a man she hates, and giving herself to him, 'cause it's what he wants. It's what everyone in the audience wants.
>
> SPENCER: And what does she want?
>
> ETTA (beat): Bigger tits.
>
> SPENCER: And what do you want?
>
> ETTA : A raise (33–34)

He agrees, and with the agreement, Etta gives up on the dream of becoming a movie star. The play, in positioning choice and the promise of sexual possibility against the material practices against the body, explores the decisions made by its female characters that occur from a misreading of the sign system in which they are engaged as both readers and signs. Etta fundamentally misunderstands Hollywood's focus on the female and reads the female body's visibility as the sign of its, and her, empowerment.[3] As a spectator seduced by the glamorous image of women's bodies that Hollywood promotes, Etta understands her body as a site of power and tangible sign of her existence. Her body, because it is hers to sell, confers agency upon her. She conceives of herself as a free agent within the system of pornographic exchange instead of a bodily being who exists as a commodified object within that system. Etta's eventual articulation of the pornographic image of her body, and her recognition of that body as an abjected object, reveals the illusion of that premise.

So if sexual desire and unconstrained sexual possibility initially appear as choices, the play's focus on women and pornography deconstructs the terms of that choice. As Shelly, who was "taken" by her stepfather at age twelve, says, "Look, I think it's kind of a turn on to be naked in front of men, I mean . . . they like me and I can make them think I like them, I do it all the time. Not that it's possible to like them 'cause they're, you know, maggots" (59). Like Etta, Shelly believes that her body is a desirable object that gives her a power over men. *Etta Jenks* insists that that female subjectivity and the constraint of agency is produced by the mechanism of its production, and that the dematerialization Sheri longs for is already in place. Shelly's "turn on," then, can never be the expression of individual desire, but only the produced effect from a system that constructs that desire as a component of its regulatory mechanism.

But even as it articulates this negation of the female body, the play explores its women characters' focus upon it. For Etta, the need for tangible measurement of existence is greater than the need for anything else. Hollywood distributes the image of the ultimate woman, so women like Etta want Hollywood not for fame or money but for the dream of being the ultimate object of male desire, and gaining the subjectivity conferred by that desire. The women's decisions stem from responses they have gotten to their bodies. We never quite know why Etta wants to be a movie star, but when Burt presses her as to why she makes porn movies, she says "It makes me feel like I'm really here" (22).

The feminist debate about pornography opposes two views of its stakes; those opposed to pornography view its sexuality as sexual violence and victimization, while defenders of pornographic expression insist that feminists must not echo society's repressive stance on women's sexuality and must affirm women's right to have sexual pleasure detached from reproduction.[4] While anti-pornography activists would legislate against the creation and distribution of pornographic materials, pro-pornography feminists argue that feminism should support women's choices and sexual autonomy and fight against the ideologies that create a restrictive field within which those choices are forced to operate. In line with the tenets of this latter movement are a women's pornography and feminist pornographic films such as those by Candida Royalle and Monica Treut.[5]

With its focus on the brutalized female body and the illusory quality of female agency, *Etta Jenks* allies itself on the anti-pornography side of the debate. Sexual desire motivates none of the female characters. In an early scene, Etta muses on her changed attitude toward sex after starring in pornographic films:

> ETTA: You know, I used to really enjoy sex? (Beat) Now every time I
>   make love even if it's somebody I like I get this terrible urge that
>   seems to come out of nowhere and it's all I can do to keep from
>   gouging his eyes out or slitting his throat . . .
> KITTY: Or hitting him over the head with a crystal ashtray you had to
>   work two days to pay for.
> ETTA(Curious): Yeah, yeah . . . what is that?
> KITTY (Pause); thoughtfully: It's like some kind of rage.
> SHERI: I'm not angry.
> KITTY: Me either.
> ETTA: I don't think I'm angry.

And toward the end of the play, Etta tells a man who expresses interest
in her, "I hate sex" (48). Furthermore, the shift in her attitude toward
her body and sexuality shifts her sense of identity. When Spencer
dismisses the effect of pornography on women by calling the
participants "self-hating greedbags who would do anything for money,"
Etta replies, "like me" (56). He says, "I meant other women," and Etta
tells him, "I am other women" (56–57).

Etta Jenks also allies itself with anti-pornography sentiments by
constructing for Etta, and Shelly, an abusive past. While little is ever
known about Etta before she arrives at the train station, the self-
actualized ingenue, the audience gleans a history from her occasional
offerings in language so spare it disappears almost immediately. She
mentions that she is the child of an incestuous relationship between her
mother and her mother's father, and that she has a child who is growing
up in a good home.

But if the play allies with the anti-pornography activists, it further
makes the point that the pornographic depiction of female sexuality and
sexual desire mirrors the Hollywood representation of the female as
object of desire. It suggests that Hollywood depends on the
pornographic image of female sexuality in order to produce its fantasy
of the desirable body, which is regulated by the same objectifying gaze
and system of exchange. In this latter presumption, the play allies itself
with the pro-pornography argument that feminists should focus on
exposing the regulatory mechanisms that produce bodies signed as
sexual objects and thus a pornography that can oppress women who
choose to participate in it.

The pornographic film industry is what keeps safe the powerful
Hollywood interest in maintaining the female as the site of spectacle
and the sign of sex. Hollywood profits from the public conception of

pornography as immoral because it becomes metaphorically constructed as virtue to pornography's vice, and the sale of women's bodies it too promotes is masked. Of course, pornography profits by the same structure of moral opposition. Etta leaves, but finally there is no place for her to go, except into the blackness of nowhere.

NOTES

1. Feminist arguments became a pitched battle when MacKinnon and Dworkin introduced a civil rights antipornography ordinance into local and city and county politics; the Feminist Anti-Censorship Taskforce (FACT) mobilized a legal and public challenge to the law and the tenets of the antipornography feminist movment. FACT took the position that women are sexually repressed by a patriarchal society and feminists against pornography subject women who participate in pornography to further judgment and collude in their sexual repression. The 1980 anthology *Take Back the Night* contains feminist anti-pornography discussions; Andrea Dworkin's 1979 *Men Possessing Women* discusses pornography as a patriarchal institution, as does Susan Griffin's *Pornography and Silence,* published in 1981. Angela Carter's *The Sadeian Woman* addresses pornography's possibilities, if freed from the contemporary ideology, for women's sexual liberation.

2. Judith Butler's *Bodies That Matter: On the Discursive Limits of "Sex,"* a follow-up to her 1990 *Gender Trouble: Feminism and the Subversion of Identity,* links the material body with a deconstructed gender in order to explore "what has been foreclosed or banished from the proper domain of 'sex'" (23).

3. Peggy Phelan discusses the very real dangers the misreading of visibility as a sign of power holds for the racial and sexually marked Other in her book *Unmarked: The Politics of Performance.* See Chapter 3 "Spatial Envy: Yvonne Rainer's *The Man Who Envied Women"* for a discussion of the cinematic gaze, the female protagonist, and feminist responses. Teresa De Lauretis also provides a theoretical examination of the use of women in film in *Alice Doesn't: Feminism, Semiotics, Cinema.* She provides "an eccentric reading, a confrontation with theoretical discourses and expressive practices (cinema, language, narrative imaging) which construct and effect a certain representation of "woman" (5). Of particular interest to this discussion is the essay "Desire in Narrative."

4. For a very good discussion of the history of the debate, see Chapter Two of Ann Marie Russo's 1990 dissertation *The Feminist Pornography Debates: Civil Rights v. Civil Liberties* (Ann Arbor: UMI). Interestingly, if perhaps not surprisingly, the opposing theoretical frameworks bear resemblance to the early feminist response to representations of women in films. Some feminists argued that women's filmmaking and criticism should focus on exposing the system of

signs and medium of exchange that created the female body as object of desire, while others celebrated a female creativity that could be expressed through women's writing and cinema.

5. Monica Treut produced and directed *My Father Is Coming* and *Female Misbehavior,* featuring porn star Annie Sprinkle who in turn directed and starred in *The Sluts and Goddesses: Video Workshop or How to Be a Sex Goddess in 101 Easy Steps* which both sends up and celebrates female sexual stereotypes. Candida Royalle's works include *My Surrender.*

WORKS CITED

Butler, Judith. *Bodies That Matter: On the Discursive Limits of "Sex."* New York: Routledge, 1993.

Butler, Judith. *Gender Trouble: Feminism and the Subversion of Identity.* New York: Routledge, 1990.

Carter, Angela. *The Sadeian Woman and the Ideology of Pornography.* New York: Pantheon, 1978.

De Lauretis, Teresa. *Alice Doesn't: Feminism, Semiotics, Cinema.* Bloomington: Indiana University Press, 1984.

Dworkin, Andrea. *Pornography: Men Possessing Women.* New York: Putnam, 1981.

Griffin, Susan. *Pornography and Silence: Culture's Revenge against Nature.* New York: Harper & Row, 1981.

Lederer, Laura, ed. *Take Back the Night: Women on Pornography.* New York: Morrow, 1980.

MacKinnon, Catharine. *Toward a Feminist Theory of the State.* Cambridge: Harvard University Press, 1989.

Meyer, Marlane, *Plays in Process: Etta Jenks.* New York: Theatre Communications Group, 1988.

Phelan, Peggy. *Unmarked: The Politics of Performance.* New York: Routledge, 1993.

Russo, Ann Marie. *The Feminist Pornography Debates: Civil Rights v. Civil Liberties.* Ann Arbor: UMI Dissertation Information Service, 1992

Sprinkle, Annie, Beatty, Marla, directors. *The Sluts and Goddesses: Video Workshop or How to Be a Sex Goddess in 101 Easy Steps.* Film. Beatty and Sprinkle, 1992.

Treut, Monica, director. *Female Misbehavior.* Film. New York: First Run Features, 1992.

Treut, Monica, director. *My Father Is Coming.* Film. New York: First Run Features, 1990.

Index